Guide to Safety at Sports Grounds

Fourth edition

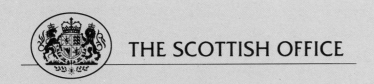

THE SCOTTISH OFFICE

Contents

List of diagrams and tables

List of paragraph headings

Preface

This fourth edition of the *Guide to Safety at Sports Grounds* is published at a time of great change, both in the sporting world and in the development of sports grounds as a whole. A considerable number of new grounds and facilities are becoming available in many sports, bringing to the public a higher standard of facilities than ever before. This has been the result of legislation, new sources of funding, and rapid advances in sports ground related technology.

Allied to these developments has been a considerable growth in the study and knowledge of design and management issues, prompted in particular by the recommendations of Lord Justice Taylor's report into the tragedy at Hillsborough, Sheffield, in 1989. Much of this newly acquired knowledge and experience, which applies to all sports grounds – not only those used for football – has been incorporated into this revised edition.

Guidance on the safety of spectators at sports grounds first became available when the Wheatley Report on Crowd Safety at Sports Grounds was published in 1972. The recommendations in the Appendix to that report were extended to include fire precautions and emergency evacuation. They formed the basis of the first *Guide to Safety at Sports Grounds*, published in 1973, and continue to do so.

Recommendations of the Working Party on Crowd Behaviour were incorporated in a new version, published in 1976, which was aimed specifically at football grounds.

Following the fire at Valley Parade, Bradford, in 1985, a working party, established under the aegis of Mr Justice Popplewell's Inquiry into Crowd Safety and Control at Sports Grounds, reviewed the *Guide* and produced a further series of recommendations. These formed the basis of an expanded second edition in 1986.

The third edition, published in 1990, incorporated further changes made following a re-examination of the guidelines in the wake of the Hillsborough disaster.

Although the most serious accidents to have taken place in this country and abroad have occurred at football grounds – most notably at Ibrox Park in 1902, Burnden Park (1946), Ibrox Park again (1971), Valley Parade and Heysel (1985), Hillsborough (1989), Bastia (1992) and Guatemala (1996) – no sports ground is immune from risk. This applies whether or not they are the subject of a safety certificate.

It is hoped therefore that all concerned with the management, design, scrutiny and certification of sports grounds will find this revised and expanded edition of the *Guide* a useful source of reference in their efforts to meet the common goal; that is, the safety, comfort and welfare of all spectators at sports grounds, at all times and in all situations.

Introduction

A   Status

The *Guide to Safety at Sports Grounds* is an advisory document for use by competent persons.

It is the distillation of many years of research and experience of the safety management and design of sports grounds.

The *Guide* has no statutory force but many of its recommendations will be given force of law at individual grounds by their inclusion in safety certificates issued under the Safety of Sports Grounds Act 1975 or the Fire Safety and Safety of Places of Sport Act 1987.

The advice given in this *Guide* is without prejudice to the application of the appropriate Building Regulations, the Health and Safety at Work etc. Act 1974, and any other relevant legislation.

B   Scope

The Safety of Sports Grounds Act 1975 defines a sports ground as:

'A place where sports or other competitive activities take place in the open air, and where accommodation has been provided for spectators, consisting of artificial structures or of natural structures artificially modified for the purpose.'

The *Guide* applies to the safety of spectators at all sports grounds which meet the above definition, whether or not the grounds are issued with a safety certificate.

The management of these grounds have a primary responsibility for the safety of spectators, and should therefore apply the recommendations in the *Guide* in order to achieve safe conditions.

The grounds to which the *Guide* applies are likely to be those which stage the following sports:

American Football	*Golf*	*Motor Racing*
Athletics	*Greyhound Racing*	*Polo*
Cricket	*Hockey*	*Rugby (Union & League)*
Equestrian events	*Horse Racing*	*Speedway Racing*
Football	*Lacrosse*	*Tennis*

The above list is not intended to be comprehensive, and there may be other sports grounds to which the *Guide* also applies.

C   Objectives and realistic aims

The objective of the Guide is to provide guidance to ground management, technical specialists such as architects and engineers, and representatives of all relevant authorities, in order to assist them in the assessment of how many spectators can be safely accommodated within a sports ground.

The document also provides guidance on measures intended to improve safety at existing grounds, in terms of both their design and safety management, while taking into account the constraints and difficulties which may exist at these grounds.

In addition, as explained in paragaph (f) below, the *Guide* now offers guidance on how to apply good practice in the design and management of new grounds or newly constructed sections of grounds.

When applying the guidance and recommendations in the *Guide*, it should be remembered that the principal objective is 'to secure reasonable safety at the sports ground when it is in use for the specified activity' (as stated in section 2(1) of the Safety of Sports Grounds Act 1975). Absolute safety, however desirable in theory, is, in reality, unattainable.

Furthermore, in all assessments, a flexible approach should be maintained to take account of the individual type, function and layout of grounds. The requirements of spectators at horse or greyhound racing tracks, for example, are in many instances fundamentally different from those attending grounds used for football or rugby.

Whatever the sport, it should also be recognised that safety concerns are often directly related to the nature of specific events and the number of spectators attending.

It should also be remembered that the greatest risk to safety is complacency.

D   Management responsibility

Responsibility for the safety of spectators lies at all times with the ground management. The management will normally be either the owner or lessee of the ground, who may not necessarily be the promoter of the event.

In discharging its responsibility, the management needs to recognise that safety should not be seen as a set of rules or conditions imposed by others, but rather as standards set from within which reflect a safety culture at the sports ground. A positive attitude demonstrated by the management is therefore crucial in ensuring that safety policies are carried out effectively and willingly.

These policies should take into consideration the safety of *all* spectators, including, for example, those with disabilities, and children.

Representatives of management cannot, however, be reasonably expected to possess all the technical knowledge and skills required to assess and apply every recommendation in the *Guide*. Management should therefore, whenever required, seek guidance from competent persons who have the relevant qualifications, skills and experience. (For a definition of 'competent person' refer to the Glossary.)

Representatives of the local authority, together with police, fire and ambulance officers, will advise management on how to discharge its responsibility, and, in certain circumstances, may require measures to be taken in order to achieve reasonable safety standards. This does not, however, exonerate the ground management from its responsibility for the safety of spectators.

Although the *Guide* is not specifically aimed at risks to spectators from the sport itself, management also have a responsibility to take all necessary precautions to safeguard spectators against the effects of accidents in, or originating from, the activity on the pitch, track, or area of activity. Particular care is needed when the sport entails the use and storage of flammable fuels.

E   Achieving a balance

Safety at sports grounds is achieved by establishing a balance between good management and good design.

In this respect, safety at sports grounds cannot be achieved simply by ensuring that individual components of a ground – such as stairways, gangways, seated areas or terraces – are satisfactory in themselves. The inter-relation of these and other components is critical. None can be treated in isolation without consideration of the effect its design and management has upon the other components. They should all be compatible and combine to form a balanced unit.

For this reason it is recommended that readers of the *Guide* familiarise themselves with all sections of the document, including those which may strictly be beyond their personal remit.

F   New construction

Although not a definitive design guide, it will be noted that this document now offers guidance on how to apply good practice in the design and management of new grounds or newly constructed sections of grounds.

Such guidance is highlighted throughout the *Guide* under the following heading:

For new construction:

The guidance is intended to ensure that new construction leads to a higher standard of safety and amenity than can be achieved at grounds already built.

In addition, unless the *Guide* recommends a higher standard, new construction should conform to the current, appropriate Building Regulations.

It should also, whenever possible and wherever specified, take into account the recommendations of other relevant advisory documents; for example, those published by the Football Stadia Advisory Design Council. These and other relevant documents are referred to in the appropriate sections, and are further listed in the Bibliography.

Although it is also recommended that, wherever possible, the refurbishment of existing structures should also seek to meet higher standards, it is recognised that this may not always be achievable. However, all refurbishment work should at least meet the standards set in the *Guide*.

G Deviating from the *Guide*

The Guide *seeks to encourage the meeting of achievable standards, particularly for new construction, but does not attempt to provide a universal minimum standard for existing sports grounds.*

It may therefore be possible to deviate from individual guidelines without detracting from the overall safety of a sports ground.

However, it is stressed that the recommendations within the *Guide* are based upon research and experience. Deviations from the *Guide* should therefore only be acceptable when considered to be necessary and reasonable. An accumulation of deviations which result in the application of lower standards in relation to any part of the ground or any aspect of its management should also be regarded as unacceptable.

It is the responsibility of ground management to ensure that any decision to deviate from the Guide *should be recorded, with supporting written evidence, including the details of a risk assessment. If the deviation is then approved (by management, and, where a safety certificate is in place, by the certifying authority), the action taken should strictly adhere to the contents of the written evidence.*

It is further stressed that unless it can be demonstrated that the alternative measures to be taken are able to achieve an equal or greater degree of safety than those recommended in the *Guide*, a capacity lower than the one which would otherwise be permitted will be required. The extent of such a reduction may be severe.

H Revisions to the *Guide*

It will be noted that this edition of the *Guide* contains certain amendments and new guidance. For quick reference Annex D contains a brief summary.

Readers familiar with the previous editions may also wish to refer to Annex E, which lists the re-numbering or deletion of all former paragraphs.

Guide to Safety at Sports Grounds

Chapter One

Calculating the safe capacity of a sports ground

1.1   **The importance of calculating a safe capacity**

As stated in the Introduction, the principal objective of the *Guide* is to provide guidance on the assessment of how many spectators can be safely accommodated within the viewing accommodation of a sports ground used for a sporting event.

This assessment is the first and most important step towards the achievement of reasonable safety.

The purpose of this chapter is to outline the main factors which must be considered in making an assessment, leading to a calculation of the final safe capacity of each section of the ground.

Clearly the assessments made will differ according to the individual ground and to the type of spectator accommodation being assessed; primarily whether it is for seated or standing accommodation. But the factors to be applied in each case are the same for every ground, regardless of the sport being staged.

Diagrams 1 and 2 on pages 24 and 25 summarise the factors to be assessed for both seated and standing accommodation.

To further illustrate the methods of assessment and calculation, worked examples are also provided in Annex A. However, the details of each step can only be fully understood by a thorough reading of the whole *Guide*.

The assessment and calculation process will require properly detailed plans of the ground, preferably drawn to a scale of 1:200.

At the majority of sports grounds, the capacities of each section will be added to establish the final capacity of the ground as a whole. However, as explained in Section 1.12, there are certain grounds – including, for example, those staging horse racing or golfing events – where it may not be appropriate to calculate the overall capacity of the whole ground. In such cases, however, the final capacities of individual sections of viewing accommodation must still be calculated.

1.2   **Applying the capacity calculation**

Once the final capacity of a section or of the whole ground is determined (as explained in Section 1.3), in no circumstances should a larger number of spectators be admitted.

If the final capacity is lower than the level management ideally require, it can be raised only after the necessary remedial work has been completed, and/or the quality of safety management improved, and the area in question then re-assessed.

Similarly, if part of the ground is required to be closed, this must be done. It must not be re-opened for spectator viewing for any reason until the necessary remedial work has been completed to remove the deficiencies which led to its closure, and not before these measures have been approved by the relevant authority.

1.3 Factors to be considered

The common factors which apply to both seated and standing accommodation can be summarised as follows.

a. **The entry capacity of the section**

The entry capacity is the number of people who can pass through all the turnstiles and other entry points serving the section, within a period of one hour.

b. **The holding capacity of the section**

This is the number of people who can be safely accommodated in each section.

In the case of seats, this will be determined by the actual number of seats, less any that cannot be used safely (owing to seriously restricted views or their inadequate condition), and an assessment of the (P) and (S) factors.

(P) and (S) factors are explained in Section 1.4.

In the case of a standing area, this will be determined by a number of features, including crush barrier strengths and layouts (see Chapter 10), areas which offer restricted views, and a further assessment of both the (P) and (S) factors.

c. **The exit capacity of the section**

This is the number of people who can safely exit from the viewing area of the section under normal conditions (see Chapter 9).

d. **The emergency evacuation capacity**

This is determined by the emergency evacuation time, which is based largely on the level of risk of the section and its associated emergency evacuation routes (see Chapter 15).

The emergency evacuation capacity is the number of people who can safely negotiate the emergency evacuation routes and reach a place of safety within that set time (see Chapter 9).

e. **The final capacity**

Having established all the above figures, the final capacity of the section, and thence of the whole ground, will be determined by whichever is the *lowest* figure arrived at for (a), (b), (c) or (d).

Diagrams 1 and 2 summarise the main stages outlined above.

1.4   The (P) and (S) factors

In order to calculate the holding capacity (as defined in Section 1.3), each part of the ground's viewing accommodation should be assessed according to its physical condition. This assessment is known as the (P) factor.

Similarly, each part of the ground's viewing accommodation should be assessed according to the quality of the safety management of that area. This assessment is known as the (S) factor.

To help in the assessment of the (P) and (S) factors, it is recommended that each should be given a numerical value. This value should be quantified as a factor of between 0.0 and 1.0, as the following examples indicate:

a.   Where the physical condition of the accommodation is of a high standard, a (P) factor of 1.0 should be applied.

b.   Where the physical condition is extremely poor, a factor of 0.0 should be applied. As explained below, this would have the effect of imposing a zero capacity on the area assessed.

c.   An intermediate assessment might result in, for example, a (P) factor of 0.6, or perhaps an (S) factor of 0.8.

While recognising that it is difficult to place specific numerical values on such assessments, it is nevertheless essential and inevitable that some form of quantified assessment be made. It may also be noted that this form of assessment is now widely used in other safety-related fields.

Owing to the wide variation of conditions and facilities to be found at sports grounds, the *Guide* does not seek to place specific values on any of the elements that are likely to be considered when assessing (P) and (S) factors. This is because the assessments should not aim to create a cumulative scoring system in which values for individual elements are simply added together.

Instead, the assessment should reflect a considered and reasonable overall judgement of the physical condition or safety management of the area in question, taking full account of all circumstances and the wider guidance in this document.

For example, Sections 11.16 and 11.17 explain the assessment of (P) and (S) factors for seated accommodation. Sections 12.23 and 12.24 provide similar guidance for the assessment of standing accommodation. Worked examples of capacity calculations in Annex A also show how (P) and (S) factors are applied.

1.5   Carrying out (P) and (S) factor assessments

It is the responsibility of ground management to ensure that (P) and (S) factors are assessed and, where a safety certificate is in place, that those assessments are agreed in consultation with the certifying authority.

It is recommended that (P) and (S) factors should be assessed by competent persons with knowledge and understanding of the ground concerned, its operation and the general principles of safety.

It is further recommended that written records of all assessments be kept.

Written records of the assessment should identify any deficiences found, so that these can be acted upon by the ground management, thereby leading to a potential increase of the (P) or (S) factors (which in turn may lead to an increase in the holding capacity).

Similarly, the records will enable any other deficiencies to be monitored, which may in turn require a reduction of the (P) or (S) factors.

1.6 Seated accommodation – calculating the holding capacity

As stated in Section 1.3, one of the figures needed in order to calculate the final capacity is the holding capacity. It should be noted that the holding capacity of a seated area will not automatically correspond with the number of actual seats provided. The following factors must also be considered:

a. seats that offer a seriously restricted view (as defined in Section 11.4) should be discounted from the holding capacity.

b. seats that exceed the numbers permitted between radial gangways in each row (see Section 11.14) may be discounted from the holding capacity.

c. seats that are damaged or whose dimensions fall below the specified minimums for seating row depths, seat widths and/or clearways (see Sections 11.11 and 11.12) should be discounted from the holding capacity.

Having established the number of usable seats, (P) and (S) factors must then be applied (see Sections 11.16 and 11.17).

Having established values for both the (P) and (S) factors, the holding capacity of the seated area can thus be calculated as follows:

holding capacity = the number of usable seats
x (P) or (S), whichever is lower

It is stressed that the (P) and (S) factors should not be multiplied by each other, but that the lower of the two factors applied to the calculation.

1.7 Standing accommodation – the calculation process

The calculation of the holding capacity for standing areas is considerably more complicated than for seated areas. As shown in Diagram 2, three stages are involved:

Stage 1: To establish the **available viewing area** (A)

Stage 2: To establish the **appropriate density** (D)

Stage 3: Using both the above figures, to establish the **holding capacity.**

The three stages are explained in the following sections.

Reference should also be made to the worked examples in Annex A. Further guidance may also be found in *Terraces – Designing for Safe Standing at Football Stadia* (see Bibliography). Although written primarily for football, the publication includes much general advice applicable to all sports grounds.

1.8 Stage 1 – calculating the available viewing area

The available viewing area (A) is not the entire area available for standing spectators. Rather, it consists only of the areas immediately behind crush barriers, less those areas from which only seriously restricted views are possible (see Section 12.13).

The extent of the areas behind crush barriers depends on the strength of those crush barriers, and how far the crush barriers are spaced apart in relation to the angle of slope. For further guidance on the inter-relation of these factors, see Table 2 in Chapter 10.

Once the crush barriers have been tested, and the spacings between barriers and the angle of slope measured, the available viewing area can then be measured, as follows:

a.   If, as recommended, the crush barriers are provided continuously between radial gangways, and are designed for the correct loads and spacings according to Table 2, all areas behind the crush barriers will be considered as the available viewing area (see Section 10.8, Diagram 8 and worked example 1 in Annex A).

b.   If the crush barriers are not continuous between radial gangways, only the areas behind individual crush barriers should be counted, according to the strength of each individual barrier. All other areas must be discounted, even though in practice they will be occupied by standing spectators (see worked example 2 in Annex A).

c.   The available viewing area must be limited if there is excessive spacing between barriers (see Table 2 and worked example 3 in Annex A).

d.   Areas immediately behind those crush barriers which have failed the testing procedures outlined in Chapter 10 must also be discounted from the available viewing area.

e.   If the crush barriers are not continuous and there are no clearly marked gangways, further areas must be discounted, calculated on the basis of how much space – measured at 1.1m wide – the required number of gangways would take up if provided (see worked example 2 in Annex A).

f.   Standing areas without crush barriers cannot be considered as safe unless the capacity is set at such a level that the risks are minimised.

If the standing area has no crush barriers, but has a front barrier (be it a barrier, rail, wall or fence) which meets the horizontal imposed load requirements of a crush barrier, the available viewing area will be limited to the space immediately behind the front barrier, depending on the strength of the barrier (see Table 2 of Chapter 10, and worked example 4 in Annex A).

g.   Where there are no crush barriers, and the front barrier (be it a barrier, rail, wall or fence) does not meet the horizontal imposed load requirements of a crush barrier, it is recommended that the available viewing area does not exceed a depth of 1.5m behind the front barrier. In practical terms this is the equivalent of approximately four persons deep.

A similar depth limitation should apply to areas of level standing, regardless of the loading of any front barrier. This is because the view of any spectator standing beyond this depth is likely to be too seriously restricted (see worked examples 5 and 6 in Annex A).

h.   It is recognised that there are standing areas and enclosures at certain sports grounds – such as lawns in front of stands at race courses – which are used for both general circulation and viewing, and where the recommendations provided in paragraphs (f) and (g) above may not be appropriate. These areas might not have any crush barriers or even a front barrier which meets the loading requirement of a crush barrier. However, because the nature of the sport requires that spectators are able to move freely, it is likely that crowds will be spread throughout the area, rather than being concentrated behind the front rails.

In such circumstances, the available viewing area may extend beyond 1.5m behind the front rail, and may cover those parts of the enclosure from which viewing is possible, provided that in order to allow for circulation a significantly reduced (P) factor is applied (as explained in Section 12.21 and worked example 7 in Annex A).

If this approach is taken, however, adequate safety management measures will be essential to prevent concentrations of spectators behind the front rail or in any other part of the enclosure.

It is also stressed that the calculation of capacities for such enclosures should be separate from the calculation of capacities for any seated or standing accommodation adjoining them. Where there is a free movement of spectators between, for example, a lawn area and a standing terrace, ground management must ensure that neither area is filled beyond its capacity.

It should be noted that in all cases any areas affected by seriously restricted views must still be discounted from the available viewing area.

1.9   **Stage 2 – calculating the appropriate density**
Having established the available viewing area (A), this must then be considered in conjunction with the appropriate density (D). The appropriate density (referred to as the 'appropriate packing density' in previous editions of the *Guide*) is expressed in terms of a number of spectators per 10 square metres.

For the purposes of calculating the capacity of standing areas at sports grounds, the maximum number that can be applied is 47 persons per 10 square metres.

This maximum figure will then be subject to the assessment of the physical condition of the area (P), and the quality of the safety management of the area (S).

As stated in Section 1.4 it is recommended that (P) and (S) factors be quantified as a factor of between 0.0 and 1.0. Guidance on the assessment of (P) factors can be found in Section 12.23, and on (S) factor in Chapters 2, 3, and Section 12.24.

Having established both the (P) and (S) factors, the appropriate density (D) of the standing area is then calculated using the following formula:

appropriate density (D) = (P) or (S) factor (whichever is lower) x 47

Thus, if both the (P) and (S) factors are 1.0, the appropriate density will be 47 persons per 10 square metres.

If the (P) factor is 0.6 and the (S) factor is 0.9, the appropriate density will be 28.2 persons per 10 square metres; that is, the lower of the two factors (0.6) x 47.

Further examples of the application of (P) and (S) factors are provided in the worked examples in Annex A.

1.10 Stage 3 – calculating the holding capacity

Having established the available viewing area (A) and the appropriate density (D), the holding capacity of the standing area can then be calculated using the following formula:

$$\text{holding capacity} = \frac{A}{10} \times D$$

It should be noted that at grounds staging different types of sport, the holding capacity may vary for each sport. For example, the free movement of standing spectators between different areas of viewing accommodation may be permitted at one sporting event but not at another, resulting in a different appropriate density being applied to the calculation (see Section 12.16).

1.11 Establishing the final capacity

As stated in Section 1.3, whether for seated or standing areas, having established the holding capacity of the area, a comparison must then be made between:

a. the holding capacity

b. the entry capacity

c. the exit capacity

d. the emergency evacuation capacity.

The final capacity of the section or whole ground will be determined by whichever is the lowest figure of the four criteria.

As stated in Section 1.2, once the final capacity of a section, and thence of the whole ground, is determined, in no circumstances should a larger number of spectators be admitted without remedial work and the approval of the relevant authorities.

Diagram 1.
Calculating the capacity of seated accommodation

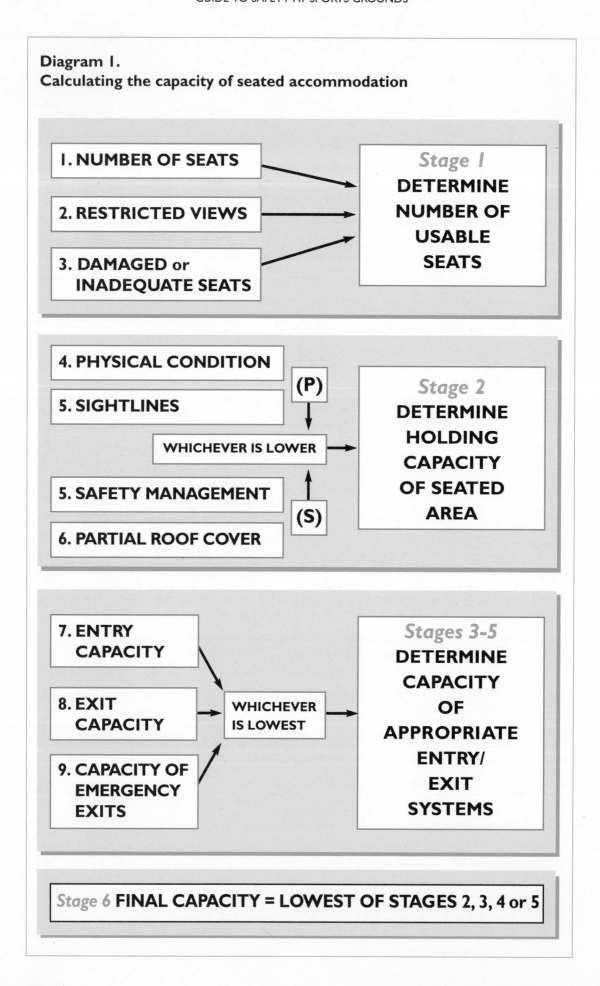

Diagram 2.
Calculating the capacity of standing accommodation

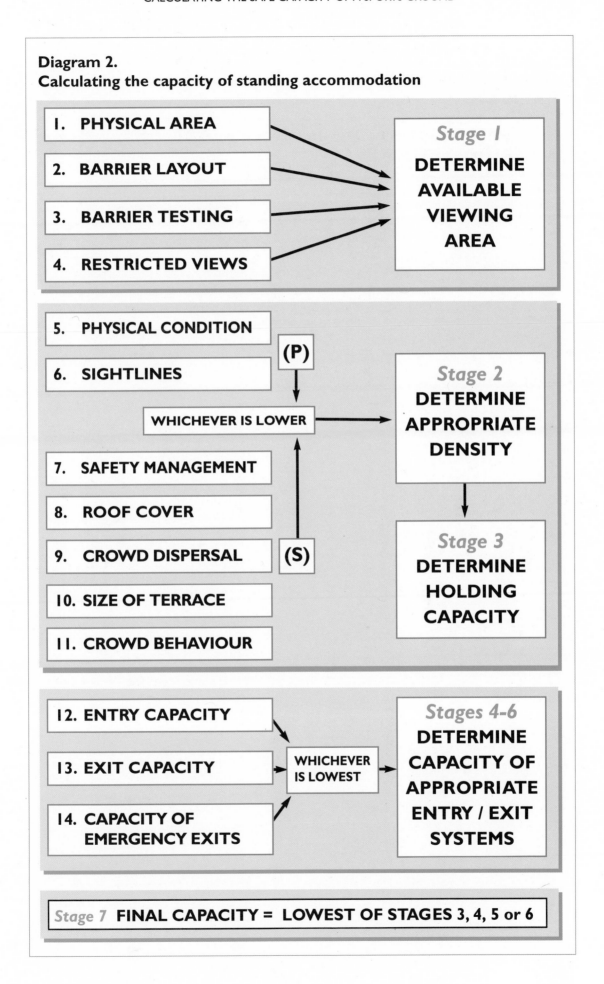

1. **PHYSICAL AREA**

2. **BARRIER LAYOUT**

3. **BARRIER TESTING**

4. **RESTRICTED VIEWS**

Stage 1
DETERMINE AVAILABLE VIEWING AREA

5. **PHYSICAL CONDITION**

6. **SIGHTLINES**

(P)

WHICHEVER IS LOWER

7. **SAFETY MANAGEMENT**

8. **ROOF COVER**

9. **CROWD DISPERSAL**

(S)

10. **SIZE OF TERRACE**

11. **CROWD BEHAVIOUR**

Stage 2
DETERMINE APPROPRIATE DENSITY

Stage 3
DETERMINE HOLDING CAPACITY

12. **ENTRY CAPACITY**

13. **EXIT CAPACITY**

WHICHEVER IS LOWEST

14. **CAPACITY OF EMERGENCY EXITS**

Stages 4-6
DETERMINE CAPACITY OF APPROPRIATE ENTRY / EXIT SYSTEMS

Stage 7 **FINAL CAPACITY = LOWEST OF STAGES 3, 4, 5 or 6**

1.12 Grounds where overall capacities do not apply

As stated in Section 1.1, there are certain sports grounds – including, for example, those staging horse racing or golfing events – where it may not be appropriate to calculate the overall capacity of the whole ground.

Such grounds may contain large areas of open land to which entry by members of the public is not controlled, and where spectators may view the event from areas not strictly designed as viewing accommodation.

In such cases, the capacities of individual, enclosed sections of viewing accommodation must still be calculated, and the number entering each section strictly controlled and monitored (see Chapter 6).

Furthermore, although not required to calculate the capacity of the open-access areas, it is still the responsibility of ground management to ensure the safety of spectators in those parts of the ground at all times during the event.

Chapter Two

Management –
Responsibility and planning for safety

2.1 Management responsibility for safety

As emphasised in the Introduction, responsibility for the safety of spectators at sports grounds lies at all times with the ground management.

The management will normally be either the owner or lessee of the ground, who may not necessarily be the promoter of the event.

Representatives of the local authority, together with police, fire and ambulance officers, should – preferably through a co-ordinated approach – advise management on how to discharge this responsibility and, in certain circumstances, may require measures to be taken in order to achieve reasonable safety standards. This does not, however, exonerate the ground management from its responsibility for the safety of spectators.

2.2 Demonstrating that responsibility

Safety should not be seen as a set of rules or conditions imposed by others, but rather as standards set from within which reflect a safety culture at the ground.

A positive attitude demonstrated by the ground management is therefore crucial in ensuring that safety policies are carried out effectively and willingly.

2.3 Meeting that responsibility

The detailed management responsibilities described in this chapter and referred to in later chapters fall into the following basic categories, each of which management should address in establishing a safety management structure:

a. **Legislation:**
   Management should be aware of:

   i.   the requirements of the safety certificate (if applicable)

   ii.   Safety of Sports Grounds legislation

   iii. fire safety legislation

   iv.   Health and Safety at Work legislation

   v.   legislation relating to people with disabilities

   vi.   any other specific pieces of legislation that may have relevant safety implications.

b. **Staffing:**
Management should:

    i.   identify those to whom it intends to allocate safety duties

    ii.   draw up job descriptions for all posts holding safety duties and resource such posts

    iii.   appoint a safety officer and deputy

    iv.   ensure all safety-related posts are held by appropriately trained and competent persons.

c. **Planning**
Management should:

    i.   draw up a written safety policy for spectators

    ii.   draw up contingency plans

    iii.   agree an emergency procedure plan

    iv.   agree a statement of intent

    v.   agree procedures for accommodating all categories of spectators, including children, semi-ambulant and disabled people, and, where appropriate, supporters of visiting clubs.

d. **Monitoring and records**
Management should:

    i.   using standard forms, record all incidents and circumstances which have the potential to cause accidents, and monitor subsequent remedial actions

    ii.   conduct periodic safety audits and reviews

    iii.   ensure that no other management decisions or policies compromise safety at the sports ground

    iv.   maintain records of each event in respect of the event, stewarding, the fabric of the ground and first aid and medical provision.

e. **Risk assessment**
Throughout the *Guide* reference is made to the need for management to conduct risk assessments (see for example Sections 15.2 and 16.17).

Although risk assessment may be a relatively new area of responsibility at sports grounds, responsible managements will already carry out *de facto* risk assessments on a day-to-day basis as part of their routine safety management procedures. They will come across faults as they appear and take the necessary corrective actions.

Risk assessment requires this process to be approached more systematically, and for the results to be recorded.

It is recommended that the assessments should be undertaken by competent persons with the appropriate skills and experience. Specialist advice may need to be sought, but members of the management's safety team should contribute their own experience and knowledge of the ground being assessed, including its operation during events.

The intention of risk assessment is not to impose a bureaucratic burden upon management but to encourage the formulation of practical and systematic action plans to reduce the level of risk to spectators.

As stated in Section 2.5, risk assessments will also be required as part of the management's responsibility to employees, under Health and Safety at Work legislation.

Risk assessment should consist of the following steps:

i.   to identify hazards to which spectators may be exposed

ii.   to determine the level of risk to which spectators may be subject from the hazards identified

iii.   to assess whether existing safety management procedures (including staff training) are adequate to eliminate the hazards, where possible, and where this is not possible, to reduce the risk to an acceptable level

iv.   to plan preventative and/or protective measures

v.   to assess and review the adequacy and effectiveness of such measures.

It is recommended that when conducting risk assessments, management should consult with the relevant authorities. Further guidance is also available from the Health and Safety Executive (see Bibliography).

2.4   Safety management and the (S) factor

As explained in Section 1.4, the assessment of a ground's capacity should take into account the quality of safety management – that is, the (S) factor. An important indicator to be used when determining the (S) factor is the standard to which the safety management structure, as outlined in this chapter, is implemented.

For example, it is not enough to have a written safety policy for spectators. That policy must be fully implemented and understood by all staff. Similarly, a safety officer may have a detailed job description, but may fail to meet its requirements on event days. Contingency plans may have been drawn up, but never tested.

If all the management's safety-related responsibilities are fully met, and the stewarding is of a high standard (see Chapter 3), an (S) factor of 1.0 should be applied. Where there are deficiencies in any aspect of the safety management, the (S) factor should be reduced accordingly. If appropriate, the (S) factor could be set as low as 0.0, and therefore the capacity of the area in question will be zero.

Management should therefore be aware that its own performance in safety-related matters will have a direct effect on the calculation of the sports ground's capacity.

2.5 Health and Safety at Work legislation

The safety management of a sports ground and its spectators should not be viewed in isolation, but as part of a total, integrated system for managing health and safety within the organisation as a whole (see Bibliography).

In particular, ground management should be aware of two complementary requirements:

a. written statement of policy

Under Health and Safety at Work legislation, organisations with five or more employees must prepare a written statement of their general policy, organisation and arrangements for health and safety at work. While the legislation and its accompanying guidance concentrate on employees, there is an added clause requiring provision for 'other persons resorting to the premises'. This may include contracted staff and media personnel (see Chapters 3 and 19).

b. risk assessment

Regulation 3 of the Management of Health and Safety at Work Regulations 1992 requires all employers to assess the risk to workers and any others who may be affected by their undertakings. In carrying out such a risk assessment ground management may find it helpful to utilise the recommendations of this *Guide*. (See also Section 2.3.e.)

2.6 A written safety policy for spectators

Every ground management should have in place a written safety policy for spectators. (In effect, this policy will be an extension of that drawn up in respect of employees under the Health and Safety at Work legislation referred to in Section 2.5 above.)

Such a policy demonstrates that management has devoted thought and effort towards the safety and welfare of spectators. Having to write down the policy helps concentrate the mind. It also shows whether the policy has been fully thought out in practical terms.

The safety policy should:

a.   explain the management's safety objectives and the means of achieving them

b.   be agreed by the management and disseminated and explained to all members of staff, contract staff, part-time and voluntary workers

c.   demonstrate that from the highest level of management downwards there is a positive attitude to public safety

d.   be reviewed by management on an annual basis and revised as necessary.

It is important that the safety policy does not conflict with any conditions of the sports ground's safety certificate (where applicable). For this reason, consultation with the certifying authority is recommended in the formulation of a safety policy.

2.7   Drawing up a safety policy document

The safety policy document should clearly indicate:

a.   the ground management's philosophy on safety

b.   with whom lies ultimate responsibility for safety at the ground

c.   to whom responsibility is delegated

d.   the chain of command

e.   how the safety policy is to be implemented and communicated

f.   how the safety policy is to be audited, by internal or external means, and reviewed.

Advice on how a safety policy document can be drawn up is available from the Football Licensing Authority and the Health and Safety Executive (see Bibliography).

2.8   Chain of command

In order for the ground management's safety policy to be implemented, it is essential that the policy outlines a personnel structure, or chain of command. This is to ensure that:

a.   those having to implement the policy recognise their role within the chain of command and have a clear understanding of the decision-making process in safety matters

b.   ground management is able to control and supervise the safety management operation

c.   spectator safety at the event can be quickly and accurately monitored

d.   liaison with other agencies follows agreed procedures

e.   follow-up action on structural or safety management issues can be co-ordinated efficiently.

2.9   Appointing a safety officer

Ground management should appoint a safety officer. This person must be given a detailed job description, clearly identifying the functions of his or her post. It is essential that a safety officer is not given any additional duties on an event day which might reduce his or her effectiveness in the principal role. Nor should the safety officer take on such duties during an event.

Although the appointment of a safety officer may be on a part-time basis, experience has shown that employment on event days only can result in too onerous a workload.

If it is judged that the safety officer cannot, for any reason, carry out his or her duties in full and effectively, the (S) factor should be reduced.

2.10 **Requirements of a safety officer**

In order to discharge properly his or her responsibilities, a safety officer should meet the following requirements:

a. **Competence**

A person will be regarded as competent for the role of safety officer when he or she has sufficient training and experience, or knowledge, to be able to implement the functions required, as detailed in the job description.

b. **Status**

On event days, a safety officer should be able to establish his or her status in the chain of command, in relation to all staff and safety personnel, and, where applicable, in relation to representatives of the emergency services. On non-event days, the safety officer should be regarded as a principal adviser to the ground management on all spectator-related safety issues.

c. **Authority**

On event days, a safety officer should have the authority to make safety-related decisions without having to refer to senior management or board members.

d. **Accountablity and access to management**

A safety officer should be accountable to the most senior management, to whom the right of direct access is essential.

e. **Identification and communication**

On event days it is essential that the safety officer is easily identifiable, and can be contacted immediately at all times. If it is necessary during an event for the safety officer to leave the control point (see Chapter 16), a competent person should be left on duty in the control point. The safety officer should also remain in direct contact with that person, either by radio or mobile telephone.

2.11 **Deputising**

Because of the key role played by a safety officer, it is essential that he or she has a suitably trained and competent deputy, to serve in the safety officer's absence and to share duties on event days.

Deputies should also be appointed for other key supervisory roles in the chain of command.

2.12 **Staffing numbers**

While members of the public are inside the sports ground, it is the responsibility of management to ensure that sufficient safety staff are on duty.

Staffing numbers will vary considerably at each ground, according to its size and configuration, and the nature of the event. However, experience has shown that by ensuring the availability of staff for the following categories, management should meet the needs of most sports grounds, matches or events:

a.   Supervisory staff; for example, the deputy safety officer, chief steward(s) and supervisors

b.   Static posts; for example, crowd monitoring points, exits, fire points, pitch perimeter gates or openings, and other strategic points or areas

c.   Stewards; typically a ratio of one per 250 of the anticipated attendance

d.   Specialist stewards; for example, for areas used by children or spectators with disabilities

e.   Additional stewards: needed for deployment in particular circumstances or for particular events.

Other staff, such as car park attendants and turnstile operators, may also be deployed for stewarding and other safety duties, provided that the conditions set out in Section 3.3 are met.

However, unless they form a recognised part of the safety management structure, individuals such as members of ground staff, security guards, hospitality staff and commissionaires should not be counted among the safety staff.

Further information on stewarding is provided in Chapter 3.

2.13   Responsibility for training and competency

Ground management has the responsibility for ensuring that all safety personnel (not only stewards) receive sufficient training to enable them to carry out the duties and responsibilities assigned to them.

Stewards in particular should be trained to a recognised national standard.

At sports grounds where safety personnel from an outside agency are on duty, it is still the ground management's responsibility to ensure that such personnel have also been trained to carry out the duties and responsibilities assigned to them, to a recognised national standard.

2.14   Contingency plans

Ground management should assess the risk of any incident occurring at the sports ground which might prejudice public safety or disrupt normal operations; for example, fire, power cuts, bomb threats, delayed starts or crowd disorder. (For a suggested list of headings, see Section 2.15.)

Such incidents often arise with little or no warning and may not be capable of being dealt with by the management resment operating under normal conditions. Management should therefore prepare contingency plans to determine specific actions and/or the mobilisation of specialist resources.

Contingency plans should lay down a structured and graduated response with clear guidelines on the measures to be adopted in particular circumstances, bearing in mind both internal and external factors specific to the individual sports ground.

Exercises should be staged at least once a year to test contingency plans in consultation with the relevant authorities and emergency services.

The procedures set out within contingency plans should be made familiar to all staff at the sports ground, not only to those with specific safety-related duties.

Guidance on contingency planning for football clubs is available from the Football Licensing Authority (see Bibliography).

2.15 Suggested headings for contingency plans

The contents of contingency plans will vary according to the type of sports ground, its location and the nature of matches or events being staged. However, experience has shown that the following headings can be adopted to suit most situations:

a. Fire

b. Bomb threat, suspect package

c. Buildings and services

     i.   damage to structures
     ii.   power cut or failure
     iii. gas leak or chemical incident

d. Safety equipment failure

     i.   turnstile counting mechanism
     ii.   closed circuit television
     iii. public address system
     iv. electronic information boards
     v.   stewards' radio system
     vi. internal telephone systems

e. Crowd control

     i.   surging or crushing
     ii.   pitch incursion
     iii. late arrivals or delayed start
     iv. lock-outs
     v.   disorder inside the ground
     vi. large-scale ticket forgery

f. Emergency evacuation

g. Ticketing strategy in the event of an abandoned fixture

h. Features/considerations specific to the location.

2.16 Emergency plan

An emergency plan (also known as an emergency procedure plan or major incident plan) is prepared and owned by the emergency services for dealing with a major incident occurring at the sports ground or in the vicinity (for example, an explosion, toxic release or large fire).

Although contingency plans are prepared by the ground management and the emergency plan is prepared by the emergency services, the two plans should be compatible.

Consultation should therefore take place between ground management, the police, fire and ambulance services, the local health authority and local authority, in order to produce an agreed plan of action, including access for emergency vehicles, for all foreseeable incidents (see also Section 18.8).

2.17 Safety audit

In addition to the inspections and tests recommended in Chapter 4 and the routine monitoring of safety performance through inspection and surveillance, it is the responsibility of management to ensure that a safety audit is carried out at least once a year. The intention of an audit is to make a deeper and more critical appraisal of all elements of the safety management systems.

Such audits should be conducted by persons who are, preferably, independent of the systems being audited, but who may be from within the organisation.

When assessing the (S) factor of a sports ground, the relevant authority may wish to be aware of the safety audit report.

2.18 Keeping records for each event

Management is responsible for keeping records of each event, including:

a.   details of all pre-event inspections (as listed in Sections 4.9 and 4.10)

b.   details of the pre-event briefing given to stewards and, where appropriate, training (see 3.11)

c.   the number of spectators admitted to the ground, and, where appropriate, to each section of the ground (see Chapter 6)

d.   the numbers and posts of all first aiders and doctor(s) in attendance (see Chapter 18)

e.   incident forms recording any accident or incident which might have led to an accident (see 3.13 and 18.9)

f.   details of all first aid or medical treatment provided, while preserving medical confidentiality regarding the identity of those treated (see 18.9)

g.   details of all emergency drills or evacuation exercises

h.   details of any non-routine opening of an exit door or gate

i.   details of any assumption of control by the police

j.   details of any defects relating to the safety of the ground arising from the event, plus details of any remedial action taken

k.   details of all fire alarms sounding, whether or not activated by an automatic fire detection system.

The above list is for guidance only and is not intended to be comprehensive in all circumstances.

2.19   Policing

While responsibility for the safety of spectators lies at all times with ground management, at certain sports grounds and for certain matches or events the presence of the police may be required to maintain public order and prevent the commission of offences.

Management should give all possible assistance to the police and provide reasonable facilities for the police within the control point.

Dependent on the sports ground it may be beneficial to provide other additional facilities, such as a detention room and an area for briefing.

Where a police presence is required, the number and disposition of the police shall be determined by the Chief Police Officer in whose area the ground is located.

However, the determination of policing resources may be influenced by the quality of the ground management's own safety structure, and the management's proven ability to discharge effectively their safety responsibilities.

If the management's own safety structure is inadequate, the capacity should be reduced accordingly, as explained in Section 2.4. The presence of police officers on an event basis should not in itself be a justification for raising a ground's capacity.

Whether there is a police presence or not, responsibility for the enforcement of ground regulations remains with the management.

2.20   Statement of intent

If there is to be a police presence in or at the sports ground, management should discuss with the police the division of responsibilities and functions between the two parties; for example, whether particular posts are to be staffed by stewards or by police officers, and who will assume responsibility in particular circumstances.

The outcome of these discussions should be recorded in a statement of intent.

It is emphasised that the statement of intent is a management statement and not a legal document.

2.21 Accommodating visiting supporters

At sports grounds where supporters of visiting clubs attend, advance planning between the ground management, the visiting club and the police is essential to ensure that such supporters are:

a. directed and welcomed to the ground

b. directed to the appropriate entrances

c. accommodated safely

d. always kept clearly informed of any special arrangements made for them inside the ground and on their departure.

Liaison between the management and police may be necessary to ensure that the likely numbers of visiting supporters is known. In consultation with the police, management should also determine clear policies on the accommodation of home and visiting groups of supporters, and on appropriate ticketing arrangements, There should be debriefing meetings to evaluate these arrangements and, if necessary, formulate changes for future events.

2.22 Segregation

If ground management adopts a policy of segregating groups of supporters, the arrangements for admitting spectators should be drawn up in consultation with the local authority and police, and be carefully controlled to ensure as far as possible that segregation is effective.

Where considered necessary, a neutral or sterile zone may be provided between groups of supporters. However, in all cases it is recommended that the method of segregation used should be flexible (see Section 11.17).

Management should ensure that each segregated area offers full access to toilet and catering facilities. It should not be necessary for spectators in segregated areas to cross barriers or seek special permission to use such facilities (see also Chapter 8).

2.23 Ejection and detention

Ground management should, in consultation with the police, draw up clearly defined procedures for the ejection and/or detention of spectators who commit offences within the sports ground. There should be adequate vehicular access for the unobtrusive removal of detainees.

2.24 Safety in the wider management context

As stated in Section 2.2 safety should not be seen as a set of rules or conditions imposed by others, but as standards set from within which reflect a safety culture at the ground. In addition, the safety management of a ground and its spectators should not be viewed in isolation.

By a process of consultation, therefore, all branches of the ground management and event day personnel should be aware, or be made aware, of the safety implications arising from their own actions and policies.

The main areas of policy are outlined in the following four sections.

2.25 Ticketing

Ticketing policies adopted by the ground management can have a direct effect on the safe management of spectators.

a. where a capacity or near-capacity attendance is expected for an event, admission should normally be by ticket only

b. tickets for seats which offer restricted views or are uncovered should be marked accordingly, and the buyer forewarned (see Sections 11.4, 11.6 and 12.12–12.14)

c. tickets for seats with severely restricted views should not be sold

d. that part of the ticket retained by the spectator after passing through a ticket control point or turnstile should clearly identify the location of the accommodation for which it has been issued

e. a simplified, understandable ground plan should be shown on the reverse side

f. colour coding of tickets, corresponding to different sections of the ground, should be considered (see also Sections 6.9 and 16.29)

g. stewards should be familiar with the ground plan and able to direct spectators to any other section of the ground (see Chapter 3)

h. management should ensure that all sections of the ground, all aisles, rows and individual seats, are clearly marked or numbered, as per the ground plan and ticketing information.

For further details of ticket-related matters, see Sections 6.10 and 11.17.

2.26 Sale of refreshments

In order to ensure that circulation areas are kept clear of trip hazards, and to minimise the risk of fire, adequate receptacles should be available for the disposal and collection of all waste and litter resulting from the sale of refreshments.

All refreshments sold in general spectator areas should be served in soft containers. This is because hard containers such as glasses, bottles or cans can constitute a danger in congested areas, and may even be used as missiles.

Hot drinks should be dispensed in suitable containers, so as to minimise the risk of scalding or burns to spectators.

2.27   Alcohol

The possession and consumption of alcohol is controlled by current legislation (see Bibliography) at the following sports grounds:

Any ground in England and Wales used for an international association football match, or for a match involving a Premier League or Football League club, and;

Any ground in Scotland used for an international association football or Rugby Union match, or by clubs in the Scottish Football League and Highland League.

At these grounds it is an offence to:

a.   possess alcohol or to be drunk whilst entering, or trying to enter, the ground

b.   to be drunk inside the ground

c.   in general spectator areas, to possess alcohol in any part of the ground that offers sight of the pitch during the period commencing two hours before the start of the match and finishing one hour after the end of the match

d.   in hospitality boxes and other rooms which overlook the pitch, to possess alcohol during the period commencing 15 minutes before the start of the match and finishing 15 minutes after the end of the match

e.   to be in possession of bottles, cans or other portable containers which are for holding drink and which, when empty, are normally thrown away or returned to the supplier and which are capable of causing injury to a person struck by them. This applies to any spectator entering or trying to enter the ground, and any spectators in any area of the ground from which the event may be directly viewed.

2.28   Commercial or non-sporting activities

Management has a direct responsibility to ensure that commercial or non-sporting activities do not in any way compromise safety at the ground, either by creating any physical obstructions, hindering the safety operation or endangering spectators.

Areas of concern include:

a.   advertising hoardings, loudspeakers, media installations or any other item, permanent or temporary, whose height, bulk or placement might obstruct sightlines and/or block emergency gates or openings

b.   high volume and lengthy musical presentations which interrupt normal communications between safety personnel at key moments

c.   firework and other pyrotechnic presentations

d.   excitation of a structure by the activities of spectators (see Section 4.5).

Guidance on the safety implications of media provision is provided in Chapter 19. The use of grounds for events other than sporting events is covered in Chapter 20.

2.29   Other management responsibilities

In addition to the responsibilities for safety outlined in this and the following two chapters on management, the attention of ground management is also drawn to the following:

a.   the requirements of fire safety (see Chapter 15)

b.   first aid and medical provision (see Chapter 18)

c.   the specific requirements and criteria of particular international and national sporting bodies and tournament organisers. Note, however, that the advice in the *Guide* should take precedence over such requirements and criteria.

2.30   Notifying the certifying authority

If a safety certificate has been issued in respect of the sports ground or stand(s) within the ground, the management should ensure that details of all consultations, arrangements and plans between them and the police, fire, ambulance services and with the local health authority are notified to the certifying authority.

Chapter Three

Management – Stewarding

3.1 The need for stewards

Effective safety management requires the employment, hire or contracting of stewards in order to assist with the circulation of spectators, prevent overcrowding, reduce the likelihood and incidence of disorder, and provide the means to investigate, report and take early action in an emergency. In carrying out these duties, stewards should always be aware of, and ensure the care, comfort and well-being of, all categories of spectators.

3.2 Agreement on responsibilities

Where an event requires the presence of police officers, the duties and responsibilities of stewards should be agreed between the ground management and the police. This agreement should form part of the written statement of intent (see Section 2.20).

3.3 Definition of a steward

A steward (also referred to at certain sports grounds as a marshal) is a person trained, or being trained, to a recognised national standard, employed or contracted by management to act in accordance with the general recommendations of the *Guide*, and, where appropriate, the specific requirements of the safety certificate.

As stated in Section 2.12, other staff, such as car park attendants and turnstile operators, may also be deployed for stewarding and safety duties, provided that:

a.   they have received training to a recognised national standard (see Sections 3.6, 3.15 and 3.16)

b.   are appropriately attired and equipped

c.   minimum stewarding numbers are maintained at all times.

Individuals such as members of ground staff, security guards, hospitality staff and commissionaires should not be considered as stewards, unless suitably trained.

3.4 Appointment of stewards

Stewards should be fit, active, aged not less than 18, and preferably not over 55, and have the character and temperament to carry out the duties required of them.

Applicants should be interviewed and, where necessary, tested before appointment to ascertain that they meet these requirements.

3.5 Stewards' status and remuneration

Although stewards are appointed on a part-time basis, they are an integral part of the safety management team, a status which should be made known to them and reinforced by the positive attitude of ground management.

Experience shows that the standard and quality which management can expect from stewards is likely to be linked to the remuneration and general level of consideration they receive. This may affect not only the stewards' performance on event days but also their willingness to attend training sessions.

Stewards' responsibilities are considerable, and at times onerous. The level of payment should reflect this. In return, management can expect a higher standard of applicant and a greater level of commitment.

3.6 Duties of stewards

While these may vary, depending on the size and configuration of the ground and the nature of the event, the basic duties of stewards (whether directly employed, hired or contracted) should be to enforce the management's safety policy, the requirements of the safety certificate, where appplicable, and all ground regulations.

There are ten basic duties for stewards, summarised as follows:

a. to understand their general responsibilities towards the health and safety of all categories of spectators (including those with disabilities and children), other stewards, ground staff and themselves

b. to carry out pre-event safety checks

c. to control or direct spectators who are entering or leaving the ground, to help achieve an even flow of people in, to and from the viewing areas

d. to assist in the safe operation of the ground, not to view the activity taking place

e. to staff entrances, exits and other strategic points; for example, segregation, perimeter and exit doors or gates which are not continuously secured in the open position while the ground is in use

f. to recognise crowd conditions so as to ensure the safe dispersal of spectators and the prevention of overcrowding, particularly on terraces or viewing slopes

g. to assist the emergency services as required

h. to provide basic emergency first aid

i. to respond to emergencies (such as the early stages of a fire); to raise the alarm and take the necessary immediate action

j. to undertake specific duties in an emergency or as directed by the safety officer or the appropriate emergency service officer.

This list is for guidance only and is not intended as a substitute for training leading to a recognised national standard. For details of such training and further references for stewards' duties, see Bibliography.

3.7 Code of conduct for stewards

Stewards are representatives of the management, and during many events are the only point of contact between the management and the public. It is therefore recommended that management draw up a code of conduct for all stewards.

A code of conduct might include the following matters:

a. Stewards should at all times be polite, courteous and helpful to all spectators, regardless of their affiliations.

b. Stewards should at all times be smartly dressed. Their appearance should be clean and tidy.

c. Stewards are not employed, hired or contracted to watch the event. They should at all times concentrate on their duties and responsibilities.

d. Stewards should never:

    i. wear any team colours while on duty

    ii. celebrate or show extreme reaction to the sporting event

    iii. be seen eating, drinking or smoking in view of the public

    iv. consume alcohol before or during the event

    v. use obscene or offensive language.

3.8 Control and communication

The stewarding operation should be co-ordinated from the ground's control point, which should maintain an efficient means of communication with the stewards and/or their supervisors (see Chapter 16).

3.9 Identification

Experience shows that spectators react more favourably towards stewards who are readily identifiable. It is also important that stewards are easily identifiable by fellow stewards and safety personnel. All stewards should therefore be provided with high-visibility, weather-proof jackets or tabards. Armbands are not acceptable.

The stewards' jackets or tabards should clearly indicate the duty performed by the steward; for example, safety officer, chief steward, supervisor, steward or car park steward.

The jacket or tabard should also carry a number, by which each steward can be identified.

3.10 Visiting stewards

There are certain matches or events where it may be beneficial to invite stewards from visiting clubs or organisations. It is recommended that such stewards arrive before the ground is open to the public and in time to be fully briefed as to the construction and configuration of the ground, the safety arrangements and their specific duties.

It is emphasised that the role of visiting stewards is to assist the home stewards and not to replace them.

3.11 Briefing

The briefing of stewards forms a necessary component of effective safety management. Arrangements for this will vary according to the number of stewards involved. If the total number does not exceed 50 it may be possible for all stewards to be briefed together, by the safety officer or chief steward. Where there are more than 50 stewards on duty, experience shows that it may be more beneficial to conduct briefing sessions in smaller groups. In such cases, the safety officer or chief steward would brief supervisors, who would then brief their individual sections.

An accurate record of briefings should be kept. For this reason it is recommended that they are scripted by the safety officer and retained with the post-event summary (see also Sections 2.3.d and 2.18).

3.12 De-briefing

A de-brief of stewards is also necessary, to ensure that any incidents or problems are referred to the safety officer for follow-up action. As advised in Section 3.11 above, the arrangements for the de-briefing will vary according to the number of stewards involved.

As part of the de-briefing procedure, incident forms should be completed by stewards and handed to the supervisor, chief steward or safety officer.

3.13 Stewards' documentation – safety handbook

Every steward should be fully appraised in writing of his or her duties and responsibilities. This can be achieved by the issue of a safety handbook.

A suggested list of headings is as follows:

a.   introduction to the sports ground; its lay-out and management

b.   general requirements of stewards

c.   communication and radio call signs

d.   duties before event

e.   duties during event

f.   duties after event

g.   emergency procedures

h. training

i. contingency plans (see Section 2.15 for headings)

j. ground regulations

k. fire precautions and fire-fighting

l. specific responsibilities (according to rank or duties)

m. code of conduct

n. plans of ground

o. positioning of key point telephones and fire safety points

p. notes.

3.14 Stewards' documentation – check list

The duties and responsibilities of a steward should also be summarised on a simple check list or 'aide-memoire' card, to be issued to all stewards for carrying during the event. The contents of this check list should follow a standard format, as established in the Safety Handbook. All such stewards' documentation should be available for inspection.

3.15 Training

It is the responsibility of management to ensure that training and supervision is provided so that all stewards, whether regular or casual, are competent to carry out their duties. Training should ensure that stewards and their supervisors are fully aware of, and practiced in, the part they are to play in the management's contingency plans. Awareness of the needs of disabled spectators and children should also form part of the training programme.

Training should be conducted by competent persons, and ideally take place at the sports ground.

During the training programme, stewards need to be assessed to measure their competence. The responsibility for this lies with management, who may wish to use outside assessors. If the assessment is carried out by the safety officer, every effort should be made to maintain records and standards that would satisfy any outside body's accreditation of the management's training system.

When considering training programmes, reference may be made to the publications referred to in the Bibliography.

3.16 Training exercises

Exercises should be carried out on a regular basis, and at least annually, to ensure that procedures laid out in the contingency plans operate smoothly. Records should be kept of the duration of the exercise, of the instruction provided and of the personnel involved. At least 14 days' notice of the intention to hold such exercises should be given to the relevant authority (if a safety certificate is in force), and the emergency services.

3.17 Keeping records

It is important to retain an accurate record of all training sessions, assessments and briefings. In addition, a records or profile form should be maintained of each steward. The type of information to be recorded should include:

a. name, age, address, and contact numbers

b. relevant professional qualifications (for example, fire-fighter or first aider)

c. training sessions attended

d. matches or events attended

e. duties or position in the ground for each event

f. assessment of progress.

Such records should be readily available for inspection by authorised persons.

3.18 Stewarding and the (S) factor

As explained in Sections 1.4 and 2.4 the assessment of a sports ground's capacity should take into account the quality of safety management – that is, the (S) factor.

An important indicator to be used when determining the (S) factor is the standard of stewarding.

It is the responsibility of management to assess the stewarding, and, where a safety certificate is in place, agree that assessment with the certifying authority. The assessment should be based on the requirements outlined in this chapter.

Where the safety management structure meets the requirements set out in Chapter 2, and the stewarding is of a high standard, an (S) factor of 1.0 should be applied. Where the stewarding is poor – for example, there are insufficient numbers of stewards in attendance or stewards are not attending to their duties – the (S) factor should be reduced.

Records should be carefully kept so that:

a. deficiencies which have been identified and recorded can be acted upon and the stewarding operation improved, thereby increasing the (S) factor

b. further deficiencies can be identified and monitored, thereby possibly entailing a reduction in the (S) factor.

Chapter Four

Management –
Structures, installations and components

4.1   Definitions

For the purpose of this *Guide* the term structures includes seated and standing accommodation, whether permanent or temporary, roofs, floodlight pylons, stairways, barriers, boundary walls and fences.

Examples of installations include mechanical and electrical systems, public address systems and fire detection systems.

Examples of components include seats, signs, fixtures and fittings.

4.2   Maintenance and the (P) factor

As stated in Sections 1.4 and 1.5, it is the responsibility of management to assess the (P) factor for each section of viewing accommodation, and, where a safety certificate is in place, agree those assessments with the certifying authority. An important indicator to be used when determining the (P) factor is the standard of maintenance.

If all structures, installations and safety-related components at the ground are maintained in good condition and working order, a (P) factor of 1.0 should be applied.

Where there are deficiencies, the (P) factor should be reduced accordingly.

If appropriate, the (P) factor could be set as low as 0.0, and therefore the capacity of the area in question will be zero.

It is imperative therefore that maintenance procedures for both new and existing structures are properly understood. It is further recommended that a system of planned maintenance be adopted. Where necessary, professional advice on this matter should be sought from competent persons.

It is also essential that maintenance is carried out in accordance with the written instructions provided by the designer or manufacturer.

> **For new construction:** the provision of maintenance manuals detailing the expected life-cycles of components should be a necessary part of the completion of any new project. This is notwithstanding any separate tests and inspection periods which may be recommended below or form part of the annual inspection.
>
> The maintenance of new structures may be as onerous as, or even more onerous than, that of existing structures. Management should be aware that the provision of a new structure does not reduce its responsibility for the maintenance of a safe structure.

4.3 Good housekeeping

In addition to maintenance, several of the recommendations listed in this chapter might otherwise be described as elements of 'good housekeeping'.

As stated in Section 2.2, it is emphasised that safety should not be seen as a set of rules or conditions imposed by others, but rather as standards set from within which reflect a safety culture at the sports ground.

Good housekeeping is a fundamental part of fostering and maintaining a safety culture at the sports ground.

Management should therefore demonstrate a positive attitude in this respect and, in doing so, encourage a conscientious, co-operative and vigilant attitude among all members of staff.

In particular, all staff should be encouraged to identify and report to management at an early stage any problem which might compromise safety, be it relating to the structures at the ground, its systems, facilities or equipment.

Their efforts and, if appropriate, suggestions, should always be acknowledged, and they should be informed of any resultant remedial action.

Wherever practical and appropriate, this positive attitude towards good housekeeping should also be communicated to spectators, visiting personnel and outside contractors (see also Section 4.6).

4.4 Structures

All structures at sports grounds should be safe, serviceable and durable at all times during their use and, where necessary, fire-resistant. They should comply with statutory requirements, including those for health and safety at work.

In order to be safe, structures should be capable of resisting all loads imposed by their foreseeable use (including non-sporting use), with adequate margins of safety.

Specialist advice from chartered engineers with the appropriate skills and experience should be sought to assess the adequacy of all load-bearing elements in a sports ground.

Designers should pay particular attention both to minimising the risk of progressive or disproportionate collapse from unforeseen incidents, and to the dynamic response of structures (see also Sections 4.5, 14.4 and 14.5). In doing so, designers should:

a.   systematically assess conceivable hazards to structures and design the structures to be stable and robust in the light of a risk assessment

b.   adopt structural forms which minimise the effects of the hazards identified

c.   provide ground management with manuals which define the key elements and components of the structure requiring regular inspection and maintenance.

4.5   Structural dynamics for permanent structures

In addition to the ability to resist static loading, structures at sports grounds may also need to resist dynamic loading. Permanent structures particularly sensitive to dynamic loading include those with long spanning or cantilevered seating decks.

In such cases, specialist advice from chartered engineers with the appropriate skills and experience should be sought to assess the dynamic behaviour of the structure.

Dynamic load effects may be caused by:

a.   Excitation by wind.

b.   Excitation by the activities of spectators. Where a seating deck has a vertical frequency of less than 6 Hz or a sway frequency of less than 3 Hz, a dynamic evaluation of the structure should be carried out, giving due consideration to the mass of the spectators.

c.   Excitation by the activities of spectators at grounds staging pop concerts or other events involving rhythmic activity, in which case the design loads may be greater than for category (b) above (see also Chapter 20).

References to the structural dynamics of temporary demountable structures can be found in Chapter 14.

4.6   Construction work at existing grounds

It is the responsibility of management to ensure that construction work taking place at an existing ground does not prejudice the safety of spectators occupying any part of the ground during an event.

The management should also ensure that any partly constructed structure, if brought into use before completion, complies with the recommendations of the *Guide*.

4.7   Anti-vandalism

Precautions should be taken to prevent people from climbing on to roofs, pylons, hoardings and other structures. Where possible such structures should be fitted with unclimbable devices; for example, stout barriers or close-boarded enclosures.

Where fitted, anti-vandal devices such as spikes and barbed wire should preferably be fitted at least 2.4m from the base of the structure.

Spikes or other similar devices should not be installed on pitch perimeter fences (see Section 10.16).

4.8   The importance of inspections and tests

Regular and detailed inspections and tests are a necessary and important function of safety management. Where applicable, they are also an essential part of the safety certification process.

Inspections and tests should seek to eliminate or minimise the potential risks to spectators and staff, and to ensure that all structures, installations and items of equipment are safe and fit for the purpose for which they were intended.

As outlined in this chapter, it is the responsibilty of management to:

a.   ensure that proper maintenance is carried out

b.   encourage attitudes and establish procedures which lead to good housekeeping

c.   draw up and adhere to a programme of inspections and tests

d.   ensure that such inspections and tests are carried out by suitably qualified persons

e.   record the details of inspections, tests and any remedial work carried out, including the dates of completion

f.   allocate adequate resources to carry out these tasks.

It should be noted that the guidance on inspections and tests which follows refers only to structures, installations and components. Inspections and tests concerning such matters as stewarding, fire safety, first aid and medical provision are covered in the relevant chapters.

It should also be noted that the lists which follow are for guidance only and are not intended to be comprehensive or applicable to all sports grounds. Nor is any order of importance intended.

For further references relating to inspections and tests, see Bibliography.

4.9   Inspections and tests 24 hours before an event

Management should ensure that at least 24 hours before each event, the following structures, installations and components are inspected and tested by competent persons, and the test results recorded.

a.   automatic fire detection and fire warning systems, including repeater panels (see Section 15.12)

b.   stewards' radio systems (see 16.10)

c.   emergency telephones (see 16.12)

d.   public address system and back-up loud hailers (see 16.13)

e.   closed circuit television system (see 16.15)

f.   video or electronic information boards (see 16.22)

g.   auxiliary power supplies (see 17.11)

h.   emergency lighting systems (see 17.13)

i.   temporary television camera platforms and gantries and other media installations (see 19.3).

If any of the above systems are not operating properly and if the faults cannot be rectified before the event, contingency plans (see Sections 2.14 and 2.15) should provide for the use of acceptable substitute measures or, if necessary, the closure of the relevant areas of spectator accommodation.

4.10   Inspections and tests before an event

Management should ensure that before each event, structures, installations and components are inspected and tested by competent persons, to check that:

a.   all structures are free from any damage, corrosion or deformation which might create a potential danger to the public

b.   exit doors, emergency exit doors, gates and pitch perimeter gates, whether operated manually or electronically, are functioning (see Sections 9.15 and 9.16)

c.   all entry and exit routes are clear of obstruction, free from trip hazards, and their surfaces are not slippery; and all such routes can be safely and effectively used (see Chapters 5 and 9)

d.   turnstiles and metering or entry monitoring systems are functioning (see Chapter 6)

e.   there are no accumulations of combustible waste or litter, particularly in voids and other areas vulnerable to fire; and all areas to which the public have access are generally clean

f.   containers used to store combustible waste or litter are secure (see 15.9)

g.   hazardous materials have been removed, or safely stored, well away from public areas (see 15.9)

h.   fire-fighting equipment is in position and in good order (see 15.15)

i.   areas to which public access is prohibited are appropriately locked or sealed off

j.   where appropriate, the ground does not contain any accessible items which could be used as missiles

k.   directional signs are in place and, where appropriate, illuminated (see 16.27)

l.   temporary signs and fittings are secure and in their appropriate positions

m.   cutting equipment for pitch perimeter fences is in place (see 10.16).

In each case, if problems are identified, remedial action should be taken before the public is allowed access to the affected area.

4.11   Inspections during the event

During an event, management should ensure that:

a.   litter and waste are not allowed to accumulate, and are removed to secure containers whenever possible

b.   materials are not allowed to accumulate or be stored in circulation, exit or escape routes

c.   all aisles, exits, emergency exits and escape routes are kept clear.

4.12   Inspections after the event

Following each event, management should ensure that:

a.   a general visual inspection of the ground identifies any signs of damage or deformation which might create a potential danger to the public, with particular attention to the condition of seats, terraces, viewing slopes, barriers and stairways

b.   combustible waste and litter are cleared (particularly from voids) and either removed or stored in secure containers

c.   any outstanding matters of concern are recorded and arrangements made for remedial action before the next event.

4.13   Annual inspection

Management should arrange a detailed annual inspection of all structures, components and installations.

This inspection should:

a.   ensure that all standing surfaces, seats, stairs, ramps, doors, gates, boundary walls, fences and claddings are fit for their intended purpose

b.   ensure that load-bearing elements are capable of withstanding the loads to which they are likely to be subjected and that they perform properly their required functions

c.   assess which barriers should be tested in accordance with the guidance found in Chapter 10

d.   ensure that all mechanical and electrical installations are in good order, and, if required, serviced (see Chapter 17).

The annual inspection should be carried out by competent persons with the appropriate qualifications and experience. In particular, it is recommended that the inspection and testing of structures be carried out by chartered engineers, architects or surveyors with the appropriate skills and experience.

The appraisal methods described by the Institution of Structural Engineers in the publication *Appraisal of Existing Structures* are recommended (see Bibliography).

The extent to which a structural appraisal is necessary for existing structures cannot be prescribed. Much will depend upon the type of structure, its size, condition, location, the materials used in its construction and the standard of maintenance.

Other periodic tests, other than annual ones, may also be required; for example, under the terms of the designer or manufacturer's written instructions, or as specified by the local authority.

4.14 Keeping records

Responsibility for the keeping of comprehensive and accurate records lies with the management.

The quality of these records may also be regarded as a good indicator of the overall quality of the safety management structure.

Records should be kept in a specified place at the ground or in the management's office, for a period of six years, and should indicate:

a. the level of competence required of those carrying out inspections and tests

b. the qualifications and status of the persons responsible for carrying out inspections and tests

c. the results of inspections and tests, and any remedial action taken.

The documentation should be available for inspection by representatives of the relevant authority.

4.15 Plans and specifications

Management is advised to retain clear, up-to-date plans and specifications. Any symbols used should be shown on a key.

Plans and specifications may include the following:

a. a general plan of the sports ground

b. a general plan of approach roads and car parks

c. the general arrangements of each stand, by floor level

d. the principal means of ingress and egress

e. the names of each stand, terrace or section, its capacity and any relevant information regarding categories of spectators

f.   the location of:

    i.   the central control point

    ii.   key telephones

    iii.   stewards' posts

    iv.   fire points

    v.   public address speakers and zoning

    vi.   emergency exits and escape routes

    vii.   first aid room

    viii.   places of safety and of comparative safety

    ix.   high risk areas (such as plant or boiler rooms, or fuel stores)

g.   general constructional specifications.

Management is also advised to retain, or have accessible, plans and specifications relating to all recent constructions.

Where appropriate, the plans and specifications should include any other details required by the certifying authority.

Chapter Five

Circulation – General

5.1 Planning and management of circulation

Circulation routes provide the means for spectators to move in and out, and around the ground, under both normal and emergency conditions.

As a necessary function of a sports ground, circulation routes must be planned and managed safely. However, it should also be recognised that such routes, and circulation areas in general – their design, efficiency and related facilities – are closely allied to the comfort and enjoyment of spectators.

Safe circulation is achieved by:

a. physical means – primarily good design and construction, reinforced by technical aids and clear signposting

b. human resources – primarily good stewarding, reinforced by technical aids, communications, maintenance and good housekeeping.

Although conditions vary considerably at grounds, largely depending on the type of sport being staged, planning and management must also take into account the fact that circulation routes and circulation areas in general function differently according to the nature of the event, the numbers attending, and the categories of spectators attending. For example, certain events may attract higher numbers of children, semi-ambulant people, or people unfamiliar with the general lay-out of the sports ground.

5.2 Creating a balanced system

Circulation cannot be planned or managed simply by ensuring that individual sections of a ground, such as stairways, concourses or gangways, are satisfactory in themselves. The inter-relation of these and other components is critical.

All parts of the circulation system should be compatible and combine to form a balanced whole.

5.3 Multi-functional circulation areas

Circulation areas – that is, areas where spectators both gather and pass through – should perform properly all their intended and actual functions.

For example, concourse areas in stands may form part of the ingress and egress systems, but also provide access to catering outlets and toilets, together with holding areas where spectators can gather to eat and drink, and/or view television monitors (see Chapter 8).

If not designed or managed properly, or if too small, such multi-functional circulation areas can become over-congested at key times. The aim of management in such circumstances should be, wherever possible, to introduce measures which channel people into other areas; for example, by offering additional or alternative stairways, catering outlets or toilets, and by improved signposting.

5.4 Zoning of circulation routes

New construction: wherever possible, new grounds should be planned so that there are continuous circulation routes around the spectator accommodation, linked to both ingress and egress routes. Diagram 3 illustrates the basis for such planning.

5.5 Design of circulation routes and areas

Detailed guidance on specific areas of circulation follows in Chapters 6–9.

However, it is stressed that the following requirements apply to all circulation routes and areas. Where deficiencies exist, the (P) and/or (S) factors should be reduced accordingly.

a. **Maintaining safe conditions**

Circulation routes and areas should be kept unobstructed where there is a direct movement of spectators, be free of trip hazards, and have slip-resistant floor surfaces.

b. **Design**

Circulations routes and areas should be designed to be free from obstructions and fire risk.

c. **Width**

For new construction: circulation routes (including stairways and gangways) should be a recommended minimum of 1.2m wide.

For existing construction: circulation routes (including stairways and gangways) should be a minimum of 1.1m wide.

(Where handrails are fitted, see Section 7.8.)

d. **Headroom**

All parts of the ground to which the public have access should have a minimum headroom of 2.0m. Wherever possible, this should be raised to 2.4m in circulation routes and viewing areas (particularly the rear of covered seated areas).

e. **Signs**

Circulation routes and areas should be identified by clear signs, illuminated where necessary (see Section 16.27).

f. **Lighting**

Circulation routes and areas should be well lit, by natural and/or artificial light, under both normal and emergency conditions (see Sections 17.10 and 17.13).

Diagram 3. New construction – zonal planning

When planning certain types of sports grounds or rebuilding existing ones (excluding racecourses), it may be helpful to plan the circulation areas in terms of four different but linked zones, as follows:

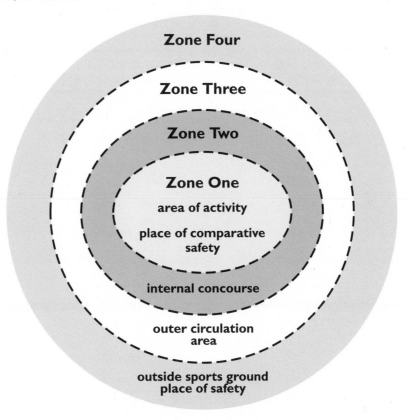

Zone One: the pitch or area of activity. This may be considered a place of comparative safety, to which spectators can be evacuated before using other emergency exits (but see Sections 9.13.b and 15.16). Although protected from Zone Two, Zone One should still be accessible to spectators via gates or openings in the pitch perimeter barriers.

Zone Two: spectator accommodation, including internal concourses and hospitality areas. If this area needs to be evacuated in an emergency, it should preferably be to Zone Four.

Note: at the majority of sports grounds, Zones Two and Three will form a single area, usually underneath or part of the stands.

Zone Three: the outer circulation area. Zone Three may, in certain situations, be considered a place of comparative safety, to which spectators can be evacuated before exiting to Zone Four. In planning terms, Zone Three can serve as a vital access area for emergency and service vehicles, without disrupting circulation in Zone Two.

Zone Four: a buffer zone outside the sports ground perimeter, used for the public to gather before entry and for links to car parks and public transport. The public should be able to circumnavigate the perimeter in this zone, in order to find an appropriate point of entry. Zone Four should be the designated place of safety in the event of an emergency.

5.6   Management of circulation routes

In order to maintain a free, unimpeded flow of people, management should ensure that circulation routes are kept as clear as possible of all non-essential items and personnel. This will require:

a.   regular clearance of waste and litter

b.   the monitoring of all circulation areas by stewards and/or CCTV

c.   preventing non-essential personnel (such as off-duty staff) from gathering around key areas, such as stairways, gangways and vomitories.

Where there is a free flow of spectators between different viewing areas, further management controls may also be necessary, as detailed in Sections 12.16 and 12.21.

5.7   Management policies and circulation

Management should recognise that a number of apparently non-safety-related policies and practices can have both positive and negative effects on the efficiency of circulation systems. These might include:

a.   ticketing or entry arrangements (see Section 6.9)

b.   the distribution and positioning of vendors

c.   the distribution and positioning of television monitors, scoreboards and other points of interest

d.   commercial or media-related activities which involve placing vehicles, temporary structures, cables or extra personnel in key areas (see Chapter 20)

e.   commercial activities or promotions which encourage spectators to gather in strategic areas or involve the distribution of handouts, refreshments or gifts

f.   the opening or closing of catering or commercial outlets before, during or after an event, in such a pattern that the loading of circulation systems becomes either greater or lesser at key times

g.   segregation arrangements which necessitate extra barriers, divided concourses, sealed-off areas or dead-end situations.

5.8   Access for emergency vehicles

In addition to monitoring circulation areas for spectators, management should ensure that adequate access is provided for emergency vehicles to all buildings within the sports ground. Wherever possible such access routes should be separate from those used by spectators for ingress and egress or, alternatively, provide for the parking of emergency vehicles so that spectator routes are not obstructed.

The police, fire and ambulance authorities should be consulted about the suitability of access roads and access to the ground generally.

Chapter Six

Circulation – Ingress

6.1

The need to count

Spectators entering all sections of the ground, including VIP and lounge areas, should be accurately counted at their time of entry, and their number controlled in order to ensure that overcrowding does not occur. This applies even if entry to the event is by ticket only.

If the procedures for accurately counting spectators are deficient, or if the entry procedures themselves lead to congestion, delays, or any breakdown of the safety management of spectators, the (S) factor should be reduced accordingly when calculating the capacity (see Section 1.4).

6.2

Counting on entry

Each section of spectator accommodation should be served by metered turnstiles or other means of counting, in order to keep a tally of the number of spectators admitted to that section.

Where one section of a ground is served by a bank or banks of turnstiles, the metering system should be capable of recording an overall total for all the turnstiles. This total should be quickly available at any given time so that appropriate action can be taken once a pre-determined figure – for example, 90 per cent of the total capacity – has been reached.

This is important for two reasons:

a. The management will need to assess how long it will take for the remaining people outside the ground (if any) to be admitted before the start of the event. If the number queuing is greater than can be admitted at the prevailing rate of admission, wherever possible extra turnstiles should be opened to cope with the demand. If this is not possible, consideration should be given as to whether or not the start of the event should be delayed.

b. When entry is other than by tickets for reserved seats, the management will need to know when the section is near capacity so that:

   i. the turnstiles can be closed before the capacity is exceeded

   ii. people queueing or approaching the turnstiles can be warned, and where appropriate, re-directed to entrances serving other sections of the ground.

As stated in Sections 2.14 and 2.15, contingency plans to cater for the above situations should be prepared. For further guidance on counting spectators on entry, see Section 16.20.

6.3 Computerised monitoring

In order for the ground's safety management to have instant access to the figures being metered or counted at each turnstile or entry point, and for rates of admission to be accurately assessed, it is recommended that a computerised monitoring system should be installed wherever practicable.

Where installed, however, management should also prepare contingency plans to deal with the system's failure (see Sections 2.14 and 2.15).

6.4 Entry capacity

As stated in Section 1.3, one of the calculations required to determine the capacity of a sports ground, or one section of the ground, is the entry capacity.

The entry capacity is the number of people who can pass through all the turnstiles or entry points serving either the whole ground or one section, within a period of one hour.

6.5 Factors affecting the entry capacity

The rate at which people can pass through each turnstile will vary according to a number of local factors. The rates of entry should therefore be measured at least once a year and recorded.

The main factors affecting the rate of entry are:

a.   the number and dispersal of turnstiles / entry points

b.   the adequacy of directional information and communications

c.   the means of entry; for example, cash payment, ticket or voucher

d.   the division of entry categories; for example, adult, juvenile, senior citizen, or family

e.   the design and condition of turnstiles / entry points

f.   the capabilities of turnstile operators.

6.6 Calculating the entry capacity

As stated in Section 6.4, the entry capacity is the number of people who can pass through all the turnstiles or entry points serving either the whole ground or one section, within a period of one hour.

However, for the purposes of calculation, and in order to ensure that spectators are admitted at a rate which is compatible with dispersal arrangements for them inside the ground, an upper limit has been set on this number.

For the purposes of calculating the entry capacity, the upper limit is set at 660 persons per turnstile (or other entry point) per hour.

Where the recorded rate of entry proves to be less than 660 persons per turnstile per hour, that lower figure is the figure which should be used for the purposes of calculating the entry capacity. Where the recorded rate of admission proves to be greater than 660 persons per turnstile per hour, the upper limit of 660 should still apply when calculating the entry capacity.

If the entry capacity is lower than the holding capacity of the section served by those turnstiles, the final capacity of that section should be reduced accordingly, as explained in Chapter 1.

6.7 Providing a sufficient number of turnstiles or entry points

Although the entry capacity is determined by the number of spectators who can be admitted within a period of one hour, in practice many grounds admit spectators well in advance of the start of a sporting event. Furthermore, for many events, large numbers of spectators arrive close to the starting time.

These variations should be recognised when determining the number of turnstiles or entry points to be provided, or staffed on particular event days.

For example, providing the exact number of turnstiles to serve one section purely on the basis that each one will theoretically admit 660 persons per hour may result in a build-up of queues outside the ground, as latecomers arrive shortly before the start.

It is also inevitable that certain turnstiles will operate more slowly than others; for example, those which admit large numbers of children.

For all spectators to be admitted in time for the start, therefore, a larger number of entry points may be required than might otherwise be the case if the number were based purely on the application of the 660 figure.

6.8 Design and management of entrances and entry routes

The design and management of entrances and entry routes should take into consideration the following:

a. Entrances to each part of the ground should, wherever practicable, be designed and located so as to allow for the even distribution of spectators and to prevent local pressure building up outside the ground.

b. Walls, fences and gates should not provide the opportunity for hand- or foot-holds which might assist climbing. They should be regularly inspected.

c. The installation of closed circuit television should be considered in order to assist in the monitoring of crowd densities outside the ground and throughout the ingress/egress routes (see Sections 16.15–16.19).

d. The design of the turnstile and its housing should allow for the operator to see and communicate clearly with entrants.

e.   Entrances should be sited so that the flow of people from them to the spectator accommodation is, as far as possible, evenly distributed. Where this distribution is uneven and gives rise to congestion at an entrance, consideration should be given to changing the turnstile or entry point arrangements, and if possible, to direct more people to under-used entrances. Additional measures might include improved signposting and increased stewarding, both inside and outside the ground.

f.   Entry routes should not be obstructed. Amenities such as refreshment kiosks or toilets should be located away from the immediate area of the turnstiles and entry routes.

g.   Entry and exit routes are often common to each other and in such cases the considerations which apply to exit routes therefore apply also to entry routes (see Chapter 9).

6.9   Providing clear information

Spectators should be provided with clear, consistent information on all aspects of entry. Wherever practical, the following measures should be considered:

a.   All entrances and entry routes should be clearly signposted and, if used in non-daylight hours, adequately lit (see Section 17.10).

b.   All turnstiles and entry points should be numbered. These numbers should be identifiable, and should be recorded in all documentation relating to the ground, including ground plans and contingency plans.

c.   Clear ground plans showing all entrance points should be displayed at strategic points outside the ground, ideally so that people approaching the ground can decide which entrance to use as early as possible.

d.   Tickets, where issued, should satisfy the following requirements:

i.   they should clearly identify the location of the accommodation for which they have been issued

ii.   they should have a ground plan reproduced on the back of that part of the ticket retained by the spectator

iii. information on the ticket should correlate with the information provided both inside and outside the ground.

For further guidance on ticketing and admission policies, see Sections 2.25, 6.10 and 16.29.

e.   Event programmes or race cards, where issued, should include a clearly labelled plan of the ground, indicating the entry/exit routes to and from different parts of the ground, and details of emergency evacuation procedures (see Section 16.29).

f.   The public should be made aware of the ground regulations, and in particular of any articles which are prohibited from the ground. This can achieved by the use of posters, and by repeating the information on ground plans and tickets, and in event programmes.

For further guidance on the communication of information, see Chapter 16.

6.10   Admission policies

As stated in Sections 2.25 and 11.17, policies adopted by the ground management can have a direct effect on the rates of admission and the management of entrance areas and spectator accommodation in general.

Specific points to consider include:

a.   **Cash sales**

To ensure a steady flow of spectators into the ground when entry is by cash, the admission price should ideally be set at a round figure which avoids the need for large amounts of small change to be handled.

The turnstile operators should also be provided with adequate amounts of change, topped up if necessary by staff assisting the operators.

b.   **Ticket-only sales**

The advantages of confining entry to ticket-only are that the rate of admission should be higher than for cash sales, and the system allows different categories of spectator (for example, parent and child) to purchase adjacent seats and enter the ground together.

If tickets are sold on the day of the event, wherever possible separate sales outlets should be provided. These outlets should be clearly sign-posted, and positioned so that queues do not conflict with queues for turnstiles or other entry points.

c.   **Reserved (or numbered) seat ticket sales**

Selling tickets for specific numbered seats has the advantage that the seats are more likely to be sold in blocks. This policy helps to avoid random gaps and ensures that in the key period preceding the start of the event there will be less need for stewards to have to direct latecomers to the remaining seats, or move spectators who have already settled.

Another advantage of this ticketing policy is that it makes it possible for management to sell the total seated capacity of the ground, or section of the ground (as opposed to a policy of unreserved seat sales, as explained below).

d.   **Unreserved seat sales**

Selling unreserved seats, whether by cash or ticket, has the advantage of being easier to administer. However, spectators are prone to occupy seats in a random pattern, and, as stated above, it can be hard to fill unoccupied seats in the key period before the start of the event.

For this reason, when seats are sold unreserved, a reduction in the number of seats made available for sale is likely to be necessary. This reduction may be in the region of 5–10 per cent of the total capacity of the section, according to local circumstances.

e. No ticket or cash entry on the event day

If all tickets have sold out in advance, or if the management decides not to sell tickets or allow cash entry on the day of the event, every effort should be made to publicise this fact in the local press and media. In addition, signs advising the public of the situation should be placed along all approaches to the ground, in order to avoid an unnecessary build-up of crowds outside the ground and its entrances.

f. Ticket design

The design of tickets can have a direct effect on the rate of admission. For example, clear, easy-to-read information will speed the ability of the turnstile or entry-point operator to process the ticket. Similarly, if anti-counterfeiting features are incorporated (as is recommended), simple procedures should be in place for the operator to check each ticket's validity.

For more guidance on ticketing, see 2.25, 6.9 and 11.17.

6.11 Crowd build-up

Dangerous overcrowding can be caused if spectators are able to force their way into a ground already full or nearly full, for example by scaling or breaking through boundary walls, fences, gates or turnstiles.

To avoid this danger boundary walls, fences and gates should be of the appropriate height and strength, should not provide the opportunity for climbing, and should, where possible, be monitored by CCTV. Turnstile areas should be stewarded wherever there is a potential threat of forced entry.

Contingency plans should be drawn up in order to deal with situations where unduly large crowds gather outside. Local knowledge of the ground and crowd patterns should be taken into account in drawing up such contingency plans.

These plans may include provision for the opening of additional or under-used entrances, but should also ensure that those who enter in such situations can still be accurately counted, and that adequate stewarding arrangements are in place for their dispersal once inside the ground.

Under no circumstances should there be uncontrolled admission into the ground.

Chapter Seven

Circulation – Stairways and ramps

7.1 Introduction

The disposition, design and management of stairways and ramps at sports grounds should be such as to provide smooth and unimpeded circulation for spectators under all conditions.

This chapter should therefore be read in conjunction with Chapters 5, 6, 8 and 9 on circulation and Chapters 11–14 on spectator accommodation.

7.2 Definitions of stairways and gangways

It is emphasised that for the purposes of design and assessment, the criteria applying to stairways at sports grounds are, in part, different to those pertaining to radial gangways.

The following definitions should therefore be noted:

a. **Stairway**

A stairway is that part of a structure which is not a radial gangway but which comprises of at least one flight of steps, including the landings at the head and foot of stairways and any landings in between flights.

b. **Radial gangway**

A radial gangway is a stepped or sloping channel for the circulation of spectators through viewing accommodation, running between terrace steps or seat rows.

c. **Lateral gangway**

A lateral gangway is a level channel for the circulation of spectators through viewing accommodation, running parallel with terrace steps or seat rows.

Further guidance on the provision and design of gangways can be found in Section 11.7 (for seated accommodation) and Sections 12.4–12.6 (for standing accommodation).

7.3 Design of stairways

Movement on stairways, especially downward movement, poses a considerable potential risk to crowds both in normal circumstances, such as at the end of an event, or in an emergency. The effects of stumbling, pushing, jostling and congestion are potentially dangerous if, as a result, the crowd suddenly surges forward or if, for any reason, any individuals suddenly change direction.

For new construction: in order to minimise hazards the design of stairways should comply with all the relevant requirements of the current Building Regulations.

For new and existing construction: the specific needs of sports grounds require that stairways should meet the following basic specifications:

a.   the stairway width should be uniform (see Section 7.5)

b.   all goings and risers on each stairway should be uniform

c.   open risers should not be used

d.   winders (that is, tapered treads) should not be used

e.   stair treads should be slip-resistant, have durable edgings, and, where appropriate, have adequate drainage

f.   all nosings should be clearly marked

g.   adequate separation should be provided between channels so that there is no overspill from one channel to another

h.   stairways should be positioned to take advantage of natural light and ventilation, but where the natural lighting is deficient the stairway should be adequately illuminated by artificial light (see also Sections 17.10 and 17.13).

Further guidance on flights of stairways, and certain of the above requirements (including specific dimensional criteria), can be found in the following sections. Note also that the requirements for stairways to be used by semi-ambulant spectators may differ (see Section 13.6).

7.4   Flights of stairways

Flights of stairways should not provide long, uncontrolled paths down which crowd pressures and surges can be created. For this reason:

a.   individual flights should consist of no more than 16 risers

b.   if there are more than 36 risers in consecutive flights, the path of the stairway should change direction of travel by at least 30°.

7.5   Dimensions of stairways

The design of stairways (and stairway channels) at sports grounds should comply with the following dimensions:

a.   Widths

For new construction:
Recommended minimum width: 1.2m   Maximum width: 1.8m

For existing construction:
Minimum width: 1.1m   Maximum width: 1.8m

Existing stairways and stairway channels of between 1.8m and 2.2m wide should, wherever possible, be narrowed to no more than 1.8m by the installation or relocation of suitable barriers.

Existing stairways and stairway channels wider than 2.2m should be divided into channels in order to meet the width requirements above.

b. **Goings**
Minimum depth: 280mm   Preferred depth: 305mm

c. **Risers**
For new construction:
Minimum height: 150mm (this is also the preferred height)
Maximum height: 180mm

For existing construction:
Minimum height: 150mm (this is also the preferred height)
Maximum height: 190mm

d. **Landings**
The going of each landing, at the head and foot of stairways, and between flights, should be not less than the width of the channel of the flight.

e. **Headroom**
Minimum headroom dimensions are provided in Section 5.5.

7.6   Barriers and handrails – definitions

It is emphasised that in terms of their dimensions and design loadings, barriers are not handrails, even though in certain situations – see Section 7.7.b – in practice they might be used by people as handrails.

For the purpose of the *Guide*, a barrier is any element, whether permanent or temporary, intended to prevent people from falling, and to retain, stop or guide people (see 7.7).

A handrail is a rail normally grasped by hand for guidance or support (see 7.8).

Further guidance on barriers is provided in Chapter 10. Further guidance on handrails used in gangways in seated areas can be found in Section 11.9.

7.7   Barriers on stairways

As illustrated in Diagram 4, barriers are used for two different purposes on stairways.

a. **Barriers to stop people falling**
Where stairways are situated next to, or in the middle of, open wells, or open spaces, barriers designed to prevent people from falling should be provided on the open side or sides. These barriers should be not less than 1.1m high.

At grounds where small children are likely to be in attendance, consideration should be given to the provision of additional guarding which is non-climbable and has no openings through which a 100mm sphere can pass.

b.   Barriers to divide stairways into channels
Stairways separated into channels must be divided by the provision of barriers. Such barriers may be designed to a height of 1.0m, in which case they can also function as a handrail.

If installed to a height of greater than 1.0m, however, separate provision for handrails should be made in the design, as specified in Section 7.8 and shown in Diagram 4.

In both the above situations, the barrier heights should be measured from the pitch line, or from the surface of the landing. The barriers should also be designed to resist a horizontal imposed load as specified in Table 1 of Chapter 10.

7.8   Handrails for stairways and ramps
As stated in Section 7.6, a handrail is provided for people to grasp, for guidance or support. If the handrails are to serve only as handrails for stairways or ramps – that is, they are not barriers as described in Section 7.7.b – the design should meet the following requirements:

a.   Handrails of the same height should be provided on both sides of stairways, landings and ramps.

b.   **For new construction:** handrails should be a minimum height of 900 mm, and a maximum height of 1.0 m, measured vertically from the pitch line or from the surface of the landing.

For existing construction: handrails should be a minimum height of 840 mm, and a maximum height of 1.0 m, measured vertically from the pitch line or from the surface of the landing.

c.   Wherever possible, handrails should project no more than 100 mm into the width of the stairway or ramp. If the projection is greater than 100 mm the usable width of the stairway should be measured between the handrails, and should be at least 1.1 m (1.2 m recommended for new construction).

d.   Handrails should extend by at least 300 mm beyond the top and bottom of any stairway, measured from the vertical of the first and last risers, or from the start and finish of the ramp.

e.   Handrails should be robust, securely fixed, and their fixings designed to be fit for purpose.

f.   The surfaces of handrails should be smooth, with no sharp projections or edges.

Diagram 4. Barriers and handrails on stairways

This diagram illustrates a
stairway with a wall
on one side and
an open space
(or well) on
the other.

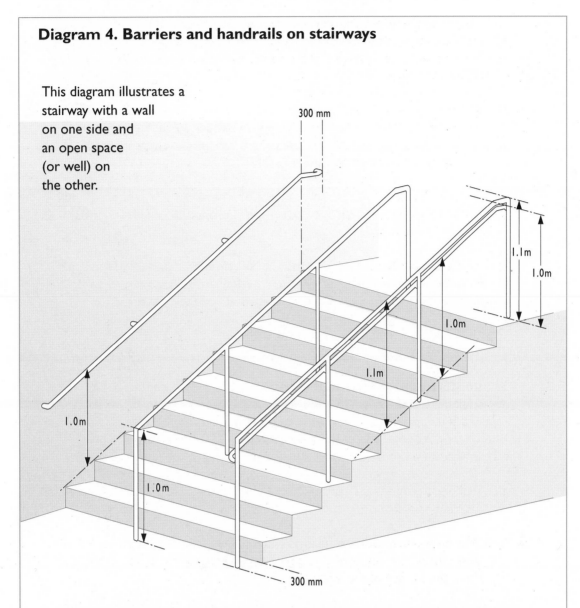

A barrier is installed to prevent people from falling over the open side. Because this barrier has to have a height of 1.1m, a handrail is attached at a lower level for guidance or support. The handrail's height is 1.0m measured from the datum (that is, from the pitch line). Note that each end of the handrail bends around the ends of the barrier, and that if small children are likely to use the stairway, additional guarding should be provided (see Section 7.7.a).

Another handrail is fixed to the wall. This too is fixed at a height of 1.0m above the datum. Particular care has to be taken when fixing such a handrail, in order to prevent it pulling away from the wall.

Finally, the central barrier, which divides the stairway into channels, is classed as a barrier, and is therefore subject to the loading requirements of Table 1 in Chapter 10. As stated in Section 7.7.b, a barrier in this location may be designed to a height of 1.0m, thus enabling it to be used also as a handrail.

Whatever the design of the central barrier, the handrails on either side of any stairway channel should be the same height.

7.9 Controlling the flow at the head of stairways

In order to ensure a free flow of people, and avoid crowd pressures building up, the head of each stairway should be designed so that flow onto the stairway is uniform across its width. Similarly, where a stairway is divided into channels, the approach should be designed to ensure a uniform flow down each channel.

The design of approaches to the head of each stairway should meet the following requirements:

a.   The approach should be level.

b.   It should be designed so that people can approach the stairway only by walking towards the direction of the stairs, and/or from its sides.

c.   In areas of spectator accommodation, any approach from directly behind a stairway (that is, from higher up the seating deck or standing area) should be controlled using the same methods as recommended for vomitories; by the routing of gangways or, in standing areas with no gangways, by the positioning of barriers around the entrance to the stairway (see Section 8.8).

d.   No part of the approach should be less than 1.1m in width (1.2m recommended for new construction).

e.   Where the approach to the head of a stairway is greater than 3m in width, the flow of spectators should be strictly controlled by barriers, as illustrated in Diagram 5.

7.10 Discharge from exit stairways

The flow of spectators as they move away from the foot of exit stairways should be controlled so that the exit routes discharge either:

a.   at ground level, and lead directly to a place of safety in the open air, or

b.   onto walkways or concourses of adequate dimensions at any level, provided these also lead directly to a place of safety in the open air.

For the purposes of the *Guide*, a place of safety is a place where a person is no longer in danger from fire or other types of emergencies (see Section 15.16).

7.11 Escalators

Although escalators may form an integral part of the entry and exit systems at certain sports grounds, they should not be used for the purposes of calculating the emergency evacuation capacity.

Escalators should discharge into a space sufficiently large and clear to avoid people being unable to step off the escalator in congested situations. Consideration should also be be given to the consequences of any breakdown of the escalators, leading to possible congestion.

Diagram 5. Approaches to the head of stairways

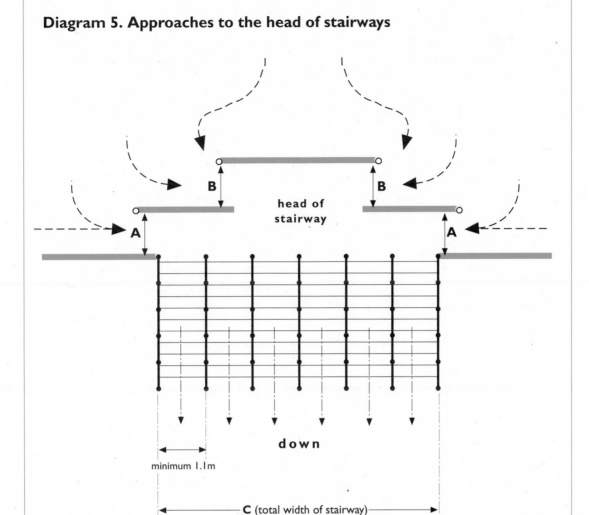

As stated in Section 7.9, in order to control the flow of spectators as they approach the head of a stairway, it is necessary to position barriers as shown above. The barriers should be designed on the following basis:

The minimum width of A or B should be 1.1m (1.2m for new construction), but the aggregate width of A + B on one side of the stairway should be not more than 3m.

To establish the correct widths for A and B, the following calculation should be used, where C = the total width of the stairway:

$$2\,(A + B) = \frac{2C}{3} \quad \text{or} \quad (A + B) = \frac{C}{3}$$

From this calculation, it can be seen that stairways wider than 9m would require the addition of more barriers at the head of the stairway.

To achieve visibility in crowded conditions, consideration should also be given to extending selected vertical posts (marked above with a black circle) to above head height.

(For guidance on the rates of passage to be applied to stairways see Section 9.6.)

71

7.12   Ramps

Ramps can be a useful alternative to stairs, but there is concern about their suitability for negotiating small changes of level within sports grounds, because they may not be easily seen by spectators during an emergency evacuation.

In addition, steep ramps can cause or exacerbate uncontrolled forward movement and lead to an accident.

Where provided, ramps should therefore meet the following requirements:

a.   **For new construction:**
The maximum gradient should not exceed 1 in 12.

    For existing construction:
The maximum gradient should not exceed 1 in 10.

b.   The preferred gradient for ramps to be used for spectators in wheelchairs is 1 in 20 (see Sections 13.14 and 13.17).

c.   The gradient of any ramp should preferably be constant and not broken by steps.

d.   The surface should be uniform and slip-resistant.

e.   Handrails should be provided using the same criteria as those applying to stairways (see Section 7.7).

Chapter Eight

Circulation – Concourses and vomitories

8.1 Concourses and vomitories

This chapter provides guidance on the safe circulation of spectators in those areas which do not exactly fit into categories outlined elsewhere in the *Guide*, but which may also serve as integral parts of ingress, egress and emergency evacuation routes. The chapter should therefore be read in conjunction with Chapters 5, 6, 7 and 9 (circulation), Chapters 11–14 (spectator accommodation) and Chapter 15 (fire safety).

For the purpose of the *Guide*, a concourse is defined as a circulation area that provides direct access to and from viewing accommodation, via stairways, ramps, vomitories or level passageways, and which serves as a milling area for spectators for the purposes of refreshment and entertainment. It may also provide access to toilets.

A vomitory is an access route built into the gradient of a stand which directly links spectator accommodation to concourses, and/or routes for ingress, egress and emergency evacuation. Passage through a vomitory can be either level, or via stairways, and can flow either parallel or transverse to the rows of terraces or seats.

8.2 Concourses and safety

The safety management of many sports grounds tends to concentrate attention and resources on ingress and egress routes and viewing areas. However, it should be recognised that concourses are an integral part of the circulation system and must therefore be monitored and managed at all times when spectators are in the ground.

Increasingly, concourses also form an important access route to facilities provided for the comfort and enjoyment of spectators. As such, it is important that neither the design nor management of concourses adversely affects the safety of spectators. This is a particular concern at existing grounds where concourses, originally designed for general circulation only, have been fitted with additional facilities which considerably add to the concourses' usage during peak times.

Key concerns are the size of the concourse, the travel routes between the concourse and vomitories, and between the concourse and ingress, egress and emergency evacuation routes. In general, these routes should be as direct as possible.

8.3 Concourses and fire safety

The presence of commercial and catering facilities in concourses – particularly when these have been added to existing structures – also raises concerns about fire safety. For this reason, under no circumstances should any significant modifications be carried out, nor any commercial or catering outlet be installed, nor any changes to wall or floor surfaces be effected, without prior consultation with the local authority. This consultation should be recorded in written form.

8.4   Size of concourses

The ease of circulation and the comfort of spectators will be largely determined by the width and spatial arrangements of the concourse.

For new construction: It is difficult to recommend precise dimensions in order to ensure the safe circulation of people, or to calculate appropriate holding capacities for concourses.

Clearly, however, the width should take into account the entry, exit and emergency evacuation capacities required, as for any circulation route. The width should then be increased to take into account the additional anticipated usage of related facilities. Experience shows that this usage may be greater than is often expected.

In addition, consideration should be given to the potential usage of concourses by spectators at events other than the sport for which the ground is primarily designed. This usage can be considerable if the event spans several hours, if inclement weather conditions prevail, and if large numbers are in attendance (as, for example, at a concert, for which the pitch or area of activity is used for viewing).

For existing construction: where concourses have been upgraded with additional facilities, leading to greater usage at peak times, management should allocate extra stewarding, and where appropriate, extra CCTV coverage, in order to monitor the circulation and milling of spectators. Where necessary, the management's contingency plans (see Sections 2.14 and 2.15) should include a response to the problem of overcrowding in concourses.

If congestion in concourses is a regular occurrence, consideration should be given to resiting or providing additional facilities in other areas.

8.5   Circulation on concourses

Concourses should be designed to allow for the smooth, unimpeded passage of people through the ingress and egress routes. In addition, careful design should ensure that during periods of peak use circulation is not impeded.

In order to achieve this, the following requirements should be considered:

a.   The positioning of travel routes – for general ingress, egress or access to toilets or catering outlets – should be determined, and should not create cross flows; that is, people moving along the concourse should not be impeded by large numbers crossing their path.

b.   Similarly, the positioning of catering outlets and toilet entrances should be such that queues do not impede the circulation of people along the concourse, nor the entry of spectators into the concourse direct from turnstiles.

c.   Catering outlets and toilet entrances should not create any unacceptable risk, or be positioned immediately next to the foot of vomitories or stairways leading from spectator accommodation. This is to avoid congestion in the vomitories owing to the potential build-up of queues.

d. To avoid congestion and discomfort, there should be an adequate number of toilets and catering outlets provided. These should be spaced sufficiently apart in concourses to avoid queues for each becoming disorderly, thereby creating additional potential congestion. (Advice on the design and provision of adequate toilets may be found in the FSADC publication *Toilet Facilities at Stadia* – see Bibliography.)

e. The siting of television monitors, or any other forms of display which might encourage large numbers of people to mill around, should be such that congestion is not created around key areas in the concourse; for example, close to the foot of vomitories, or close to toilet entrances.

8.6 Design of concourses and related facilities

The design of concourses should, wherever possible, take the following factors into consideration:

a. Signs should be provided at such a level and in positions which enable people to read them during periods of peak usage. The signs should also be placed facing both lateral and transverse directions to enable people entering the concourse from any ingress point or from a vomitory to make a quick decision as to which direction to take in order to reach their intended destination.

b. Where possible, natural lighting should be maximised in order to assist in the safe and efficient flow of people towards exits, and to create a more comfortable environment.

c. Where natural lighting levels are low or cannot be provided, artificial illumination should be sufficient to facilitate normal circulation and activity.

d. The flooring of concourses should be slip-resistant, in particular in areas where spillage is likely (for example, around catering outlets), and in areas where rainwater can be tracked in from vomitories and external areas.

e. Where concourses form part of an emergency evacuation route they should be designed as areas of very low fire risk, having at least a one hour fire separation from catering and other outlets which may contain a fire risk. Consideration may also need to be given to the provision of smoke containment and/or extraction measures (see also Section 9.10).

f. At grounds where areas of spectator accommodation are segregated, the design of concourse areas should ensure that any divisions do not exclude the provision of amenities in one part of the concourse.

g. The planning of concourses, whether new or for refurbishment, should take into account the service needs of all facilities, and other management details such as the location and type of litter bins and the provision of shelving for refreshments. These should not be sited in such a way as to impede passage through egress routes.

8.7 Management of concourses

Owing to their considerable use during peak periods, it is essential for management to allocate resources and manpower to the management of concourses, before and during events. The following factors should be considered:

a. management should ensure that concourses are properly stewarded and, where necessary, monitored by the use of CCTV cameras

b. the siting of any temporary fittings or kiosks should not impede the circulation of spectators through the concourse

c. the delivery of supplies and services to catering outlets or toilets should not impede spectator circulation

d. waste and litter should be collected and removed at regular intervals.

8.8 Vomitories

Vomitories are a common means of reducing travel distances in stands. They are also an aid to safety management, allowing stewards and other personnel to gain direct and easy access to particular areas. There are several different designs and layout of vomitories but, in general, the following requirements should be met:

a. If passage through the vomitory is by steps, the design, dimensions, barriers and handrails should meet the requirement for stairways (see Chapter 7).

b. Whether passage through the vomitory is by steps or by level passage, its approaches should also be controlled as for any stairway at a sports ground; that is, people should be able to approach the vomitory only from the front and/or from its sides. The approach to the vomitory may only be from behind if it is controlled by the routing of gangways.

c. In standing areas where there are no gangways routed around the vomitory, it is recommended that such gangways be provided. If this is not practical, however, barriers should be positioned at each side of the vomitory's entrance. This is to ensure that spectators approaching from behind have to pass around the ends of the barriers and therefore approach the vomitory entrance from the sides.

    These barriers should be protected (by infill or screening), to prevent spectators climbing through and approaching from behind.

d. In all areas of spectator accommodation, where appropriate, consideration should also be given to providing protection against objects being accidentally knocked onto spectators passing through the vomitory.

e. Management should ensure that no spectators or non-essential staff are allowed to stand in vomitories during an event. Similarly, during ingress and egress, stewards should position themselves away from, or to the side of, the vomitory, in order to allow a free flow of spectators.

Chapter Nine

Circulation –
Egress and emergency evacuation

9.1 Safety issues

It is generally recognised that a period of great risk to crowd safety is at the time of leaving the sports ground. It is important, therefore, to provide exit systems capable of accommodating safely the passage of people within an acceptable period of time, and to avoid congestion and psychological stress.

Exit systems may comprise gangways, stairways, passageways, ramps and other means of passage.

Management should ensure that exit routes are planned and managed safely, to provide for spectators a smooth, unimpeded passage through an exit system until they reach the boundary of the ground, or, in emergency situations, a place of safety.

In order to achieve this, management should ensure that:

a. there are sufficient numbers of exits in suitable locations

b. all parts of exit routes are of adequate width and height

c. people do not have to travel excessive distances in order to exit from the ground

d. provision is made for the control of spectators entering an exit system

e. all exits are identifiable in both normal and emergency conditions.

This chapter offers guidance on the design and management of exit systems both under normal conditions and for emergency evacuation. However, it is stressed that congestion and accidents can occur under normal conditions, and that people react and respond in diverse ways according to their perceptions of risk.

Furthermore, pressures that can arise during the time of exit must be contained and controlled by attention to the detailed design of elements which form part of the exit systems, such as stairways (Chapter 7), barriers (Chapter 10) and gangways (Chapters 11 and 12).

9.2 Basic design principles

Smooth, unimpeded flow through an exit route is best achieved by ensuring that the exit system does not narrow along its length.

If, at any point along the route, there are elements narrower than those preceding, constriction can occur, causing people to converge in the narrower points.

In addition, controlling the crowd flow at the beginning of the route – that is, within the viewing accommodation – is vital to ensure that people enter the exit system at an acceptable rate.

In order to achieve this, the first element of the exit route from the spectator accommodation should be no wider than any subsequent element.

For new construction: exit routes in new construction should comply fully with the above principles.

For existing construction: narrowing in the exit routes may occur at existing constructions. However, this should be acceptable only when the narrowing is preceded by an open space or 'reservoir area', where the holding capacity is sufficient to contain those people held up because of the difference in the flow rate into and out of the reservoir area.

Guidance on the calculation of capacities for reservoir areas follows in Section 9.4.

Management should conduct a risk assessment of any reservoir area to ensure that there are no potential hazards to people passing through.

Reservoir areas are not acceptable within, or in close proximity to, any combustible structure (for example, a timber stand).

If deviations from the recommendations in the *Guide* create potential dangers in any part of the exit route, that section of the route should be closed and the final capacity of that section of the ground reduced accordingly.

In areas of standing accommodation, the exit routes used for the purposes of calculating the exit capacity of a section should include only designated gangways. Notional gangways between staggered crush barriers cannot form part of the calculation.

9.3 Factors in design and management

When considering the design and safe management of exit systems and emergency evacuation systems, four factors have to be considered:

a. The **widths** of each part of the exit, or emergency exit route (see Section 9.4).

b. The **rate of passage** of people through the exit, or emergency exit system. This is a pre-determined figure (see 9.5).

c. The **egress time**. This is normally a maximum of eight minutes for calculation purposes (see 9.7).

d. The **emergency evacuation time**. This is a variable, maximum time, between two and a half minutes and eight minutes, based on a number of factors (see Section 9.9).

The above factors are used to help calculate the final capacity of a ground, or section of a ground (explained in Chapter 1).

9.4   Exit route widths and reservoir areas

The capacity of an exit system is limited by its narrowest element. It makes no difference to the efficiency of the system where the most restrictive element is located; the capacity is always determined by it.

Exit route widths should meet the following requirements:

a. **For new construction:**
The recommended minimum width of an exit route is 1.2m.

b. **For existing construction:**
The minimum width of an exit route should be 1.1m.

Where reservoir areas are used as part of an exit system, their capacity should be calculated on the basis of the appropriate rate of passage (see Section 9.6) and the appropriate emergency evacuation time (see Section 9.9).

A density of 40 persons per 10 square metres of the area available for standing within the reservoir area is the maximum permitted for safety. It is the responsibility of management to ensure that this density is not exceeded.

Doors providing passage from executive boxes and some hospitality areas may form part of exit systems at sports grounds. In these locations, the minimum width of an exit door should not be less than 750mm.

9.5   Rates of passage – method of calculation

The rate of passage is the number of people who can pass through a particular point in an exit system, or emergency evacuation system, in a given time.

The rate of passage therefore forms a fundamental part of the calculation of the capacity of both exit and emergency evacuation systems.

It will be noted that previous editions of the *Guide* expressed rates of passage in terms of a number of people per unit width per minute. The unit width – in effect, the width occupied by people moving in single file – was set at 550mm (that is, half of 1.1m).

In situations where the widths of exits were not whole multiples of 550mm, however, the previous edition of the *Guide* (published 1990) indicated that the calculation of rates of passage should reflect the actual width of the exit; that is, in practice, the rate of passage could be expressed as the number of spectators per metre width per minute.

This is now the recommended method to be adopted in all situations, as detailed in the following section.

9.6   Recommended rates of passage

The recommended maximum rates of passage for both normal egress and emergency evacuation, to be used as the basis of calculation, should be as follows:

a.   **On all routes within seated accommodation (including gangways, concourses and ramps)**

and on all stairways within the ground

73 spectators per metre width per minute.

b.   **All routes in other parts of the ground (including within standing accommodation)**

109 spectators per metre width per minute.

It is stressed that these rates are the maximum. Where it is clear that spectators cannot exit within the prescribed normal egress time (see Section 9.7) or emergency evacuation time (see 9.9), it will be necessary to reduce the capacity accordingly.

For new construction: when designing new grounds or sections of grounds, consideration should be given to applying rates of passage lower than the maximum. This is because research and experience show that, in certain situations, maximum rates can be sustained only over a short period of time.

Factors affecting the rates of passage may include the following:

c.   the presence of children, semi-ambulant or disabled spectators

d.   the location and level of use of commercial, catering or other spectator facilities situated along the exit route

e.   the design and physical condition of the exit system; for example, the number of stairways, the quality of directional signs, lighting levels and underfoot conditions.

Examples of how to apply rates of passage can be found in Annex A.

9.7   Egress time

It is emphasised that there is a difference between egress times and emergency evacuation times.

The egress time is the total time taken for all spectators, in normal conditions, to leave an area of viewing accommodation and enter into a free flowing exit system. It does not include the time taken to negotiate the entire exit route.

(For a definition of emergency evacuation times, see Section 9.9.)

The normal maximum egress time for sports grounds is eight minutes.

If for any reason – for example, there are not enough exits – spectators cannot exit within eight minutes, a reduction of the final capacity may be required (see Chapter 1).

The limit of eight minutes has been set as a result of research and experience, which suggests that within this period spectators are less likely to become agitated, or experience frustration or stress, provided they enter an exit system at an acceptable rate, or are familiar with the sports ground and/or can identify their point of exit.

In certain circumstances it may be appropriate to apply a shorter egress time than eight minutes; for example, if the design or management of the viewing accommodation is such that regular observation shows that spectators become agitated or experience frustration or stress in periods of under eight minutes.

It should also be recognised that in many circumstances spectators will willingly take longer than eight minutes to leave; for example, in order to watch scoreboards, hear additional announcements or simply wait for the crowds to disperse. This practice must not be considered a factor in the determination of the egress time, however.

9.8 Design and management of exit systems

The design and management of exit systems should take into account the following:

a. **Movement**
    Once spectators have passed into the exit system they should be able to keep moving throughout its length.

b. **Alternative exits**
    In the event of an incident which renders the usual exit route unusable, spectators should be able to use an alternative exit route or routes.

c. **Direct exit routes**
    Where there is a simple exit route; that is, a direct passage from the viewing area to the exit gate from the ground, every part of that route should be able to accommodate the flow from the terrace or stand exit.

d. **Complex exit routes, or networks**
    For a more complex exit system which combines a number of exit routes and/or offers a choice of alternative routes, the system should be analysed in the form of a network. This is in order to check that the capacity of the exit route from the viewing area is sufficient to ensure a free flow of spectators to the various exits from the ground. Where branching of routes gives spectators a choice of paths, the proportion of the crowd likely to use each path should be assessed; for example, the exit closest to a railway or bus station may be likely to attract a higher proportion of spectators.

    Grounds which have complex exit systems should have clear, illustrative plans of the network system which serves each section, identifying the capacity of the routes within the system. These plans should be kept with the drawings of the section of the ground to which they relate. Any changes to the ground which affect the entry/exit routes should be identified on the network plan. (A network plan is illustrated in worked example 1 in Annex A.)

e. Number and disposition of exits

As stated in Section 9.1, in order to ensure a smooth, unimpeded passage for spectators through an exit system, there must be a sufficient number of exits in suitable locations (although no simple calculation of the number can be given which would apply to all situations). To avoid inconvenience and confusion, it is also important that the exits are not inconveniently located or spaced too widely apart.

f. Keeping exit routes clear

Exit routes should be kept clear of obstructions. Catering, sales or toilet facilities should be located in such a way that neither they, nor any queue or waiting they attract, obstruct an exit route. Where exit routes pass through car parks or other areas affected by vehicular movements, consideration should be given to suitable methods of traffic control.

g. Signposting

All elements of the exit system should be clearly signposted in accordance with the requirements of the Health and Safety (Safety Signs and Signals) Regulations 1996 (see Sections 16.27 and 16.28). Directional signs should be provided to encourage crowds in any particular section to flow in one direction when leaving the ground and should, wherever practicable, provide information on the destination of the exit route (for example, 'Station', 'Town Centre' or 'Visitors' Coach Park') so as to provide confidence to people using them.

9.9 Emergency evacuation time

As stated in Section 9.7, there is a difference between egress times and emergency evacuation times.

The emergency evacuation time is a calculation which, together with the rate of passage, is used to determine the capacity of the emergency exit system from the viewing accommodation to a place of safety in the event of an emergency. (For the definition of a place of safety see Section 15.16.)

The maximum emergency evacuation time for sports grounds varies between two and half minutes and eight minutes.

The time set depends largely on the level of fire risk present. Spectator accommodation which has a high fire risk should have an emergency exit capacity based on an emergency evacuation time of not more than two and a half minutes. A longer emergency evacuation time, of between two and a half minutes and eight minutes, is acceptable for grounds or parts of grounds where the fire risk is reduced. For guidance on varying levels of fire risk, see Sections 15.3–15.6.

However, as stated in Section 15.1, rather than relying solely on a short emergency evacuation time, the aim should always be to introduce measures which will minimise the outbreak and spread of fire.

For new construction: while in practice spectators may evacuate onto the pitch or area of activity in an emergency, this should not form part of the calculation of the emergency evacuation time for newly constructed grounds or sections of grounds.

9.10   Design of emergency evacuation routes

Evacuation routes for use in emergencies may need to be provided in addition to normal exits. In all cases, the following points should be considered:

a.   there should be more than one emergency evacuation route from a viewing area

b.   the system should be designed in such a way that the loss of one emergency evacuation route does not prevent access to an alternative

c.   where a stairway or any other circulation route passes up, down or through any area used by spectators, unless it is in the open air, it should be in a fire-resistant enclosure separated from the remainder of the building by a structure having a fire resistance of not less then one hour (see also Sections 8.3 and 15.10)

d.   emergency evacuation routes should discharge into a place of safety, preferably in the open air

e.   where emergency evacuation is possible only by passing through an enclosed concourse (for example, from the upper tier of a stand), consideration should be given to the provision of fire separation to individual routes of escape (see also Section 8.3).

If the capacity of the exit route is considered insufficient for emergency evacuation purposes the final capacity of the section served may have to be reduced.

Where appropriate, the design of emergency evacuation routes should also take into account the needs of spectators with disabilities.

9.11   Management of emergency evacuation routes

Management is responsible for ensuring that emergency evacuation routes are capable of being safely and effectively used at all times when the ground is occupied. This requires such routes to be maintained as sterile areas, free from any blockages, temporary fittings or stored equipment.

In addition, as stated in Sections 2.15 and 2.16, management should prepare contingency plans. These plans should provide for the evacuation of people in the event of an emergency from all areas of the ground to a place of safety. Such plans will require the designation of exits and emergency evacuation routes.

CCTV is a useful means of monitoring the exit and emergency evacuation routes (see Section 16.16).

All such routes should also be clearly signposted (see Section 16.27).

9.12   Use of the pitch or area of activity for emergency evacuation

In certain cases, forward evacuation onto the pitch or area of activity may form part of the emergency evacuation route, provided that it leads directly to an exit which itself leads to a place of safety.

The following requirements should also be taken into account:

a. Whether or not the emergency evacuation of spectators onto the pitch or area of activity forms part of the agreed emergency evacuation plan, wherever there is a pitch perimeter barrier in front of spectator accommodation, other than in exceptional circumstances it must be fitted with a sufficient number of suitably designed gates or openings (see Sections 9.13 and 10.17).

b. Where the playing surface is made of synthetic materials, advice from the fire authority should be sought to establish whether it can be properly considered as an emergency exit route in the event of a fire. This is because some forms of artificial turf might constitute a hazard in the event of fire.

c. If the pitch or area of activity is wholly surrounded by covered accommodation, with no breaks in the roofing (see Section 15.10), it may not be a suitable route for emergency evacuation in the event of fire. In such cases advice from the fire authority should be sought.

As stated in Section 9.9, for new construction, the use of the pitch or area of activity for emergency evacuation should not form part of the capacity calculation.

9.13 Provision of gates or openings in a pitch perimeter barrier

As stated above, where a pitch perimeter barrier is in place in front of spectator accommodation, other than in exceptional circumstances it must be fitted with gates or openings allowing access onto the pitch or area of activity.

If a viewing area is divided by structural means (see Section 12.15), each division must have sufficient gates or openings to evacuate all the spectators in that division within the emergency evacuation time set for that part of the ground.

Such gates or openings should:

a. be a minimum width of 1.1m (1.2m recommended for new construction)

b. align with radial gangways (where provided) and measure not less than the width of those gangways

c. be appropriately stewarded.

Where gates are fitted, they should:

d. open away from spectators

e. be kept unlocked

f. only be fitted with catches that can be released from both sides

g. be clearly marked and painted a different colour from the rest of the pitch perimeter barrier.

9.14 Discounting an exit route for calculation purposes

There are no hard and fast rules as to whether or not an exit route should be discounted when calculating the emergency exit capacity of a sports ground or section of a ground. Each case needs to be determined in the light of local circumstances, taking into account the importance of a particular exit from an area of spectator accommodation and an assessment of the level of fire risk present.

If the fire risk assessment determines that there is a need to discount an exit, the exit to be discounted should be the widest one serving the area. If the fire risk is minimal and all elements of the exit system are suitably protected from the effects of fire, it may be unreasonable to discount an exit. (For guidance on fire risk assessment, see Sections 15.2–15.8.)

9.15 Exit doors and gates

Exit doors and gates should meet the following requirements:

a. All final exit doors and gates, unless secured in an open position, should be staffed at all times while the ground is used by the public.

b. No door or gate forming part of an exit route should be locked or fastened in such a way that it cannot easily and immediately be opened by those using that route in an emergency.

c. All final exit doors on a normal exit route should be secured in the fully open position before the end of the event. When open, no door should obstruct any gangway passage, stairway or landing.

d. All exit doors and gates on an exit route should always be capable of opening outwards so that crowds can escape in an emergency without obstruction. In situations where the opening of the doors or gates would cause an obstruction on a public highway, the doors or gates should be resited (that is, put further back) within the exit route they serve.

e. Where practicable exit doors and gates should be sited adjacent to entrances. There should be no obstructions and no changes in level at exit doors.

f. Sliding or roller-shutter gates should not be used because they are incapable of being opened when pressure is exerted in the direction of crowd flow, and they have mechanisms or runways which are vulnerable to jamming.

g. Reversible turnstiles or, preferably, pass doors should be provided in order to allow anyone to leave the ground at any time (including those ejected for breaching ground regulations). Such openings should be limited to allow the passage of only one person at a time.

h. Reversible turnstiles are not acceptable as a means of escape and should not form any part of the normal or emergency exit system.

i. Each exit door and gate should be clearly marked on both the inside and the outside with its identifying number.

9.16 Electronic securing systems

Where they are in place, electronic securing systems on exit doors and gates should meet the following requirements:

a. As stated in Section 9.15, no door or gate forming part of an exit route should be locked or fastened in such a way that it cannot easily and immediately be opened by those using that route in an emergency. This applies equally to exit doors and gates that are electronically secured.

b. All electronically secured doors and gates should be staffed by stewards at all times when spectators are in the ground.

c. The doors or gates should be capable of being de-energised individually by the steward.

d. The stewards should be specifically authorised to open their gates without further instructions in the event of a sudden local emergency.

e. Emergency telephones should be provided for instant communication, directly between the stewards staffing the exit doors or gates and the operator of the control panel (see below). All such telephones should be instantly accessible to the stewards without the use of a key.

f. The operation of each door or gate should be tested both electronically and manually immediately before each event and the result of each test recorded. The record should include all tests, any faults found, and any opening of any door or gate while spectators are present in the ground.

g. The control panel for the system should be located in the ground's control point and should be staffed continuously by a suitably trained and authorised person, who should have no other duties.

h. The base emergency telephone in the control point should be positioned so that the panel operator can answer it without having to leave his or her post.

i. Each gate should be clearly marked on both the inside and the outside with its identifying number. This identification should correspond to the identification of the switch on the control which releases it.

j. The doors or gates should be designed so that, in the event of a power failure, they are automatically de-energised and capable of being opened manually.

k. Electronically secured doors and gates should ideally be monitored by CCTV.

Before approving an electronic securing system, ground management or, where there is a safety certificate in force, the local authority, should consider carefully and take full account of the hazards associated with such a system. In particular, they should consider carefully what would happen if there was a major emergency and spectators had to force the doors open themselves.

Chapter Ten

Barriers

10.1 **Definition and categories of barriers**

A barrier (also referred to as a 'guard' or 'guard rail' in the Building Regulations) is any element of a sports ground, permanent or temporary, intended to prevent people from falling, and to retain, stop or guide people. This chapter is concerned with barriers in the following situations:

a. barriers used in areas of seated accommodation and on stairways and ramps (see Sections 10.2–10.5, Table 1 and Diagrams 6 and 7)

b. barriers used in areas of standing accommodation, known as crush barriers (see Sections 10.6–10.12, Table 2 and Diagrams 8–10)

c. barriers used in spectator galleries (see Section 10.13 and Table 3)

d. barriers used to separate spectator accommodation from the pitch or area of activity, known as pitch perimeter barriers (see Sections 10.14–10.17)

e. barriers such as boundary walls, fences or gates used to enclose the sports ground or individual sections (see Section 10.18).

Sections 10.19–10.26 provide guidance on the risk assessment and testing of barriers.

When applying the recommendations in this chapter, the distinction between a barrier and a handrail, as outlined in Section 7.6, should be noted.

10.2 **Barrier design and loading**

Barriers at sports grounds should be designed to resist safely the minimum horizontal imposed loads specified in Tables 1, 2 or 3. It should be noted, however, that in all situations professional judgement should ensure that the loadings are sufficient for the barrier's intended purpose.

Regardless of the height of the barrier (see Section 10.4), the horizontal imposed load should be considered to act at a height of 1.1m above the datum, when applied as a static load at right angles to the longitudinal axis.

Designers should ensure that any construction or structure acting as a support for barriers is of adequate strength and stability to resist safely all applied loads, without excessive stress, deflection or distortion.

When using limit state design, the partial factors for loads and materials should be those recommended by the appropriate British Standard for the relevant material.

Table 1. Horizontal imposed loads for barriers

types of barrier	horizontal imposed load
1. Crush barriers for standing accommodation	See Table 2
2. Barriers for spectator galleries	See Table 3
3. Barriers for gangways of seating decks, aligned at right angles to the direction of spectator movement	3.0 kN/m length
4. Barriers for gangways of seating decks, parallel to the direction of spectator movement	2.0 kN/m length
5. Barriers for seating decks, adjacent to the end row of seats and protecting spectators from falling sideways	1.0 kN/m length
6. Barriers for seating decks, behind a rear row of seats and protecting spectators from falling backwards	1.0 kN/m length
7. Barriers positioned within 530mm in front of seats	1.5 kN/m length
8. Barriers for stairways, landings and ramps, aligned at right angles to the direction of movement of spectators	3.0 kN/m length
9. Barriers for stairways, landings, and ramps, aligned with the direction of movement of spectators	2.0 kN/m length
10. Barriers for gangways in standing areas, aligned at right angles to the direction of spectator movement	5.0 kN/m length
11. Other barriers, including walls, boundary walls, fences and gates, that may be subject to crowd loading	See Section 10.18

Table 2. Horizontal imposed loads for crush barriers

angle of terrace or viewing slope	horizontal distance between crush barriers				
5°	5.0m	4.0m	3.3m	3.0m	2.0m
10°	4.3m	3.4m	2.9m	2.6m	1.7m
15°	3.8m	3.0m	2.6m	2.3m	1.5m
20°	3.4m	2.7m	2.3m	2.0m	1.3m
25°	3.1m	2.5m	2.1m	1.8m	1.2m
horizontal imposed load	5.0 kN/m length	4.0 kN/m length	3.4 kN/m length	3.0 kN/m length	2.0 kN/m length

Table 3. Horizontal imposed loads for barriers in spectator galleries

distance	3.4m	2.3m	1.7m
horizontal imposed load	3.0 kN/m length	2.0 kN/m length	1.5 kN/m length

General notes to Tables 1, 2 and 3

■ All barriers should be capable of resisting proof loads equivalent to 1.2 times the horizontal imposed loads listed in the tables.

■ Barrier testing methods and the criteria to be met are given in Sections 10.20–26.

■ Barrier foundations should be designed to resist the overturning moments and sliding forces induced by the horizontal imposed loads with a factor of safety of 2.

■ Loads specified in these tables should be treated as unfactored or characteristic loads for design purposes.

Notes to Table 1

■ This table should be read in conjunction with Diagrams 6 and 7.

■ All references to seats are to fixed seats (that is, any seat, tip-up or otherwise), attached to the main structure.

Notes to Table 2

■ Interpolation may be made between these figures.

■ Angles of slope in excess of 25° are potentially hazardous and should be avoided. Where they exist they should be subject to a risk assessment.

■ The maximum horizontal imposed load on a crush barrier should not be greater than 5 kN/m. This is because a transient load greater than 5 kN/m on the spectator immediately behind a crush barrier risks physical injury.

■ The horizontal distances specified are the maximum recommended according to the barrier strength and angle of slope, and should not be exceeded in new construction. If the distances at existing constructions exceed the maximum, the available viewing area (which forms part of the capacity calculation) should be limited to the area behind the barrier which falls within the maximum distance. The remaining space behind should be discounted, even though in practice spectators may stand in those areas (see worked examples 2 and 3 in Annex A).

Notes to Table 3

■ Interpolation may be made between these figures.

■ The required horizontal imposed load should be calculated according to the distance between the barrier and the gallery's rear wall, or any other restraint.

■ If the spectator gallery also forms part of an escape route, the barrier's horizontal imposed load should be no less than 2 kN/m length.

Diagram 6. Barrier design loads, heights and positions

This diagram illustrates the types of barriers used in seating decks, stairways and gangways. The type numbers correspond with those listed in Table 1.

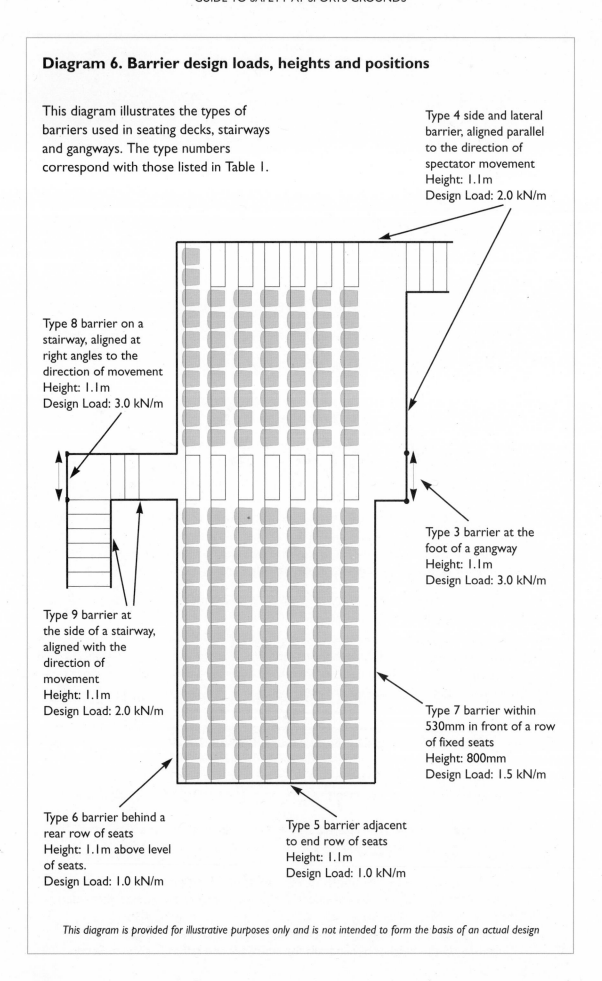

Type 4 side and lateral barrier, aligned parallel to the direction of spectator movement
Height: 1.1m
Design Load: 2.0 kN/m

Type 8 barrier on a stairway, aligned at right angles to the direction of movement
Height: 1.1m
Design Load: 3.0 kN/m

Type 3 barrier at the foot of a gangway
Height: 1.1m
Design Load: 3.0 kN/m

Type 9 barrier at the side of a stairway, aligned with the direction of movement
Height: 1.1m
Design Load: 2.0 kN/m

Type 7 barrier within 530mm in front of a row of fixed seats
Height: 800mm
Design Load: 1.5 kN/m

Type 6 barrier behind a rear row of seats
Height: 1.1m above level of seats.
Design Load: 1.0 kN/m

Type 5 barrier adjacent to end row of seats
Height: 1.1m
Design Load: 1.0 kN/m

This diagram is provided for illustrative purposes only and is not intended to form the basis of an actual design

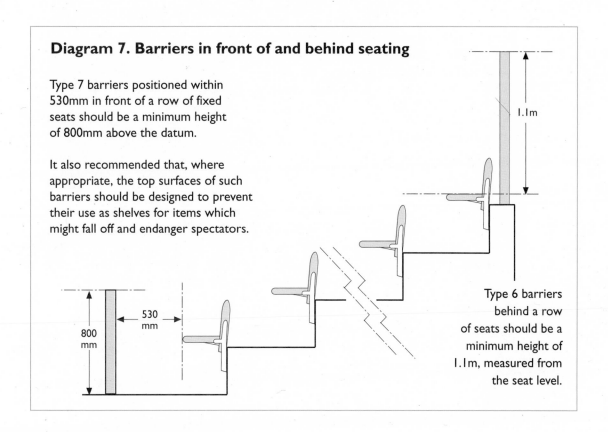

Diagram 7. Barriers in front of and behind seating

Type 7 barriers positioned within 530mm in front of a row of fixed seats should be a minimum height of 800mm above the datum.

It also recommended that, where appropriate, the top surfaces of such barriers should be designed to prevent their use as shelves for items which might fall off and endanger spectators.

1.1m

800 mm

530 mm

Type 6 barriers behind a row of seats should be a minimum height of 1.1m, measured from the seat level.

10.3 Barrier fixings

The strength of all fixings and joints should be adequate for the loading to which the barrier will be subjected. The design should avoid reliance wholly on the pull-out strength of a single fixing. It is also essential that fixing design takes account of the material into which the fixing is placed, the spacing between fixings, the edge distance and, where appropriate, the position of reinforcement in the concrete. The fixings should not create a trip hazard for spectators.

10.4 Barrier heights

Barriers used in areas of seated accommodation and on stairways and ramps should be designed to a height of not less than 1.1m, measured from the datum, unless they fall into one of the following three categories:

a.   Barriers within 530mm in front of fixed seating should be a minimum height of 800mm above the datum (see Diagram 7).

b.   Barriers immediately behind a row of seats should be a minimum height of 1.1m above the datum, which in this case is the level of the seat (see Diagram 7).

c.   Barriers designed to separate stairways into channels may be a minimum height of 1.0m above the datum (see Section 7.7.b and Diagram 4).

In all cases, as stated in Section 10.2, regardless of the height, the horizontal imposed load should still be considered to act at a height of 1.1m above the datum.

Further guidance on the height of crush barriers is provided in Section 10.10. Guidance on the heights of handrails for stairways and ramps is given in Section 7.8.

10.5   Barriers and sightline considerations

As stated in Section 11.2, all spectators in seated areas should have a clear, unobstructed view of the whole pitch or area of activity. However, it is recognised that even barriers meeting the height requirements listed in Section 10.4 may obstruct sightlines.

Careful consideration should therefore be given to the design and construction of any barrier forming part of a seating deck. This applies particularly to barriers placed within 530mm of fixed seating.

10.6   Crush barriers – main design criteria

This section and Sections 10.7–10.12 on crush barriers should be read in conjunction with Chapter 12, concerning the overall design and management of standing areas. Detailed reference should also be made to Table 2.

At sports grounds where standing accommodation is provided, many of the hazards arising from crowd pressure on terraces and viewing slopes can be eliminated by the provision of crush barriers that are appropriately designed and constructed.

The main considerations concerning the design and construction of crush barriers are detailed in the following sections, and can be summarised as follows:

a.   the angle of slope of the terrace or viewing slope, which in turn will determine the appropriate spacing of the crush barriers and the required horizontal imposed load for each crush barrier (see Section 10.7)

b.   the configuration of the crush barriers in relation to gangways (see Sections 10.8 and 10.9)

c.   the height and positioning of the crush barriers in relation to the treads or surfaces of the standing area (see Section 10.10)

d.   the construction and condition of the crush barriers (see Section 10.11).

Section 10.12 summarises the consequences of any deficiencies or deviations from the requirements outlined in Sections 10.7–10.11.

10.7   Crush barriers – factors determining the horizontal imposed load

As stated in Section 10.6 above, the required horizontal imposed load for crush barriers is determined by the angle of the terrace or viewing slope, in relation to the horizontal distance between the crush barriers, as shown in Table 2.

Table 2 indicates that the steeper the angle of slope and the greater the horizontal distance between crush barriers, the greater the horizontal imposed load required for those crush barriers.

a.   Angle of slope

The angle of slope (or gradient) is the first factor to be considered when determining the required horizontal imposed load for crush barriers.

For new construction: the angle of slope for newly contructed areas of standing should be designed according to the calculations for sightlines (see Section 12.11). Although for seated areas the angle can be as steep as 34°, for standing areas it should not exceed 25°.

For existing construction: the angle of slope will be pre-determined. However, it is recommended that the angle should not exceed 25°, and in no circumstances should exceed 30° (see Section 10.12).

b. **Horizontal distance between crush barriers**
Having established the angle of slope, the spacing between crush barriers should then be considered.

For new construction: designers should use the figures in Table 2 to determine the appropriate crush barrier loadings and spacings according to the desired angle of slope.

For existing contruction: the horizontal spacing between crush barriers will be pre-determined, in which case the horizontal imposed load of the crush barriers must be in accordance with the requirements specified in Table 2. If the spacing proves to be excessive, the available viewing area should be reduced to those areas immediately behind each crush barrier, measured to a depth appropriate to the crush barrier's strength (see Table 2 and Section 10.12).

Any crush barrier which fails to meet the horizontal imposed load requirements specified in Table 2 should be removed and replaced, or strengthened and then re-tested (see Section 10.11).

10.8 Crush barriers – continuous crush barrier configuration
The configuration of crush barriers – that is, their lay-out in relation to each other and to the gangways – has a crucial influence on the safe management of spectators in standing areas.

Experience at sports grounds indicates that the safest configuration is to provide crush barriers along the full width of a terrace or viewing slope, with gaps only at the radial gangways.

For new construction: at all new sports grounds where standing areas are to form part of the viewing accommodation, or at grounds where new standing areas are to be constructed, a continuous crush barrier configuration should be provided between radial gangways.

For existing construction: at all sports grounds where standing accommodation is already provided, consideration should be given to the conversion of existing standing areas so that they incorporate a continuous crush barrier configuration between radial gangways.

An example of a continuous crush barrier configuration is illustrated in Diagram 8.

Diagram 8. Continuous crush barrier configuration

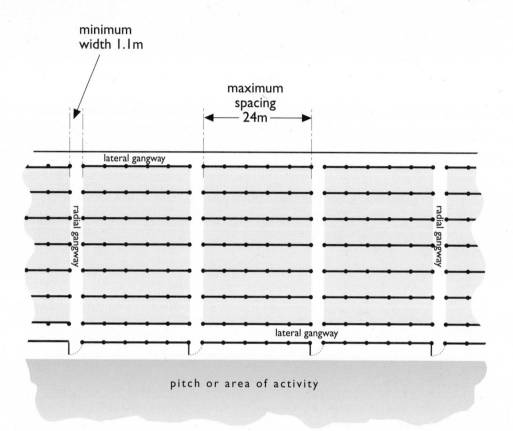

A continuous crush barrier configuration is recommended for all areas of standing accommodation and is the principal method by which ground managements can aim to achieve the highest permissible capacity levels for a standing area.

Note that all spectators should be within 12m of a gangway or exit, hence the spacing of gangways 24m apart. Note also that for new construction the recommended minimum width for gangways is 1.2m.

At sports grounds where pitch perimeter barriers are positioned in front of standing areas, gates or openings should be provided to allow spectators to escape onto the pitch or area of activity in the event of an incident.

Where gates are fitted, as illustrated these should open away from the viewing accommodation.

Wherever practicable in standing areas, as stated in Section 10.15 and shown above, there should be a lateral gangway dividing the front row of crush barriers from the pitch perimeter barrier. However, where a continuous crush barrier configuration is provided, a front lateral gangway may not always be necessary, depending on local conditions.

Because this configuration is considered to be the safest arrangement for guiding and controlling the movements of standing spectators, it is also the principal method by which ground managements can aim to achieve the highest permissible capacity levels for a standing area.

As stated in Section 1.8, provided that the strengths of the continuous crush barriers are appropriate for the angle of slope and the spacings between the crush barriers, and the standing area is both in good condition and well stewarded, there should be no reduction in the calculation of its available viewing area, nor of its (P) and (S) factors, nor of its appropriate density, which should be the maximum of 47 persons per 10 square metres (as explained in Section 1.9).

Worked example 1 in Annex A illustrates how a continuous crush barrier configuration results in a higher capacity than a standing area of an identical size but with a non-continuous configuration (as shown in worked example 2 in Annex A).

10.9   Crush barriers – non-continuous crush barrier configuration

For existing construction: although not recommended, non-continuous crush barrier configurations may still be regarded as acceptable, provided that the capacity is reduced using the calculations specified in Chapter 1, and appropriate safety management systems are also put into place.

Where non-continuous crush barriers are in place, the alignment of gaps in successive rows of barriers should form an angle of less than 60° to the barriers (see worked example 2 in Annex A).

There should be no more than two consecutive gaps in any line. These gaps should be at least 1.1m, and not more than 1.4m, in width.

10.10   Crush barriers – height and positioning

Research has shown that in order to locate the top rail of a crush barrier against that part of the body most able to tolerate pressure, and to accommodate a typical range of spectators, a reasonable height for the top rail is 1.1m.

Note, however, the need to evolve a management strategy for the safe accommodation of children, for whom the recommended barrier height might actually constitute a hazard (see Section 12.24.i).

For new construction: as illustrated in Diagram 9, to allow spectators sufficient room to stand safely and comfortably behind a crush barrier, new crush barriers should ideally be positioned immediately in front of a terrace step's riser, or if not, at the front of a step. In both cases, the 1.1m is measured from the step on which the spectator stands to the top of the crush barrier's rail.

For existing construction: previous editions of the *Guide* measured the height of crush barriers from the step to the centre line of the top rail, allowing a range between 1.02m and 1.12m. Existing crush barriers meeting this requirement should still be regarded as acceptable.

Diagram 9.

Positioning and height of crush barriers

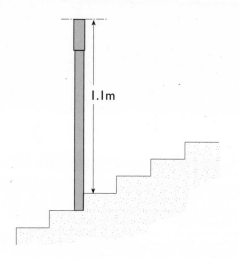

In the top two examples, the barriers are positioned, as recommended, at the front of the step. The recommended height of 1.1m is measured from the surface of the step to the top of the rail. For existing situations, the measurement can be taken from the step to the centre of the rail, and be between 1.02m and 1.12m.

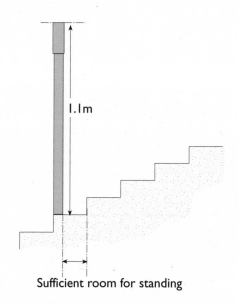

Sufficient room for standing

In this example the barrier is positioned in such a way as to make it difficult for a spectator to stand on the same step. For this reason the height measurement should be taken from the step behind. This positioning of barriers is not recommended for new construction.

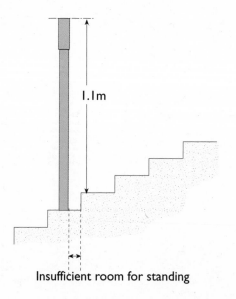

Insufficient room for standing

However, any crush barrier not meeting the height requirement should be removed and replaced, or modified.

If the positioning of existing crush barriers leaves insufficient room for standing on the same step, as illustrated in Diagram 9, the height should be measured from the step immediately behind.

10.11 Crush barriers – construction and strengthening

Crush barriers should be constructed or strengthened taking into account the following requirements:

a.   For safety and comfort, there should be no sharp projections or edges.

b.   For safety and comfort, the crush barrier's top rail should be flat and measure 100mm in vertical depth.

c.   As stated in Section 10.7, any crush barrier which fails to meet the horizontal imposed load specified in Table 2 should be removed and replaced. If this is not possible and therefore strengthening measures are to be considered, care must be taken to avoid simply transferring the problem to another part of the crush barrier or its foundations.

If strengthening the crush barrier post, portal type bracing is recommended, as illustrated in Diagram 10.

All newly strengthened barriers must be tested before use.

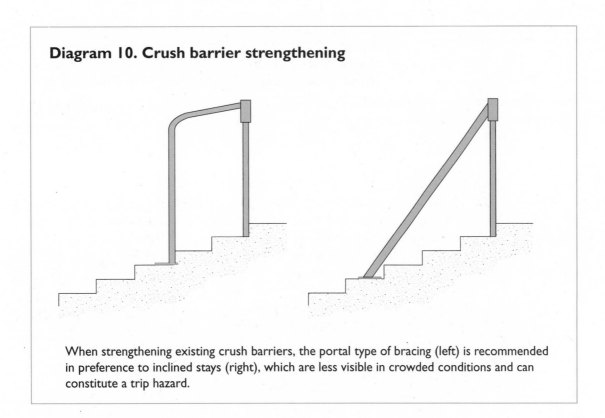

Diagram 10. Crush barrier strengthening

When strengthening existing crush barriers, the portal type of bracing (left) is recommended in preference to inclined stays (right), which are less visible in crowded conditions and can constitute a trip hazard.

10.12 Crush barriers – factors affecting the holding capacity

In addition to the reduction of the available viewing area resulting from the provision of a non-continuous crush barrier configuration (see Section 10.9), further deficiencies or deviations from the recommendations in the *Guide* may require a reduction of the holding capacity of the standing area (see Chapter 1).

A summary of the main concerns follows. Note that this list is not intended to be comprehensive, nor applicable in all circumstances.

A reduction in the holding capacity of a standing area may be necessary if:

a. the angle of slope is above 25° (thereby requiring a reduction of the (P) or (S) factors)

b. the crush barrier spacing is too great in relation to the angle of slope (thereby requiring a reduction of the available viewing area, and a possible reduction in the (S) factor)

c. after testing, the barrier fails completely (see Section 10.26) and is removed but not replaced (thereby requiring a reduction in the available viewing area, and a possible reduction in the (S) factor).

It should be noted that there may be other aspects of the standing area which also require a reduction in the holding capacity. These might include the physical condition of the standing area, its safety management, the provision of partial cover only, or the inadequacy of sightlines. Further guidance on these concerns is provided in Chapters 1 and 12.

10.13 Barriers in spectator galleries

Viewing galleries for standing spectators are generally attached to hospitality areas at sports grounds staging sports such as horse or motor racing. Although the number of spectators who have access to such galleries is normally limited by the capacity of the hospitality area, the front barrier must still be designed to withstand crowd loading.

Table 3 specifies the required horizontal imposed loads, which vary according to the horizontal distance between the barrier and either the rear wall of the spectator gallery or any other restraint.

10.14 Pitch perimeter barriers

A pitch perimeter barrier is a barrier installed to separate spectators from the pitch or area of activity. Such barriers can take the form of crush barriers, walls or rails.

The type, height and horizontal imposed load of a pitch perimeter barrier will vary according to its location and required function.

If spectators can lean on, or gather immediately behind, the perimeter barrier, it should be deemed a crush barrier and therefore meet the horizontal imposed load and height requirements as specified in Sections 10.6–10.12.

Even if a pitch perimeter barrier does not need to meet the horizontal imposed load requirements of a crush barrier, its height should ideally not exceed 1.1m (1.12m to the centre line in existing constructions). This is in order to facilitate spectator access to the pitch or area of activity in the event of an emergency. (This height requirement does not, however, preclude the need for gates or openings in pitch perimeter barriers, as stated in Section 10.17.)

10.15 Pitch perimeter barriers and standing areas

As stated in Section 12.18, wherever practicable, pitch perimeter barriers should be separated from an area of standing accommodation by a lateral gangway, to assist circulation (see also Diagram 8).

An exception to this recommendation might be a standing area which has a continuous crush barrier configuration. In such cases an assessment of the need for a lateral gangway should be made, based on local conditions.

Wherever the standing area does descend directly to a pitch perimeter barrier, however, that barrier must meet the height and horizontal imposed load requirements of a crush barrier.

10.16 Pitch perimeter fences

The term 'pitch perimeter fence' in the following paragraphs means any pitch perimeter barrier which exceeds the maximum recommended height of 1.1m (1.12m to the centre line at existing sports grounds), and which is of a non-solid construction, thus enabling spectators to see through to the pitch or area of activity.

Such fences were installed at a number of association football grounds to prevent spectators gaining access to the pitch, although many have now been removed.

For new construction: the use of pitch perimeter fences is not recommended under any circumstances. Other means of preventing spectators from gaining unauthorised access to the pitch should be utilised. These means may include high profile stewarding, clear signs, regular public address announcements, and/or the construction of sunken lateral gangways.

For existing construction: the use of pitch perimeter fences is not recommended for standing areas, and should be avoided in all cases in front of seated areas.

Where such fences are in place, however, the following requirements should be met:

a. Standing areas should not descend directly to a pitch perimeter fence. Instead, there should be a lateral gangway between the first row of crush barriers and the pitch perimeter fence. This is to assist circulation and to prevent spectators from gathering immediately behind or climbing up the fence.

b. If spectators can gather immediately behind, lean against or climb up a pitch perimeter fence, the fence should be designed to resist crowd loading.

c. The pitch perimeter fence should not impair visibility of the pitch or area of activity. If sightlines are obscured by fencing, congestion may be caused, for example because standing spectators are unwilling to move forward, or seated spectators are induced to stand up. If such problems are not resolved satisfactorily, a reduction in capacity should result.

d. The height of a pitch perimeter fence should not exceed 2.2m.

e. There should be no overhanging sections and no spikes, barbed wire or other devices installed or attached to a pitch perimeter fence.

f. As an additional precaution, consideration should be given – in consultation with the local authority if a safety certificate is in force – to the provision of suitable cutting equipment so that, if necessary, sufficient fencing can be removed in order to release any trapped spectators. Trained operators provided by the management should be available in order to use the equipment. The safety officer or a nominated senior police officer will decide when such equipment is to be used.

Even if all the above requirements are met, however, the use of pitch perimeter fences is still not recommended. Management should ideally seek to utilise other methods of preventing spectators gaining access to the pitch or area of activity, such as those listed earlier in this section.

10.17 Emergency access to the pitch or area of activity

As stated in Section 9.12, in certain cases forward evacuation onto the pitch or area of activity may form part of the emergency evacuation plan, provided that the pitch or area of activity leads directly to an exit which itself leads to a place of safety.

However, regardless of whether the pitch or area of activity forms part of the emergency evacuation plan, any pitch perimeter barrier or fence placed in front of an area of standing accommodation must be provided with gates or openings which allow spectators access to the pitch or area of activity.

Further guidance on such gates or openings is provided in Section 9.13.

10.18 Other load-bearing barriers

In addition to the barrier types already covered in this chapter, other load-bearing barriers subject to crowd loading at sports ground may include walls (including boundary walls), fences and gates.

If required to withstand crowd pressures, all such barriers should be designed, constructed and maintained to withstand those pressures safely.

Allowance should also be made for forces simultaneously and independently induced by other factors; for example, wind forces or attached installations.

10.19 Barriers and risk assessment

The previous edition of this *Guide* recommended that all barriers be inspected annually, and that, in addition to any suspect barriers, at the very least a 25 per cent representative sample of the barriers throughout all parts of the ground should be tested every year.

It is now recommended that this approach to testing be modified, as follows.

All barriers (including crush barriers) should be subject to an annual risk assessment. Every barrier identified by the risk assessment as a potential risk should be tested immediately.

The risk assessment (which, in practice, will be carried out in a similar fashion to an annual inspection) should be conducted and recorded by a chartered engineer, architect or surveyor of the appropriate skill and experience. It should take into account all relevant recommendations in this *Guide*, combined with a detailed appraisal of each of the following specific considerations:

a. any available recorded information concerning the barrier's design compliance

b. the adequacy of the barrier's construction

c. the age of the barrier

d. any visual evidence of weakening or general deterioration of the barrier, including signs of corrosion, cracks, holes, misalignment, undue distortion, missing bolts or fittings

e. the barrier's exposure to moisture

f. the barrier's location within the sports ground.

Those barriers which need to be tested immediately might include those whose theoretical strength is indeterminable, those which have suffered visible decay, and those where there is potential for undetected deterioration.

Responsibility for appointing a competent person to undertake and record the results of a risk assessment of barriers lies with the management of the sports ground.

10.20 Barrier tests – personnel and equipment

Having conducted the risk assessment and determined which barriers, if any, require testing, it is then the responsibility of management to ensure that the tests are carried out immediately.

The management is further responsible for ensuring that the testing is carried out by, or under the supervision of, a competent person of the appropriate skill and experience.

The competent person will then be responsible for ensuring that the tests are properly carried out and that all results are accurately recorded (see Section 10.21).

The competent person must be satisfied that the equipment used for the testing is suitable for the purpose and is used in the correct manner.

The equipment used should be capable of a level of accuracy of 5 per cent of the test load.

The deflection measuring equipment should be calibrated and be capable of a level of accuracy that reflects the magnitude of the deflections being measured.

10.21 Barrier tests – records

Detailed written records should be made and kept of all observations, loadings and deflection/recovery readings in respect of each barrier tested. The documentation should include a standard record sheet including the following information:

a. the identity of each barrier tested

b. its location, including a cross-reference to the ground plan

c. the date of inspection

d. all relevant results and comments arising from the test

e. a clear statement as to whether the barrier has passed or failed.

10.22 Barrier tests – methodology

The test method for barriers should be in two parts:

a. the 'bedding-in' cycle

b. the proof cycle.

Barriers that do not fulfil the requirements of both parts shall be deemed to have failed the test.

The deflection measuring equipment should be unaffected by any movement of the barriers, their supports, or the movements of personnel performing the test.

The deflections in the horizontal plane should be measured at relevant locations; for example, at the centre of a barrier rail or the top of an upright.

The loading procedure adopted shall result in each component part of any barrier being subject to levels of stress at least equal to the stresses that would occur were the structure subjected to the relevant uniformly distributed load at a design level of 1.1m.

10.23 Barrier tests – bedding-in cycle

In order to allow for bedding-in, the barrier should be loaded up to its horizontal imposed load as defined in either Tables 1 or 2. The bedding-in load should be applied in at least five equal increments and then removed. Deflections should be monitored at each increment of the load cycle and upon removal of the load. The barrier may be considered to have satisfactorily completed this part of the test if, on removal of the load, the recovery is at least 75 per cent of the maximum deflection, as measured from the original position prior to loading, or if the permanent deflection is less than 2mm.

If the barrier fails to achieve this level of recovery it shall be considered to have failed the test unless there is a satisfactory explanation for the results.

10.24 Barrier tests – proof cycle

The proof cycle is to consist of two consecutive applications of the proof load. The interval between each application shall be such as to enable complete unloading.

For crush barriers the proof load is equal to 1.2 x the horizontal imposed load specified in Table 2.

For other barriers the proof force is equal to 1.2 x the horizontal imposed load specified in either Table 1 or Table 3.

The application of the proof load should consist of five equal increments.

The full proof load shall be maintained for five minutes and then removed.

A record shall be kept of:

a. the deflection at each load increment

b. the deflection after the five-minute application of the full proof load

c. the residual deflection after removal of the load.

The procedure is then repeated.

If, on removal of the load after the second application, the recovery is at least 95 per cent in any measured deflection (as measured from the barrier position at the start of the proof test cycle – that is, after the bedding-in cycle), the barrier should be considered to have satisfied the proof cycle loading requirement.

10.25 Barrier tests – further considerations

Comparisons should be made with the records available from previous testings of the barrier.

Comparison should also be made with the performance of other barriers of a similar type subjected to the same or similar tests. This is to establish whether there are indications of a reduction in overall performance, perhaps indicative of a developing weakness that necessitates either remedial action or more regular testing or inspection.

If the barrier satisfies the requirements of the testing procedure, but during that procedure doubt arises as to its safety, for any reason (including such matters as corrosion, distortion of connections and fittings, or cracking in the vicinity of supports), a further detailed investigation should be carried out. Unless the results of this detailed investigation remove the doubt, the barrier should be deemed to have failed.

The results of tests carried out using the principles of the testing procedure recommended in previous editions of the *Guide* are valid until such time as a barrier is re-tested according to these current guidelines.

10.26 Barrier tests resulting in failure

A barrier failing the test procedure should be removed and replaced, or strengthened and then retested.

As stated in Section 10.12, if a crush barrier fails and it is not replaced or strengthened, the available viewing area of the standing area should be reduced, together with a possible reduction of the (S) factor, which in turn may lead to a reduction of the area's final capacity.

However, the non-replacement or non-repair of a failed crush barrier is not recommended.

The removal of a crush barrier – particularly one placed where a high density of spectators may congregate – is likely to lead to uncontrolled movements and increased crowd pressure. In such situations, the reduction of the area's holding capacity should be much greater than if it were related to the non-replacement of an individual crush barrier elsewhere.

The non-replacement of a crush barrier will also require a management strategy to prevent overcrowding in the affected area.

Replacement, or repair, of the failed barrier should therefore always be the preferred option.

Chapter Eleven

Spectator accommodation – Seating

11.1 The provision of seated accommodation

At sports grounds where spectators are essentially non-ambulatory during the event – such as grounds staging football, rugby, cricket, athletics, tennis, hockey or motor racing – the provision of seated accommodation for all spectators is, wherever possible, recommended.

When considering new construction at such grounds, management should take this into consideration as part of its strategy for overall safety management.

It is recognised, however, that where spectators may be ambulatory during the event – such as at grounds staging golf or horse or greyhound racing – a combination of seated and standing accommodation is a fundamental design requirement.

The provision of seats is not, in itself, a guarantee of safe conditions for spectators. It is also necessary that seated areas are designed and managed to be safe.

Moreover, as stated in Section 1.6, the safe capacity of seated areas does not automatically correspond to the number of actual seats provided. It should instead be set at a number which the management can manage safely, and must always be assessed using the (P) and (S) factors. Guidance on the assessment of (P) and (S) factors for seated accommodation is provided in Chapter 1 and Sections 11.16 and 11.17.

Newly constructed seated accommodation should conform to any applicable Building Regulations, and to the appropriate requirements of the *Guide*, such as the design of circulation routes, barrier and handrail provision and fire safety. In addition, when designing and managing seated accommodation, the comfort and amenities of spectators, and their access to amenities, should be considered at all times.

It is therefore recommended that, in all matters relating to the design of seated accommodation, management seeks professional advice from competent persons of the appropriate skill and experience.

For further guidance, reference may be made to the FSADC publication *Seating* (see Bibliography). Although written primarily for football grounds, the publication includes much general advice applicable to all sports grounds.

11.2 Viewing standards

The provision of adequate viewing standards is a key factor in ensuring that seated accommodation is both safe and serves its intended purpose.

Spectators in seated accommodation should have a clear, unrestricted view of the whole of the playing area or area of activity.

Designs should ensure that spectators are encouraged to remain seated and do not have to stretch or strain to view the event. (The only exceptions to this requirement are grounds staging such events as horse or motor racing, where clearly a view of the whole area of activity is difficult to achieve from any static viewing position.)

Viewing standards depend largely on three inter-related factors:

a.   the quality of **sightlines** (see Section 11.3 and Diagram 11)

b.   the existence of any **restrictions** (see Section 11.4)

c.   the **viewing distance** (see Section 11.17).

11.3   Sightlines

The term 'sightline' refers to the ability of a spectator to see a predetermined focal point (on the pitch or area of activity) over the top of the head of the spectators immediately in front. The better the sightline, the more likely it is that spectators will remain seated during the event. Ensuring adequate sightlines is therefore an important part of providing safe seated accommodation.

The quality of a sightline is often expressed as a 'C' value. Diagram 11 shows how 'C' values are calculated. The recommended 'C' value for spectators varies according to the sport, as does the choice of focal point.

For example, it is important for spectators at football or rugby matches to be able to see the nearest touchline, so this should form the focal point. However, a focal point further in-field may be acceptable for viewing cricket.

Because of the complex nature of sightline calculations in individual circumstances it is therefore recommended that management seeks professional advice from competent persons of the appropriate skill, and with experience of designing spectator accommodation for the sport (or sports) to be staged.

11.4   Restricted viewing

As stated previously, all spectators should have a clear, unrestricted view of the whole of the playing area or area of activity. Although there are exceptions to this requirement (see Section 11.2), the causes of potential restrictions should be considered at all sports grounds. These may include:

a.   inadequate sightlines

b.   roof supports or roof structures

c.   the flanking walls, screens or overhanging upper tiers of stands

d.   barriers serving gangways

e.   segregation barriers or fences

f.   structures such as floodlights, scoreboards or temporary camera platforms

g.   advertising hoardings

Diagram 11. Sightlines for seated spectators

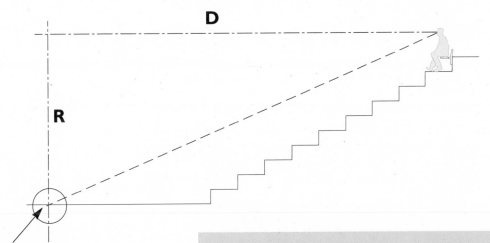

point of focus:

typically the nearest touchline,
or outside lane of a running track,
or boundary of area of activity

To calculate the appropriate 'C' value for the sport to be viewed, the following formula applies:

$$C = \frac{D\,(N + R)}{D + T} - R$$

Key to diagram:

C = the 'C' value

D = the horizontal distance from the eye to the point of focus

N = the riser height

R = the vertical height to the point of focus

T = the seating row depth

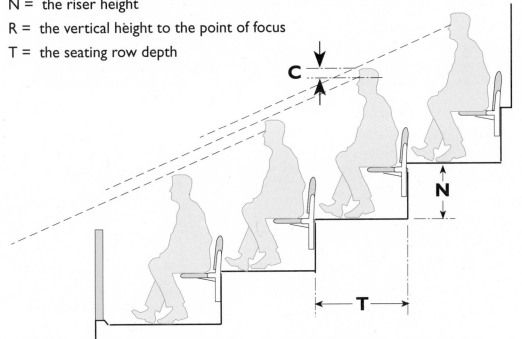

h.   the passage of other spectators or ground personnel in front of seats or in lateral gangways

i.   the positioning of media personnel (such as photographers and camera operators), stewards and any other personnel.

Note that the provision of pitch perimeter fences in front of seated areas is not recommended (see Section 10.15), unless specifically required for the protection of spectators from the activity taking place (as, for example, in hockey).

Management is responsible for assessing the effects of restricted viewing from every seat to which spectators have access, and for taking the appropriate action where necessary (see Section 11.5).

In carrying out this assessment, it is recommended that the following criteria are applied:

■   **Partial restriction**
This applies to seats from which the view may be restricted, for example by a roof support, but not to the extent that spectators have to strain or are encouraged to stand in order to gain an improved view.

■   **Serious restriction**
This applies to seats from which the view is sufficiently restricted, for example by inadequate sightlines or advertising hoardings, to encourage spectators to stand.

In assessing the level of restriction, a pragmatic and clear distinction should be made between spectators who are positively encouraged or even forced to stand up because of restrictions, and spectators who stand up briefly at key moments during an event.

11.5   Management strategies towards restricted viewing

For new construction:
No newly constructed stands should have any seats offering views with serious restrictions. Every effort should also be made to ensure that partially restricted views are eliminated.

Furthermore, it is the responsibility of both the management and designers to ensure that the viewing standards provided are adequate and appropriate for the sport (or sports) to be staged. For this reason, management may wish to request that designers provide written assurance to that effect.

For existing construction:
Where views are partially restricted and the restrictions cannot be removed, consideration should be given to marking tickets for the affected seats with the words 'Restricted View'. Management should ensure that people are advised of this before they purchase such tickets. Where there is a safety certificate in force, this course of action may be required by the local authority on safety grounds.

Where views are seriously restricted and the restrictions cannot be removed, the affected seats should not be made available to spectators and should be excluded from the holding capacity (see Chapter 1).

If, despite carrying out the measures recommended above, it is observed that spectators in certain seats continue to stand for extended periods during an event, there should be a reduction in the (S) factor, thus leading to a possible reduction of the final capacity of the stand (see Section 11.17).

11.6 Provision of cover

Although at grounds staging certain sports it is recommended that all seated accommodation be covered, it is recognised that full protection from the elements is hard to achieve in all situations and in all weather conditions; for example, because of the height of the roof or the direction of prevailing winds. For further guidance, reference may be made to the FSADC publication *Stadium Roofs* (see Bibliography).

Where the protection provided is only partial, or there is no cover at all, the following strategies should be considered:

a. **Partial cover**

Experience shows that where partial cover only is provided and spectators are able to migrate from an uncovered section to a covered section, congestion can occur. In such situations management might consider the following options:

i. To extend the roof. If such an extension adds to the number of roof supports, however, these could adversely effect the viewing standards of a larger number of spectators.

ii. To provide a new roof covering the whole area.

iii. To install appropriate barriers, to prevent or control migration, and/or

iv. To adopt appropriate stewarding strategies to control the migration.

If none of the above options are implemented, or if either options iii or iv are implemented but the problems of migration and overcrowding continue, consideration should be given to limiting the final capacity of the affected section to those seats under cover.

b. **No cover**

At sports grounds where uncovered seats are provided, management should ensure that spectators seeking shelter do not overcrowd other areas of the ground (such as covered stands and concourses).

c. **Ticketing**

As a general principle, tickets for seats which are not covered should be marked with the words 'Uncovered Seat'. Management should ensure that people are advised of this before they purchase such tickets. If a safety certificate is in force, this course of action may be required by the local authority, on safety grounds.

11.7   Gangways in seated areas – general requirements

As stated in Section 11.1, the provision of seats alone is not, in itself, a guarantee of safe conditions for spectators. It is also necessary that seated areas are designed and managed to be safe.

Although is is recognised that, compared to standing spectators, people in seated areas are generally less hurried and more orderly in terms of their circulation – largely because of the lay-out of seating rows – careful consideration must still be given to the design and provision of ingress and egress routes, including both radial and lateral gangways.

In general, the design of gangways in seated areas should meet the following requirements:

a.   They should be provided so that no spectator in any part of a seated area should have to travel more than 30m from their seat in order to enter an exit system, measured along the line of the seating row and gangway. (For example, in stands with vomitories this distance would be measured from the seat to the entrance of the vomitory.) It should also be noted that the normal maximum egress time for all areas of viewing accommodation, standing or seated, is eight minutes (see Section 9.7).

b.   As for all areas of spectator accommodation, gangways in seated areas should be a minimum of 1.1m wide (1.2m recommended for new construction); should be even and free from trip hazards; and their surfaces should be slip-resistant.

c.   Any stepped side gangway (that is, with viewing accommodation on one side only) should be provided either with a barrier which meets the requirements of Table 1 in Chapter 10 or, if a barrier is not necessary (see Section 7.7), a handrail which meets the requirements detailed in Section 7.8.

Further guidance on circulation can be found in Chapters 5–9, and in the following sections.

11.8   Lateral gangways in seated areas

The design and management of lateral gangways in seated areas requires particular attention.

a.   **Front lateral gangways**

Spectators seated in the front rows of stands which have front lateral gangways at the same level as the first row of seats may have their view restricted by the passage of people along the gangway.

Where such a situation exists, the management should make every effort to ensure that spectators are not encouraged to stand. If the restriction of views cannot be managed effectively, a reduction in the (S) factor may have to be considered, or access to the affected seats prohibited (see Section 11.17).

b. Mid-level lateral gangways

Where spectators in seats immediately behind mid-level lateral gangways have their view restricted by the passage of people along the gangway, the same considerations as above should be applied.

In addition, designers should recognise that when incorporating mid-level lateral gangways the geometry of the design should ensure that sightlines for spectators in the rows behind such gangways are not adversely affected.

11.9 Radial gangways in seated areas

As stated in Section 7.2, for the purpose of design and assessment, the criteria applying to radial gangways are, in part, different to those pertaining to stairways. The main difference is that the dimensions of the goings and risers of radial gangways will be determined by the gradient of the seating rows (although they should not exceed that achieved by the step dimensions for stairways; that is, 34°).

Taking this into account, the following requirements should apply:

a.   The goings of steps in radial gangways should not be less than 280mm, and should be uniform.

b.   The risers of steps in radial gangways should not be more than 190mm, and should also be uniform.

However, in order to provide adequate sightlines in larger tiers of stands, it is often necessary for seating rows, or series of seating rows (sometimes called facets), to be constructed with riser heights which increase incrementally from the front to the rear of the tier. Accordingly in such situations, the riser heights of steps in radial gangways will also increase incrementally.

This is acceptable practice, with one proviso. If the resultant radial gangway steps do not comply with the specified minimum or maximum dimensions, compensatory measures should be considered in order to ensure safe passage. Examples of compensatory measures may include hand-holds or intermittent central handrails.

These hand-holds or handrails should be robust, securely fixed, and their fixings designed to be fit for the purpose.

c.   In order to minimise the discomfort of spectators, it may be preferable to shorten the length of excessively long radial gangways on steeply angled upper tiers by diverting the flow along lateral gangways.

d.   The nosings of steps in radial gangways should be clearly identified for the benefit of spectators.

e.   Radial gangways in seated areas should not contain winders (that is, tapered treads).

f.   Any barrier (including walls, fences or gates) at the foot of radial gangways in seated areas should be 1.1m high and have the design load shown in Table 1 of Chapter 10 (that is, 3.0 kN/m length).

11.10 The importance of seat dimensions

As stated in Section 11.3, the provision of adequate and appropriate sightlines requires a complex calculation which, as illustrated in Diagrams 11 and 12, involves a number of different factors relating to seat dimensions.

In addition, the safety, comfort and amenity of spectators will be determined by the amount of space provided for each individual seat.

For new construction: it is the responsibility of management to ensure that sightlines and seat dimensions are provided to the highest standard that can be reasonably achieved, and that these factors are incorporated into the design by competent persons of the appropriate skill and experience.

For existing construction: although it may be difficult to improve upon the sightlines or seat dimensions in existing constructions, wherever practicable management should consider upgrading areas where the provision is clearly inadequate. If reconstruction of the particular areas is impracticable, consideration might be given the installation of more appropriate seat types, or to the adjustment or adaptation of the existing seats. In all cases, management should seek guidance from competent persons.

For an explanation of the terms used in the following sections, see Diagram 12.

11.11 Seat widths and seating row depths

For new construction:
The minimum space allotted to each seated person should be as follows:

- Seat width: 460mm (40mm greater if fitted with armrests)
- Seating row depth: 700mm

For comfort and accessibility, however, it is recommended that these measurements should be increased to at least 500mm and at least 760mm respectively.

This recommendation applies particularly in the following circumstances:

a. where spectators require, and/or the management hopes to facilitate, easy movement to and from seats during an event (for example, to purchase refreshments)

b. where the sport being staged is of a lengthy and continuous nature

c. where it is the custom of spectators to place refreshments, bags or hampers on the seating row tread

d. at sports grounds where it is intended to stage events such as concerts, for which a greater level of accessibility and comfort may be desirable.

It should also be recognised that designing new construction to the minimum recommended dimensions may preclude the upgrading of facilities in the future; for example, the provision of more advanced seat types.

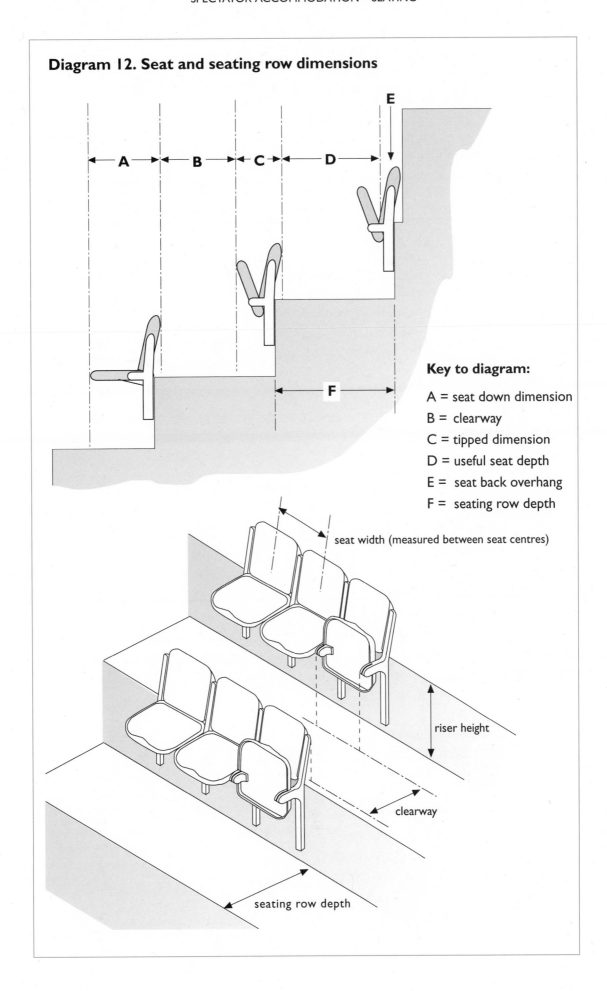

Diagram 12. Seat and seating row dimensions

Key to diagram:

A = seat down dimension
B = clearway
C = tipped dimension
D = useful seat depth
E = seat back overhang
F = seating row depth

seat width (measured between seat centres)

riser height

clearway

seating row depth

For existing construction:

The minimum space allotted to each seated person should be as follows:

- Seat width: 460mm (40mm greater if fitted with armrests)

- Seating row depth: 610mm

However, it is emphasised that the above figure of 610mm was included in previous editions of the Guide for bench seats in existing constructions. It is unlikely to be satisfactory for other types of seating.

11.12 Clearways

As illustrated in Diagram 12, the clearway (B) is the distance between the foremost projection of one seat and the back of the seat in front of it. This measurement is also known as the seatway, and is included in the seating row depth. The size of the clearway determines how safely and freely spectators and other personnel (such as stewards or first aiders) can move along rows of seats.

For new construction:

The minimum clearway should be 400mm. This may be reduced to 305mm where there are not more than seven seats in a row served by a gangway on one side, or not more than 14 seats seats in a row served by gangways on both sides.

For existing construction:

The minimum clearway should be 305mm.

The following points should also be considered:

a. Where tip-up seats are fitted, the clearway is measured with the seat in its tipped-up position.

b. Where fitted, armrests must not project into the clearway to such an extent that they reduce the clearway to below the specified minimum.

11.13 Useful seat depths

Another dimension which needs careful consideration is the useful seat depth (D in Diagram 12). This is an important factor in the comfort and accessibility of seats. The useful seat depth is the horizontal distance between the back of the seat, measured at seat height, and the rear of the seat in front.

The selection of a seat with a narrow tipped dimension (C in Diagram 12) will result in an improved useful seat depth.

11.14 Number of seats in rows

It is recommended that the number of seats in a row should not exceed:

a. 14 where there is a gangway at one end only

b. 28 where there is a gangway at both ends.

Deviations from this guidance should be permitted only if a risk assessment demonstrates the acceptability of the proposals, taking into account the requirements of both the normal egress time and the maximum recommended travel distance (see Sections 9.7 and 11.7).

11.15 Seat design

When selecting and installing seats, the following requirements should be met:

a. **Fixing**

All seats should be securely fixed in position. The fixings should not present any trip hazards on the treads. They should be vandal-proof and contain no sharp projections or edges.

b. **Flame retardancy**

All seats, irrespective of the material used, and whether upholstered or not, should satisfy the ignition source requirements specified in the current relevant British Standards.

11.16 Assessment of (P) factors for seated areas

As stated throughout the *Guide* (and in particular in Sections 1.4 and 11.1) the safe capacity of all areas of seated accommodation will be partly based on an assessment of their physical condition, or the (P) factor. It should be noted, however, that the (P) factor can be applied only after the number of usable seats has been established – that is, the actual number of seats, less those affected by seriously restricted views and those found to be inadequate or damaged (see Section 1.6).

The (P) factor is then used to calculate the holding capacity of the area, which in turn forms part of the calculation of the final capacity of the area.

The following are some of the main requirements that will need to be met if the (P) factor is not to be reduced. It is stressed that this list is neither comprehensive nor applicable in all situations. Nor is it presented in order of importance.

a. **Physical condition**

This concerns not the condition of the seats (since those which are damaged or inadequate should already have been excluded from the calculation), but the condition of all gangways, seating row treads, barriers and handrails.

(Damaged seats should be repaired, replaced or removed; whichever is appropriate to maintain safe conditions in the seated area.)

b. **Structures**

Management should ensure that any structures or parts of structures with which seated spectators could come in contact are made safe and secure. Where necessary, protective measures should be taken to avoid potential injury; for example, from low roof beams at the back of seated areas or from sharp edges of seat fixings.

c. **Sightlines**

If the sightlines are inadequate, thus encouraging spectators to stand, an assessment should be made of the risks to safety and, if necessary, the (P) factor reduced accordingly.

Wherever doubts arise as to the physical condition of a seated area, consideration should be given to a reduction in the (P) factor.

11.17 Assessment of (S) factors for seated areas

In addition to (P) factors, the calculation of a safe capacity for all areas of seated accommodation will be partly based on an assessment of their safety management, or the (S) factor.

The (S) factor is used to calculate the holding capacity of the area, which in turn forms part of the calculation of the final capacity of the area.

The following are some of the main requirements that will need to be met if the (S) factor is not to be reduced. It is stressed, however, that this list is neither comprehensive nor applicable in all situations. Nor is it presented in order of importance. (Further general guidance on (S) factors is also provided in Section 1.5.)

a. **Ticketing**

Management should ensure that tickets are issued only for usable seats, and that the information on the tickets corresponds exactly with the correct number and row. As stated in Section 11.6, management should also ensure that tickets for seats with partially restricted views and either partial or no cover are marked accordingly and the purchaser warned in advance. Reference should also be made to the recommendations in Section 6.10 concerning the sale of unreserved tickets.

b. **Seat and row identification**

Each individual seat and seat row should be clearly, neatly and accurately identified for the benefit of spectators and stewards. The seat identification marks should be fixed so as to make their removal difficult.

To avoid congestion and confusion, where tip-up seats are installed, for ease of reading, seat identification marks should, ideally, be located on the front of the back rest, rather than on the underside of the seat.

c. **Good housekeeping**

Clean and tidy seated areas are not only safer, but they also assist in promoting good behaviour and a more favourable attitude among spectators towards the facilities provided.

Each seat should therefore be cleaned before spectators are admitted. This is particularly important in exposed situations where seats may collect moisture or dust. Where seats are exposed to rain, ground staff should be provided with suitable means for wiping each seat immediately before it is occupied, so that spectators are not encouraged to stand in order to avoid coming into contact with a wet surface.

d. Stewarding

Stewards should be familiar with the lay-out of all areas of seated accommodation, the location of specific rows and seats, and the location of exits, emergency exits and amenities.

If reserved seats are sold, stewards should be trained and briefed to ensure that spectators sit in their designated seats. If unreserved seats are sold, they should be able to encourage spectators to sit in concentrated groups, so as to make it easier to direct latecomers to unoccupied seats.

While allowing for the natural tendency of spectators to stand up at key moments during an event, stewards should also be trained and briefed to deal effectively with spectators who persistently stand up.

e. Keeping gangways clear

It is essential that gangways, both lateral and radial, are kept clear, especially in areas where the passage of spectators and other personnel obtructs the views of seated spectators, including spectators using wheelchairs. In addition to the efforts of stewards, spectators should be informed of this requirement by signs and other means; for example, by announcements in the event programme and via the public address system.

f. Migration – viewing distances

As stated in Section 11.2, one of the factors determining viewing standards is the viewing distance. This is the distance between the spectator and the playing area or area of activity.

Viewing distances are not, in themselves, a safety matter. However, the distance may influence spectators' behaviour at key moments during an event. For example, management may need to ensure that spectators in areas closest to the pitch or area of activity are not encouraged to leave their seats and surge forward, particularly in response to the actions of players or participants in the event.

This should be achieved by the use of high-profile stewarding, clear signs and public address announcements. As recommended in Sections 10.15 and 11.4, pitch perimeter fences should not be erected in front of areas of seated accommodation.

If observation indicates that forward migration is a persistent problem, a reduction in the (S) factor may be necessary. Alternatively, the use of front row seats can be prohibited.

For certain sports there may also be a need to protect spectators near the front from the activity taking place.

Where the viewing distances are long, management should ensure that spectators in the rearmost rows are also not encouraged to migrate forwards at key moments of an event in order to obtain a closer view.

Guidance on optimum viewing distances for various sports can be found in *Stadia: A Design and Development Guide* (see Bibliography).

117

g.   Migration – partial cover

Management should ensure that the migration of spectators as a result of partial cover does not lead to congestion or to a breakdown of safety management procedures.

h.   Removal or control of potential restrictions

Before and during an event, management should ensure that any restrictions to viewing are removed or controlled. Such restrictions are listed in Section 11.4.

In addition, provision should be made for the accommodation of any stewards or members of staff who may not be on duty during an event. Such personnel should not be allowed to stand in vomitories or in areas where they might restrict views or obstruct gangways or exits.

i.   Segregation methods

If it is necessary to segregate tiers of seats into sections for different groups of spectators, care should be taken to ensure that the dividing methods used do not restrict views.

In all cases it is recommended that the methods used should be flexible, so that differing numbers of spectators can be segregated according to the needs of the event. Such methods may include the use of stewards and/or a line of tape or suitable fire-resistant material draped over a width of several seats from the front to the back of the tier of seating.

Care should be taken to ensure that the positioning of any temporary means of segregation does not result in more than 14 seats in a row with a gangway at one end only (see Section 11.14).

For further guidance on the segregation of seated spectators, see Sections 2.22 and 8.6.

Chapter Twelve

Spectator accommodation – Standing

12.1 The provision of standing accommodation

Standing accommodation is recognised as presenting a special safety problem at sports grounds. For this reason, although the problems have mainly been associated with football grounds, as stated in Section 11.1, wherever possible the provision of safe seated accommodation for all spectators is recommended.

When planning a new standing area, management should therefore consider the possibility of converting it to seats at a later date (see Section 12.25).

Wherever standing accommodation is provided – be it in the form of terraces, viewing slopes, level areas or spectator galleries – it should be designed and managed to be safe. The comfort and amenities of spectators – and their access to amenities – should also be considered, in as much detail as it would be for seated areas.

Account should also be taken of the nature of the event and the varying patterns of crowd movement at different types of event; for example, at horse racing compared to football.

It is therefore recommended that in all matters relating to the design of standing accommodation, management seeks professional advice from competent persons of the appropriate skill and experience.

Newly constructed standing accommodation should conform to any applicable Building Regulations, and should be designed in accordance with recommendations contained elsewhere in the *Guide*, particularly those in Chapter 10, concerning the provision of barriers (including crush barriers and pitch perimeter barriers).

For further guidance on the design of safe standing accommodation, reference may be made to the FSADC publication *Terraces – Designing for Safe Standing at Football Stadia* (see Bibliography). Although written primarily for football grounds, the publication includes much general advice applicable to all sports grounds.

12.2 The importance of good design

Owing to the complex patterns of crowd circulation and movement to which standing areas are subject – at many grounds, continuously throughout the occupancy of the area – their design cannot be considered simply in terms of their individual elements. Instead, they should be regarded as a finely balanced network of inter-related elements, including entry systems, gangways, terrace steps, crush barriers, exit systems and emergency evacuation routes. Design faults or deterioration in any one of those elements shifts additional pressures onto the others, which, as experience shows, has often led to accidents, occasionally with fatal consequences.

To provide reasonable safety, standing areas and the circulation routes which serve them should therefore be designed taking the following conditions into consideration:

a.   Spectators should be able to gain access to their desired standing position from the point of entry to the ground via a properly designed and constructed route.

b.   Spectators should be able to leave their viewing position by a clearly defined and properly designed and constructed route at any time during the event, to gain access to toilet and other facilities. They should also, within reason, be able to return to their viewing position at any time during the event.

c.   Spectators should be able to leave the viewing area and exit from the sports ground at any time during, or at the end of, the event, via a properly constructed and defined exit route.

12.3   Viewing conditions for standing spectators

Once spectators are in position, the design and management of the standing area should ensure that they are able to view all elements of the event in such a way that they are not subjected to:

a.   excessive pressures from crowd surges

b.   excessive pressure from a high density of spectators

c.   forces that cause spectators to lose control of their own movement, so that they step forward in an uncontrolled manner

d.   physical stresses caused by poorly constructed terracing, such as sloping treads, uneven surfaces or broken or damaged terracing

e.   restricted viewing, necessitating frequent changes of position or excessive movement, which might affect other spectators.

The assessment of (P) and (S) factors in all existing standing areas should start by considering whether, by design and management, the conditions listed above and in Section 12.2 are being met.

Further guidance on the assessment of (P) and (S) factors for standing areas is provided in Chapter 1 and Sections 12.23 and 12.24.

12.4   Gangways in standing areas – general requirements

As in seated areas, radial and lateral gangways should provide the means for spectators to proceed in a uniform, orderly manner into, around and out of standing areas. However, because spectators often have more freedom of movement in standing areas, the provision of suitably designed and clearly marked, designated gangways is a vital part of achieving safe standing conditions.

In general, the design of gangways in standing areas should meet the following requirements:

a. They should be provided so that all spectators are within 12m of a gangway or exit as measured along a line of unobstructed travel from the viewing position, so that they can move quickly into the exit system. It should be noted that the normal maximum egress time for all areas of viewing accommodation, standing or seated, is eight minutes (see Section 9.7).

b. All gangways in standing areas, lateral and radial, should be clearly delineated by the application of a non-slip paint in a conspicuous colour. This not only makes them easier for spectators to identify in congested situations, but also aids those who are responsible for keeping the gangways clear.

c. As for all areas of spectator accommodation, gangways in standing areas should be a minimum of 1.1m wide (1.2m recommended for new construction); should be even and free from trip hazards; and their surfaces should be slip-resistant.

d. Any stepped side gangway (that is, with viewing accommodation on one side only) should be provided either with a barrier which meets the requirements of Table 1 in Chapter 10, or, if a barrier is not required, a handrail which meets the requirements detailed in Section 7.8.

Further guidance on circulation can be found in Chapters 5–9, and in the following sections.

12.5 Lateral gangways in standing areas

Spectators should not be allowed to stand in lateral gangways because this disrupts the passage of spectators along them and may restrict the views of those standing on the steps behind, causing them to stretch or strain in order to see the event.

In order to assist management in achieving this, the following design requirements should be considered:

a. To discourage standing in lateral gangways, the surfaces should be sunk approximately 150mm.

b. Wherever possible, the front steps of standing areas behind mid-level lateral gangways should start at a level higher than the section in front, to ensure that views from the rear areas are not restricted.

c. Crush barriers should be provided behind the lateral gangway, but not immediately in front.

d. As stated in Section 10.15, in order to assist circulation, wherever practicable a lateral gangway should be provided between the front row of crush barriers and the pitch perimeter barrier.

12.6 Radial gangways in standing areas

The design and management of radial gangways is of particular importance in standing areas, owing to the tendency of spectators to stand in them for viewing, and because of the potential for crowd surges down the gangway. For this reason it is stressed that management should ensure that radial gangways are always kept clear.

This responsibilty should be much easier to discharge where continuous crush barriers are provided between radial gangways (see Sections 10.8 and 12.7).

Wherever reasonably practicable, the following requirements should apply to all radial gangways in standing areas:

a.   Whatever the crush barrier configuration, all areas of standing accommodation should have clearly marked, designated radial gangways.

b.   As stated in Section 12.4, all spectators should be within 12m of a gangway or exit. The spacing of radial gangways should also take into account the future possibility of the standing area being converted to seating (see Section 12.26).

c.   Where the gangway is stepped, the goings should be uniform and the step dimensions compatible with those for the terrace which they serve (see Section 12.9).

d.   To minimise the risk of crowd surges, it may be preferable to shorten excessively long radial gangways by diverting the flow along lateral gangways.

e.   The nosings of steps in radial gangways should be clearly identified for the benefit of spectators.

f.   Radial gangways should not contain winders (that is, tapered treads).

g.   Any wall, barrier, fence or gate at the foot of radial gangways in standing areas should be the same height as crush barriers (1.1m) and have the maximum horizontal imposed load for crush barriers (that is, 5.0 kN/m length, as shown in Table 1 of Chapter 10.)

12.7 Crush barriers

Crush barriers are vital elements in the design and management of standing areas.

As stated in Section 10.8, crush barriers should be provided along the full width of a standing area, with gaps only at the radial gangways. These barriers should be designed and spaced according to the recommendations given in Chapter 10. An example of continuous crush barrier configuration is illustrated in Diagram 8.

If the provision of crush barriers conforms to this recommendation, many of the other elements required for the design and management of standing areas should be simpler to provide as part of an integrated and smoothly functioning network.

In addition, there is a much greater likelihood that the capacity calculation can be based upon the maximum appropriate density of 47 persons per 10 square metres (see Chapter 1).

a. **For new construction:**
At all sports grounds where standing accommodation is provided, a continuous crush barrier configuration should be provided.

b. **For existing construction:**
If all other elements of the standing accommodation are in good condition and the safety management is effective, non-continuous crush barrier configurations may still be regarded as acceptable. However, as stated in Section 1.8, the capacity will still have to be significantly reduced. This reduction is explained further in worked examples 2 and 3 in Annex A. Wherever possible, therefore, the existing standing areas should be redesigned to incorporate continuous crush barriers between radial gangways.

c. **Standing areas without crush barriers:**
Standing areas without crush barriers cannot be considered as safe unless the capacity is set at such a level that the risks are minimised. For guidance on how to calculate the capacity in such situations, see Section 1.8 and worked examples 5 and 6 in Annex A.

Section 12.21 and worked example 7 in Annex A also shows how to calculate capacities in situations such as are common at racecourses, where adjoining standing areas both with and without crush barriers may form part of a larger enclosure.

12.8 Design of terrace steps
When designing new terraces, or assessing the (P) factor of existing standing areas, it should be noted that:

a. The dimensions of terrace steps, and therefore the angle of slope, have a direct correlation with the spacing of crush barriers, as detailed in Table 2 of Chapter 10.

b. Angles of slope, or gradients, in excess of 25° are potentially hazardous and should be avoided. Where they exist, consideration should be given to a reduction in the (P) factor or the provision of additional crush barriers.

c. Excessive variations in the gradient of a terrace are potentially hazardous and should be avoided.

d. The surface of terrace steps should be slip-resistant.

e. The surface of each tread should be uniform, and designed so that rain or water does not accumulate, thereby leading to deterioration. This can be achieved by creating a slight fall on each tread.

f. An excessive fall on terrace treads will reduce the comfort of spectators and possibly lead them to step forward in an uncontrolled manner.

Further guidance on the assessment of (P) factors for standing areas is provided in Chapter 1 and Section 12.23.

12.9 Dimensions of terrace steps

For new construction:
The dimensions of terrace steps for a newly constructed standing area should be as follows:

a. **Tread depth:**   350mm minimum   400mm maximum

Designing to these dimensions will also enable the terrace, if required, to be converted to seating more easily at a later date (see Section 12.25).

b. **Riser height:**   75mm minimum   180mm maximum

It should be noted that when designing new standing areas the exact dimensions of riser heights are not pre-determined. Rather, they depend on the calculation for sightlines.

For existing construction:
The dimensions of terrace steps for existing terraces should be as follows:

a. **Tread depth:**   280mm minimum   400mm maximum

b. **Riser height:**   75mm minimum   180mm maximum

If any riser height is greater than 180mm, a crush barrier should be provided at the top of the riser.

12.10 Viewing standards

As stated in Section 12.3, the provision of adequate viewing standards is a key factor in achieving safe standing conditions. Viewing standards are explained more fully in Sections 11.2 and 11.3, and in relation to standing accommodation are illustrated in Diagram 13. As for seated spectators, viewing standards for standing spectators depend largely on three inter-related factors:

a. the quality of **sightlines** (see Section 12.11 and Diagrams 11 and 13)

b. the existence of any **restrictions** (see Section 12.12)

c. the **viewing distance** (see Section 12.24).

12.11 Sightlines

The provision of adequate and appropriate sightlines for standing spectators is an important part of achieving safe standing conditions.

The better the sightline, the more likely it is that standing spectators will not have to stretch or strain in order to view the event. If the sightlines are poor, resulting in excessive crowd movement and pressure, the (P) factor for the standing area should be reduced. This in turn will lead to a reduction of the appropriate density and may result in a reduction of the final capacity (see Chapter 1 and Section 12.23).

As stated in Section 11.3, the quality of a sightline is often expressed as a 'C' value. 'C' values for seated spectators are calculated for every row. However, for standing spectators they may be calculated for every second tread. This is because standing spectators have more freedom to re-adjust their position, and the variation of eye-level is greater across the range for standing spectators than for seated spectators.

When calculating sightlines it should be noted that the maximum recommended angle of slope for standing accommodation is 25°, compared with 34° for seating.

For new construction:
If adequate and appropriate sightlines are provided for newly constructed standing accommodation, should that area be converted to seating (see Section 12.25), the sightlines for seated spectators are likely to be acceptable.

12.12 Restricted viewing

As stated in Section 12.3, all standing spectators should have a clear, unrestricted view of the whole of the pitch or area of activity. Although there are exceptions to this requirement (for example at events such as horse or motor racing), the causes of potential restrictions are likely to be the same as those listed in Section 11.4.

Management is responsible for assessing the effects of restricted viewing from every part of the standing area to which spectators have access, and for taking appropriate action (see Section 12.13). Where appropriate, this assessment should take into account the additional restrictions caused by pitch perimeter fences (although, as stated in Section 10.16, the provision of such fences is not recommended).

In carrying out the assessment, the following criteria should be applied:

a. **Partial restriction**
   This applies to areas from which partial restrictions force standing spectators to stretch or strain in order to gain an improved view, but without significantly changing their position or affecting other spectators.

b. **Serious restriction**
   This applies to areas from which standing spectators have seriously restricted, or even completely obstructed, views of part of the playing area or area of activity, necessitating significant changes of position or excessive movement, thereby risking the possibility of crowd surging.

12.13 Management strategies towards restricted viewing

For new construction:
Newly constructed standing accommodation should be designed so that it has no areas offering views with serious restrictions. Every effort should also be made to ensure that partially restricted views are eliminated.

As is the case for seated areas, it is, furthermore, the responsibility of both the management and designers to ensure that the viewing standards provided are adequate and appropriate for the sport (or sports) to be staged. Management may therefore wish to request that designers provide written assurance to that effect.

For existing construction:

Where views are partially restricted and the restrictions cannot be removed, an assessment of the potential risk of crowd movement should be made, and if considered necessary, the affected area should be discounted from the available viewing area (see Chapter 1).

Where views are seriously restricted and the restrictions cannot be removed, the affected areas should be discounted from the available viewing area and consideration given to them being prohibited for the purposes of viewing. These areas may either be sealed off, or their boundaries marked clearly on the actual terrace surface and stewarded accordingly.

If, despite carrying out the measures recommended above, it is observed that areas with seriously restricted views continue to be occupied by standing spectators, and this results in excessive crowd movement, there should be a reduction in the (S) factor, thus leading to the possibility of a further reduction of the final capacity of the standing area (see Chapter 1 and Section 12.24).

12.14 Provision of cover

Although it is recommended that at certain sports grounds all standing accommodation should be covered, as stated in Section 11.6, it is recognised that full protection from the elements is hard to achieve in all situations and weather conditions.

Where the protection provided is only partial, or there is no cover at all, the following strategies should be considered:

a. Partial cover

Experience shows that where partial cover is provided, in poor weather conditions standing spectators will, whenever possible, migrate to covered areas. In certain circumstances this can result in unacceptable local concentrations of spectators, particularly where the covered area is smaller than the uncovered area. Additional safety concerns arise when conditions under the roof are inferior to those on the rest of the standing area.

In such situations management might consider the following options:

i.   to extend the existing roof or provide a new roof covering the whole area

ii. to install appropriate barriers, to prevent or control migration

iii. to adopt appropriate stewarding strategies to manage or control the migration, preferably with the assistance of CCTV monitoring

If none of the above options are acted upon, or if either options ii. or iii. are implemented but the problems of migration and overcrowding continue, further consideration should be given to the following options:

iv.   to limit the final capacity of the whole section by restricting the available viewing area to the area under cover

v.   to limit the final capacity of the whole section by a reduction of the (S) factor.

Management and, if a safety certificate is in force, the local authority, will need to judge carefully all the circumstances before deciding which of the above options to pursue.

b.   No cover
At sports grounds where uncovered standing areas are provided, management should ensure that spectators seeking shelter do not overcrowd other areas of the ground (such as covered stands and concourses).

c.   Admission
As a general principle, people should be advised before seeking admission to standing areas which are not covered. If a safety certificate is in force, this course of action may also be required by the local authority.

12.15   Division of standing accommodation

Large areas of standing accommodation, or physically adjoining areas of standing accommodation, are subject to migration, which in turn can lead to dangerous overcrowding. In such cases it will be necessary to introduce structures and/or management controls to separate the areas into divisions.

If such areas are not divided, or if the divisions are not adequately arranged or managed as recommended below, a reduction of the capacity or capacities should be enforced by reductions of the (P) and/or (S) factors (see also Sections 12.23 and 12.24). This reduction should also apply when assessing the effect of migration in standing areas with only partial cover (see Section 12.14).

For situations where a free movement of spectators between divisions is desirable, see Section 12.16.

It is strongly recommended that any division of standing accommodation complies with the following requirements:

a.   Each division must have its capacity assessed separately.

b.   Entry to each division must be controlled either by its own designated turnstiles, or by other entry arrangements which allow management to keep an accurate count of the number of spectators admitted.

c.   As with any other separate area of spectator accommodation, in order to alert staff and stewards at the entry points when a division is nearing capacity, and then when it is full – and for the purposes of overall safety management – it should be possible to monitor the numbers of spectators in each division from the control point, by counting systems, and by stewarding and/or CCTV.

d. Once the capacity of the division has been reached, further entry should be denied and spectators re-directed to other available areas.

e. When dividing areas of standing accommodation, the siting of dividing barriers, walls or fences should be such that each division functions safely as a separate unit, in terms of its crush barrier configuration, gangways, and its means of ingress, egress and emergency evacuation (including pitch perimeter gates or openings).

f. Each division should also be self-contained in terms of its toilet and refreshment facilities.

g. Consideration should be given to providing additional access from one division to another for use in an emergency evacuation. However, such access will not normally be taken into account in any exit capacity calculation.

h. If required to withstand crowd pressures, all barriers (including walls or fences) used to divide one section from another should be designed, constructed and maintained to withstand those pressures safely.

    In situations where dividing structures might be vulnerable to crowd pressures, the use of brick, blockwork or other solid structures is not recommended. Where they are used, they should be subject to regular appraisal by competent persons of the appropriate skills and experience.

i. Where the separation is achieved by means of radial divisions, where appropriate, gangways should be provided on either side, to discourage lateral movement and prevent spectators pressing up against the dividing structures. These gangways should be suitably stewarded and kept clear at all times.

j. Dividing structures should be designed or sited in such a way that they do not restrict the views of spectators. If they do, the affected areas should be discounted from the available viewing area (see Chapter 1).

12.16 Allowing free movement of spectators between divisions

At certain sports grounds – for example those staging horse or greyhound racing – it is customary to allow spectators to move freely between various areas of spectator accommodation.

However, if free movement of spectators is to be allowed between standing areas, or between standing areas and any other areas of spectator accommodation (including circulation areas), the management should ensure that appropriate measures are taken to control and monitor the situation at all times and in all weather conditions, to ensure that the capacity of each area is not exceeded. As stated in Section 12.15.c this should be achieved by control of entry points between each section, by effective stewarding, and by monitoring from the control point (by CCTV if appropriate).

Even if all these measures are implemented, where free movement of spectators is allowed, a careful assessment should be made of the (P) and (S) factors for each individual division or separate area of viewing accommodation.

12.17 Segregation of standing accommodation

Where areas of standing accommodation are divided in order to segregate different groups of spectators, the requirements for the design and management of divided areas listed in Section 12.15 should be met in full.

It is emphasised that whichever form of dividing (or segregation) structure is used, the structure should not restrict the views of spectators.

Flexible means of segregation, such as are recommended for seated areas (see Section 11.17), can also be used in standing areas, provided that the stewarding arrangements, barrier configurations and gangway layouts are suitable.

However, all segregation methods should be the subject of consultation between the ground management, the local authority and the police.

12.18 Pitch perimeter barriers and fences

Guidance on pitch perimeter barriers is provided in Sections 10.14–10.15, and on pitch perimeter fences in Section 10.16. However, it is stressed that the use of pitch perimeter fences is not recommended, in areas of standing or seating. If necessary, other means of preventing spectators from gaining unauthorised entry to the pitch or area of activity should be utilised.

Where pitch perimeter fences do exist, the standing area should be divided from the fence by a lateral gangway, and spectators prevented from gathering immediately behind or climbing up the fence.

It should also be noted that pitch perimeter barriers and fences must be provided with gates or openings which open away from the spectators and allow access to the pitch or area of activity, or to a perimeter track or walkway, in the event of an emergency. Where standing areas are divided, as detailed in Sections 12.15 and 12.17, each division should be served by an adequate number of gates or openings.

For further guidance on emergency evacuation, see Chapters 9 and 15.

12.19 Viewing slopes

A viewing slope is defined as a non-stepped sloping area providing standing accommodation for spectators. Wherever possible their use should be avoided at grounds staging sports where spectators maintain an essentially fixed position for the duration of the event (such as football or rugby).

However, where they are provided, in order to be considered suitable for standing spectators, viewing slopes should comply with the following requirements:

a. the surface should be properly drained and such that spectators do not lose their footing or balance

b. the angle of slope should ideally be no greater than approximately 10° (compared with the maximum angle recommended for terraced areas of 25°)

c. if the angle of slope is greater than 10° continuous crush barriers should be provided between radial gangways

d. the spacing of crush barriers should be the same as for those on terraced areas (see Table 2 in Chapter 10).

12.20   Level standing accommodation

As stated in Section 1.8.g, it is recommended that whatever the loading of any front barrier, the available viewing area allowed when calculating the capacity of a level standing area should be no greater than 1.5m. This is the equivalent of approximately four persons deep. Beyond this depth viewing is too seriously restricted to be considered as part of the viewing accommodation.

An example of the capacity calculation for a level standing area is provided in worked example 6 in Annex A.

It is further recommended that level areas for standing do not form part of the spectator accommodation for new construction.

12.21   Combined standing and circulation areas

It is recognised that at a number of sports grounds where free movement of spectators is common during the event – for example, those staging horse racing – there are often non-stepped enclosures which do not exactly fit into the categories of either viewing slopes or level standing areas.

Typically these enclosures – often known as lawns – may be used for both viewing and circulation, have no crush barriers, and are occupied by personnel such as bookmakers and vendors. They often also allow a free movement of spectators between other areas of spectator accommodation, such as seated stands or terraces for standing spectators. Worked example 7 in Annex A illustrates such an area.

In such situations, it is stressed that although spectators may freely move from the enclosure into a stand or terrace, the holding capacity of the stand or terrace should still be calculated separately from the adjoining enclosure or lawn. As stated in Section 12.16, management should also ensure that the capacity of each area is not exceeded.

As is the case for any section of a sports ground where free movement of spectators is common, a reduction in the (P) factor will be necessary in order to facilitate safe movement.

This reduction may be severe where there is not only free movement but where viewing areas are used also for circulation. In this respect it should be noted that research indicates that spectators can circulate freely only when crowds are no denser than approximately 10–15 persons per 10 square metres.

In order to assess the capacity of the enclosures, or lawns, it will therefore be necessary to assess both the (P) and (S) factors, taking into account all the usual factors, but with particular attention to local circumstances.

This will require assessment of the following:

a.   When calculating the available viewing area a reasonable assessment should be made of those parts of the area in which viewing, rather than circulation, actually takes place.

b.   Those areas clearly used only for circulation should not form part of the available viewing area.

c.   Discounts from the available viewing area should be made to allow for areas occupied by bookmakers, vendors and other personnel.

d.   Those areas from which viewing does take place should be assessed as to the underfoot conditions, the quality of sightlines, the existence of any restrictions and any other relevant physical characteristics which may affect the safety of standing spectators.

e.   The ability of stewards to prevent congestion or overcrowding.

The above list is not comprehensive nor intended to apply in all circumstances or in all weather conditions.

Regular monitoring may also be required to ensure that a safe capacity limit is set, appropriate to the viewing area's particular characteristics.

12.22   Spectator galleries

Spectator galleries in which spectators stand are usually accessed from hospitality areas, whose capacities are already limited by their size and design. Clearly, these capacity limits should be strictly applied.

However, spectator galleries should still be subject to an assessment of (P) and (S) factors, and all barriers should comply with Table 3 of Chapter 10.

12.23   Assessment of (P) factors for standing areas

As stated throughout the *Guide* (and in particular in Sections 1.4 and 1.9), the calculation of capacities for all areas of standing accommodation will be partly based on an assessment of their physical condition, or the (P) factor.

The following are some of the main requirements that will need to be met if the (P) factor is not to be reduced. It is stressed that this list is neither comprehensive nor applicable in all situations. Nor is it presented in order of importance.

a.   **Physical condition of standing areas**
Management should ensure that all surfaces, treads, risers and nosings, and all gangway markings are maintained in good condition. Any alterations or repairs to surfaces should avoid creating additional trip hazards (due to unevenness) and all gangway markings should be reinstated.

All barriers and crush barriers, and their fixings, should be maintained, inspected and tested as recommended in Chapter 10.

Particular attention should be made to:

i.   crumbling of the surface due to age or poor maintenance

ii. unevenness of the terrace due to poor construction, settlement or repair work

iii. irregular terrace tread depths or riser heights

iv. poor drainage, leading to standing water and/or icing.

b.   Structures
Management should ensure that any structures or parts of structures with which standing spectators could come in contact are made safe, secure and, where appropriate, unclimbable. Where necessary, protective measures should be taken to avoid potential injury; for example, from low roof beams at the back of covered terraces.

Any structure located in a standing area, be it permanent or temporary – for example floodlight pylons or television camera platforms – should be protected from potential crowd pressures, by the provision of suitably designed barriers.

c.   Sightlines
If the sightlines are poor, thus encouraging spectators to stretch or strain, an assessment should be made of the effects upon spectator movement. If this movement is considered to be excessive, or leads to any of the pressures detailed in Section 12.3, a reduced (P) factor will in turn reduce the numbers allowed to occupy the area.

d.   Lighting
Where standing areas are to be used during non-daylight hours, they must be sufficiently lit to enable spectators to identify hazards.

Wherever doubts arise as to the physical condition of a standing area, consideration should be given to a reduction in the (P) factor.

12.24   Assessment of (S) factors for standing areas
In addition to (P) factors, the calculation of capacities for standing areas will be partly based on an assessment of their safety management, or the (S) factor (see Section 1.5). The following are some of the main requirements that need to be met if the (S) factor is not to be reduced. It is stressed that this list is not comprehensive or applicable in all situations. Nor is it presented in order of importance.

a.   Admission
Management should ensure that the number of people admitted to standing areas, or divisions of standing areas, is counted and strictly controlled, according to the capacities set for those areas.

b. **Stewarding**

Stewards should be familiar with the layout of all areas of standing accommodation and the location of exits, emergency exits and amenities. They should be trained and briefed to ensure that spectators do not stand in gangways, do not climb on barriers, fences or other structures, and do not behave in such a way as to endanger other spectators.

c. **Keeping gangways clear**

As stated above, it is essential that gangways, both lateral and radial, are kept clear. In addition to the efforts of stewards, spectators should be informed of this requirement by signs and other means; for example, by means of announcements in the event programme and via the public address system.

d. **Distribution of spectators**

Using suitably trained and briefed stewards and, where appropriate, CCTV, management should ensure that spectators are evenly distributed. This is particularly important in popular standing areas – for example, behind the goals at football grounds or close to the finishing post at racecourses – where concentrations of spectators are prone to gather.

Monitoring and controlling the distribution of spectators is also particularly important if non-continuous crush barriers are provided, because of the greater risk of crowd surges in the gaps between crush barriers, or if there are no crush barriers at all.

e. **Migration – viewing distances**

As stated in Section 12.10, one of the factors determining viewing standards is the viewing distance. This is the distance between the spectator and the pitch or area of activity. Viewing distances are not, in themselves, a safety matter. However, the distance may influence spectators' behaviour at key moments during an event. Management should therefore ensure that spectators in areas closest to the pitch or area of activity are not encouraged to surge forward, particularly in response to the actions of players or participants in the event.

Similarly, where standing spectators are a long distance from the playing area or area of activity, management should ensure that they are not encouraged to migrate forwards at key moments of an event in order to obtain a closer view.

f. **Migration – partial cover**

For guidance on safety management of standings areas offering only partial cover, see Section 12.14.

g. **Large standing areas**

Although the determination of the available viewing area (see Chapter 1) will have already taken the crush barrier strengths and configuration into account, on large standing areas with inadequate crush barriers this can still result in a considerable capacity. In such situations, special attention should be paid to the ability of the ground's safety management to cope with migration and congestion in popular areas.

h.   Removal or control of potential restrictions

Before and during an event, management should ensure that any restrictions to viewing are removed or controlled. Such restrictions are listed in Section 11.4. In addition, provision should be made for the accommodation of any stewards or members of staff who may not be on duty during an event. Such personnel should not be allowed to stand in vomitories or in areas where they might restrict views or obstruct gangways or exits.

i.   Provision for children

The presence of young children on standing areas raises particular concerns, because, in common with smaller adults and elderly people, they may have neither the strength nor stature to deal with crowd movement. They may also be vulnerable when pressed up against standard 1.1m height crush barriers.

It has traditionally been common for children to migrate to the front of terraces, with or without adults, in order to obtain a better viewing position. Where non-continuous barriers are provided, this can create additional safety concerns, because at the front children are clearly more vulnerable to maximum pressure.

Ground management should recognise these potential dangers and develop a strategy to ensure the safety of children and indeed any vulnerable adults in such situations.

The ideal strategy is to create a well-managed and appropriately designed children's or family enclosure where children can remain free from crowd pressures and movement, and obtain a clear view of the pitch. Wherever possible, these areas should have their own entry and exit points, to avoid children having to pass through other areas of terracing.

j.   Provision for spectators with disabilities

Depending upon the particular circumstances at a ground, provision for disabled spectators on standing areas may need to be considered. The fact that an area is designated for standing spectators does not mean that provision for semi-ambulant spectators, or those using wheelchairs, should not be considered. For further guidance on the provision of accommodation for spectators with disabilities, see Chapter 13.

k.   Signs

The provision of clear, informative and suitably elevated signs, illuminated where necessary, is particularly important in standing areas (see Chapter 16).

l.   Crowd behaviour

This is a factor where crowd behaviour is such that it creates safety risks on a regular basis, and the ground's safety management proves unable to deal with the problem.

Wherever doubts arise as to the safety management of a standing area, consideration should be given to a reduction in the (S) factor.

12.25 Conversion of terraces to seating

Although primarily a matter of design, as stated throughout this chapter, when planning the construction of new standing areas or the refurbishment of existing ones management and designers should take into account the possibility of future conversion to seating.

If all the recommendations listed in this chapter for new constructions are followed, the conversion should be relatively simple. For further guidance, reference should be made to the FSADC publication, *Terraces – Designing for Safe Standing at Football Stadia* (see Bibliography).

However, as is the case for all matters relating to the design of standing or seated accommodation, it is recommended that management seeks professional advice from competent persons of the appropriate skill and experience.

The following is a summary of the main considerations.

a. If the future conversion of the terrace to seating is achieved by the usual method of creating one seating row from every two terrace treads (see Diagram 13), then provided the sightlines are correctly calculated for seated spectators in advance of the terrace being constructed, sightlines for standing spectators are also likely to be correct.

b. By designing new terracing to the appropriate dimensions recommended in Section 12.9, future conversion to seating will be much simpler and meet the requirements for seating listed in Section 11.1.

c. If radial gangways provided for standing areas are to be appropriately sited for future use in a seated area, to avoid additional costs they should be spaced 13–14m apart, rather than 24m as would be the case for standing areas.

d. If a roof is already in place, advanced calculations of sightlines will be necessary to ensure that, once converted to seats, the roof will not require replacement or remodelling in order to avoid restricted views.

Diagram 13.
Conversion of terracing to seated accommodation

By designing new standing areas to the appropriate dimensions (see Section 12.9), the future conversion to seating will be much simpler.

As illustrated, this can be achieved by creating one seating row for every two terrace treads.

If this approach is taken, as stated in Section 12.25, designers should work out the sightlines for seated spectators in advance of the terrace being constructed. By doing this the sightlines are likely to be adequate and appropriate both for the standing spectators and, after conversion, for seated spectators.

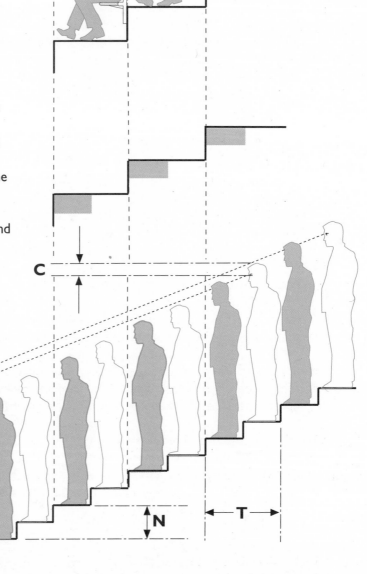

Note that, as illustrated, regardless of whether the terrace is going to be converted to seating at a later date, and when assessing existing standing areas, 'C' values for standing spectators need only be calculated for every second tread (see Section 12.11 and Diagram 11).

Chapter Thirteen

Spectator accommodation – Disabilities

13.1 Provision for people with disabilities

It is the responsibility of management to ensure that accommodation provided for people with disabilities is safe, properly designed and managed. None of the safety measures set out elsewhere in the *Guide* should be construed in such a way as to avoid this responsibility, or to place undue restrictions on people with disabilities.

It should be noted that all new construction should comply with the Building Regulations. This applies to:

a.   all new sports grounds

b.   all new stands built at existing sports grounds

c.   in certain cases, the extension of existing stands.

In addition, no alterations to any existing accommodation should reduce the level of accessibility for disabled people, or make worse any facilities to which they previously had access.

Consideration should be given to the provision of essential safety-related information to spectators with disabilities.

Account should also be taken of the likely use of hospitality and other related facilities for events other than sporting events (see Chapter 20).

It is therefore recommended that in all matters relating to the design of accommodation for disabled people, management seeks professional advice from competent persons of the appropriate skill and experience.

For further guidance, reference may be made to the FSADC publication *Designing for Spectators with Disabilities*. Although written primarily for football grounds, the publication includes much general advice applicable to all sports grounds. Guidance is also available from the Centre for Accessible Environments (see Bibliography).

13.2 Disability Discrimination Act

Management should also be aware of the Disability Discrimination Act 1995, which requires all providers of goods, facilities and services to take reasonable measures to ensure that they are not discriminating against disabled people (see Bibliography).

The Act also requires that no business which employs 20 or more staff (whether permanent, temporary or contract workers) should discriminate unreasonably against current or prospective employees who have a disability.

13.3 Definitions of disability

The term 'disability' is defined as meaning any physical or mental impairment which has a substantial and long-term adverse effect on a person's ability to carry out normal day-to-day activities.

In the context of sports grounds, attention has frequently been focused upon people who use wheelchairs. However, when designing and managing safe accommodation, other forms of disability should be considered, as follows:

a. People with impaired vision
This includes people who are totally blind or partially sighted.

b. People with impaired hearing
This includes people who are totally deaf or have a hearing impairment.

c. People with impaired mobility
People with impaired mobility include:

  i. people in wheelchairs who remain in their wheelchairs while viewing the event

  ii. people who arrive at the sports ground in a wheelchair but then transfer to a seat

  iii. people who view the event from their own special vehicle

  iv. semi-ambulant people, who can walk, either unaided with difficulty, or only with assistance.

Unless they have additional physical disabilities, people with learning difficulties will not normally have any special safety or design requirements at sports grounds.

As stated in Section 13.19 management needs to be aware that the presence of spectators who have partial impairments may not be apparent until an emergency arises.

13.4 People with impaired vision

Provision for people with impaired vision should take into account the following considerations:

a. All signs, and particularly signs relating to fire safety and emergency evacuation, should be presented and sited so that as far as possible they can be easily seen and readily distinguishable by those with impaired vision or colour perception. Advice on this matter is available from the Royal National Institute for the Blind or the National Federation of the Blind of the UK (see Bibliography). Further guidance on signage can be found in Chapter 16.

It is stressed, however, that only a minority of the general population has perfect vision, and that clear, well designed signage will therefore be of benefit to all spectators.

b. Although the need for good housekeeping and good design is emphasised throughout the *Guide*, thoughtless actions and poor design present particular hazards for people with impaired vision. Examples of this include doors or windows which open outwards into narrow circulation routes, low obstacles left lying in the path of main circulation routes, and changes in level. Management should therefore ensure that all staff and stewards are trained to take special care in areas where it is known that people with impaired vision are present.

c. Again, although clear, audible public address announcements are of benefit to all spectators, they are vital for the safety and enjoyment of people with impaired vision (see Section 16.14).

d. The use of headphone sockets for relaying commentaries is a common feature at sports grounds. However, in order to facilitate the wider dispersal of disabled spectators – as recommended in Section 13.6 – and not place any limit on the number of people with impaired vision admitted to an event, management should be aware of modern technology which allows commentaries to be relayed to any person in the sports ground equipped with the necessary receiver and ear-piece.

e. Consideration should be given to the use of tactile indicators set into the flooring at key crossing points.

f. Management should consider the possible need to accommodate guide dogs during an event.

13.5   People with impaired hearing

Provision for people with impaired hearing should take into account the following:

a. In the same way that the safety and enjoyment of people with impaired vision depends on clear, audible public address announcements, people with impaired hearing rely on the presentation of clear, informative visual information on scoreboards, electronic boards and video boards.

b. Management should consider the installation of audio induction loops in areas of spectator accommodation and in ticket offices.

c. It should be noted that many people with impaired hearing rely on lip-reading. At points where important information may be requested, such as at turnstiles and counters, lighting levels should therefore be sufficient.

d. Management may wish particular stewards or members of staff to undergo brief training in methods of communication with people who have impaired hearing (see Bibliography).

e. Although people with impaired hearing may experience difficulty in hearing messages on the public address system, they may still be sensitive to sound and to conventional alarm signals. It is also reasonable to expect spectators around them to warn those with impaired hearing in the event of an emergency. (See also Section 16.22.)

13.6   Dispersal of ambulant and semi-ambulant disabled spectators

It is recommended that accommodation for disabled spectators should be dispersed throughout the sports ground. This in order to provide a range of viewing options.

Management and designers should therefore take into account the following issues:

a.   Ambulant and semi-ambulant disabled spectators may be physically unable, or may find it difficult, to gain access to all parts of the spectator accommodation.

b.   The widespread dispersal of ambulant and semi-ambulant disabled spectators may conflict with the fundamental need for their early evacuation (see Section 13.17).

c.   The requirements for stairways for use by semi-ambulant people may vary as a result of the application of Building Regulations.

It may therefore be appropriate to identify areas to be used by ambulant and semi-ambulant disabled spectators (and their helpers) that are close to vomitories or other exits. These areas should ideally be situated where there are few steps to negotiate and where the gradient of the seating tier is not more than 20°.

Wheelchair storage space should also be provided within reasonable distance for spectators who prefer to transfer from their wheelchairs to a seat.

13.7   Dispersal of wheelchair spaces

The recommendation that accommodation for disabled spectators should be dispersed throughout the sports ground also applies to the provision of spaces for spectators using wheelchairs.

For new construction:
Reasonable provision of wheelchair access should be made in accordance with the Building Regulations.

For existing construction:
Although movement to and from accommodation at ground level is easier for spectators using wheelchairs, consideration should also be given to the means by which they can be accommodated on other levels without prejudicing their safety or the safety of others.

For practical and safety management reasons, it is recognised that it will normally be necessary to retain at least some grouping of wheelchair spaces. However, it should also be noted that the safe evacuation of smaller groups of disabled spectators may be more manageable than larger groups.

When siting wheelchair spaces it is recommended that:

a.   The areas should be accessible with the minimum of assistance.

b.   Where appropriate, wheelchair spaces should be available in both home and away areas of spectator accommodation.

13.8   Provision of wheelchair spaces

Wherever possible at existing sports grounds, it is recommended that management provide spaces for people who use wheelchairs.

For new construction:

As stated in Section 13.1, all new construction must comply with the Building Regulations. In Scotland the Building Regulations provide a formula that can be applied to determine the minimum number of wheelchair spaces required in any size of sports ground.

In England and Wales the Building Regulations require that for newly constructed sports grounds, or any completely new section of an existing ground, provision should be made for:

■   a minimum of six wheelchair spaces, or

■   one space for every 100 of the capacity of newly constructed seated accommodation

whichever is the greater.

It further states that 'in a large stadium' it is reasonable to provide a lesser number of wheelchair spaces than one for every 100 of the total seated capacity.

This *Guide* recommends that the term 'a large stadium' applies to any newly constructed sports ground with a seated capacity of 10,000 or more.

Table 4.
Provision of wheelchair spaces at a newly constructed sports ground

seated capacity of newly constructed ground	number of wheelchair spaces
under 10,000	minimum of 6, or 1 in 100 of seated capacity (whichever is greater)
10,000 to 20,000	100 plus 5 per 1,000 above 10,000
20,000 to 40,000	150 plus 3 per 1,000 above 20,000
40,000 or more	210 plus 2 per 1,000 above 40,000

Notes to Table 4

■   All circulation routes – for ingress, egress and emergency – should be designed and managed to cater for the number of wheelchair spaces provided.

■   Sufficient amenities, such as toilet provision and access to catering facilities, should also be provided in relation to the number of spaces. Where such provision is insufficient, both congestion and discomfort may be caused.

13.9   Design of wheelchair spaces

A wheelchair space should meet the following requirements:

a.   It should measure 1.4m in depth and a minimum width of 900mm.

b.   The surface should be level and uniform, and marked appropriately.

c.   The space may be one which is kept clear for occupation only by spectators in wheelchairs, or one which can be readily made available by either removing a seat or keeping the seat behind unoccupied by able-bodied spectators.

Because access and circulation areas should still be designed to accommodate the maximum number of wheelchairs that the area might accommodate, it may be most appropriate to site such flexible viewing areas at the front or the rear of a seating tier.

Note, however, the implications for sightlines when positioning spectators in wheelchairs at the front or rear (see Section 13.10).

d.   Seats for helpers should ideally be adjacent to the space (either behind or to the side). Helpers should not stand in all-seated grounds.

13.10   Wheelchair spaces and viewing standards

The provision of adequate and appropriate viewing standards for spectators using wheelchairs is as important as for able-bodied spectators. The following considerations should be taken into account:

a.   The positioning and level of the wheelchair space should be designed in such a way that the views of both the spectator in the wheelchair and, where appropriate, those of spectators behind, are not restricted.

b.   When calculating sightlines for spectators sitting behind those in wheelchairs, it should be noted that although spectators in wheelchairs sit at approximately the same height as able-bodied spectators, they will usually sit further forward on the tread (owing to the rear dimensions of the wheelchair).

c.   Where wheelchair spaces are positioned behind rows of able-bodied spectators, on a tread which is not sufficiently elevated, careful stewarding will be needed to ensure that the spectators in front do not repeatedly stand up and block the views of the spectators in wheelchairs.

d.   Because not all wheelchair users can easily adjust their position, the siting of wheelchair spaces should ideally avoid areas from which views may be partially restricted.

e.   Where the wheelchair spaces are positioned at pitch level, or behind a lateral gangway, management should carefully assess the effect of any viewing restrictions – such as advertising hoardings – and ensure that all movements of staff and personnel are kept to a minimum.

13.11 Provision of shelter for wheelchair spaces

Wherever possible, wheelchair spaces should be sited in viewing areas that provide adequate shelter. If separate shelter is provided (for example, for an area of wheelchair spaces), the roof level should not restrict views of other spectators, but should still be sufficiently high to allow able-bodied people, such as helpers and stewards, to enter the shelter and move around as normal.

13.12 Circulation

The dispersal of disabled spectators around the ground, and particularly on upper levels of stands, has considerable implications for the safe management of circulation areas, and for the design and management of exit and emergency evacuation routes.

Wherever possible, and in all cases of new construction, management and designers should take account of the current British Standard covering Means of Escape for Disabled People. This provides guidance on suitable stairs, ramps and refuges (see also Section 13.16). Where, because of constraints posed by existing buildings, it is not possible or practicable to apply the British Standard fully, alternative ways of meeting its objectives should be sought.

13.13 Horizontal circulation routes

Horizontal circulation routes used by disabled spectators should be designed to ensure smooth, safe and, where appropriate, unaided passage, with sufficient space to avoid confusion and conflict between disabled and able-bodied spectators. For this reason, the following requirements should be met:

a. Wherever possible, spectators in wheelchairs should have access to their own entrances. Normal egress should usually be the reverse of the ingress route.

b. Entrances and exits should be clearly signposted and staffed, and should, if required, be available to semi-ambulant and other ambulant disabled spectators.

c. All circulation routes used by spectators with wheelchairs should, ideally, be 1.2m wide. For new construction, this is also the recommended minimum (see also Section 9.4). Consideration should also be given to areas where spectators in wheelchairs may need to pass in opposite directions.

d. In existing construction, all doors along circulation routes should have a minimum clear width of 800mm. For new construction the minimum clear width should comply with the Building Regulations, with space on either side and to the sides of the door to avoid congestion.

e. In corridors or passages, unstaffed doors which remain closed during an event should ideally have a glazed panel enabling the wheelchair user to see through to the other side.

f. Travel distances should be kept to a minimum.

g. Surfaces should be slip-resistant, particularly in areas where there is a possibility of wetting.

13.14   Vertical circulation routes

The requirement for the reasonable provision of access to all levels of spectator accommodation in newly constructed sports grounds or newly constructed stands places upon management and designers a more onerous responsibility to consider all aspects of vertical circulation and safety management.

Where appropriate, it should also be noted that even if disabled spectators do not use the viewing accommodation provided on upper levels of a stand, access to hospitality and other related facilities should be made possible for events other than sporting events (see Chapter 20).

When considering vertical circulation routes, the following requirements should be considered:

a.   **Passenger lifts**

The Building Regulations recognise that it is not reasonable to require a lift to be provided in every instance. However, passenger lift access may be required under certain circumstances, in which cases the lifts and their approaches should be designed in accordance with the Building Regulations.

It is important to note that the design of a passenger lift may determine whether it is used in the event of an emergency evacuation (see Sections 13.17 and 17.14).

b.   **Stairs**

Where a passenger lift is not provided, internal stairs for the use of disabled people should comply with the requirements of the Building Regulations. It should be noted that in certain details the criteria differ from those for general purpose stairways, as outlined in Chapter 7. For example, recommended maximum riser heights are 170mm (compared with 180mm) and shorter flights are required (see also Section 13.15).

c.   **Ramps**

Where provided for use by spectators with wheelchairs, ramps should comply with the recommendations of current relevant British Standards. Wherever possible they should be a minimum of 1.2m in width, and no steeper than 1 in 20. Any changes of level should be identified by the use of appropriate signs.

For further guidance on ramps for general spectator use, see Section 7.12.

d.   **Wheelchair stairlifts**

Where a passenger lift is not provided but the storey has a nett floor area greater than 100 sq. m. and contains a 'unique facility', it may be a requirement to provide a wheelchair stairlift. A 'unique facility' is one that exists at an upper level and is unavailable elsewhere. Examples in a sports ground might include an executive box, a restaurant or a viewing lounge.

The installation or fittings of a wheelchair stairlift should in no circumstances impede the means of escape (see Section 13.17).

13.15 Emergency evacuation procedures

It is essential to consider practical measures for the emergency evacuation of disabled spectators. Guidance on this is provided in the Building Regulations.

Designers are recommended to provide refuges (see Section 13.16) to accommodate known numbers of wheelchair users and to subsequently plan for their evacuation from upper or lower levels by means of suitable lifts or agreed management procedures. Horizontal travel distances for disabled persons should be kept short, with separate escape routes being provided where possible.

Fire safety arrangements for emergency evacuation usually rely on the protection of escape routes, the provision of fire warning tones or signals, and the independent capability of people to use stairs for escape. This is clearly inappropriate for some disabled spectators, but satisfactory assisted escape can still be achieved by the use of fire-resisting construction and an adequate system of escape management.

13.16 Refuges

A refuge is a place of comparative safety in which a disabled person can wait either for an evacuation lift or for assistance up or down stairs. Depending on the design and fire resistance of other elements (such as catering outlets), a refuge could be a lobby, corridor, part of a concourse or stairway, or an open space such as a flat roof, balcony or similar place which is sufficiently protected (or remote) from any fire risk and provided with its own means of escape.

13.17 Emergency evacuation of disabled specators

a. Stairways

Stairways used for the emergency evacuation of disabled people should comply with the requirements for internal stairs in the Building Regulations (see Section 13.14). The normal minimum stairway width of 1.1m (1.2m recommended for new construction) should be adequate to enable wheelchairs and their occupants to be carried down the stairs, if necessary.

Contingency plans should also allow for the careful carrying of disabled spectators down stairs without their wheelchairs, should the wheelchair be too large or heavy. (For further guidance on the design of stairways used for emergency evacuation, see Chapter 7.)

b. Evacuation lifts

A lift provided for passenger use in the normal operation of the sports ground may be used for emergency evacuation purposes only if it meets the requirements of an evacuation lift, as specified in the current relevant British Standards. Among other requirements, this means that it should be able to operate in reasonable safety when there is a fire in the building.

Although evacuation lifts need not be provided in all multi-storey buildings, such lifts do reduce the need to provide physical assistance for the evacuation of disabled people by staircases.

However, evacuation lifts can fail. It is therefore crucial that, having reached a refuge by an evacuation lift, a disabled person can also gain access to a stairway as a last resort, should conditions in the refuge become untenable. An evacuation lift with its associated refuge should therefore be located adjacent to a protected staircase.

The location of evacuation lifts should be clearly indicated with signs on every floor level.

c.   Fire-fighting lifts

A fire-fighting lift is essentially an evacuation lift that is provided principally for the use of the fire service and which meets the requirements of the current relevant British Standard. Such a lift may, however, be used for the evacuation of disabled people.

For this procedure to be managed safely, consultation should have taken place with the fire service as part of the preparation of the management's contingency plans for emergency evacuation.

d.   Wheelchair stairlifts

Although wheelchair stairlifts are suitable for access, they should not be used for emergency evacuation.

Where installed in a stairway used for emergency evacuation it is essential that no parts of the lift, such as its carriage rail, reduces the width of the stairway – or any other part of an emergency evacuation route – to less than 1.1m (1.2m recommended for new construction).

e.   Ramps

Ramps can be a useful alternative to stairs, but there is concern about their use for emergency evacuation, during which small changes of level may not be easily seen by spectators. Where ramps are necessary for the emergency evacuation of spectators in wheelchairs they should be as gentle as possible; that is, preferably no steeper than 1 in 20 (see Section 13.14).

13.18   Fire and emergency warning systems

Contingency plans for emergency evacuation should take into account the special needs of spectators with disabilities. If separate emergency evacuation routes for disabled spectators are provided, as is recommended, the contingency plans will allow for able-bodied and disabled spectators to be evacuated at the same time.

If separate escape routes for disabled spectators cannot, for practical reasons, be provided, the contingency plans may be based on the use of a two-stage warning system.

The first stage should take the form of a coded message alerting stewards to an imminent evacuation. This allows for stewards to begin moving disabled spectators to refuges, from which they can be moved either by evacuation lifts or by assistance downstairs to ground level.

The second stage should be a general alert.

Warning systems may consist of an evacuation signal, announcements over the public address system, and, where appropriate, visual instructions on electronic scoreboards or videoboards.

As stated in Section 13.5, the fact that some people have a hearing impairment does not mean that they are necessarily insensitive to sound. Many people with severe impairments have enough perception of conventional audible alarm signals to require no special provision. Furthermore, in most situations it is reasonable to plan on the basis that most spectators with impaired hearing will rely on others for warning.

13.19   Management of accommodation for disabled spectators

The need for safe management of accommodation for disabled spectators is absolutely fundamental.

In addition to the guidance which precedes this section, the following management issues may be considered.

a.   **Good and safe design**
A large number of disabled spectators may not need, or want, special attention or assistance. It is therefore stressed that good and safe design should always strive to make it possible for disabled spectators to attend events safely, without the necessity for high levels of stewarding or intervention.

b.   **Stewarding**
Nevertheless, stewards should be trained and briefed in all matters relating to the safety and welfare of disabled spectators. It is further recommended that, where appropriate, individual stewards be given special responsibilities towards disabled spectators. Expert guidance on training should be sought from competent persons.

Stewards should also be alert to the effects that other spectators' behaviour can have upon disabled spectators. Such behaviour might include blocking the views of spectators in wheelchairs, unauthorised use of toilets for disabled spectators, blocking circulation routes used by disabled spectators and exerting pressure in congested areas.

c.   **Staff**
Similarly, any staff who come into contact with the public should be suitably trained and briefed on the needs of disabled spectators.

d.   **Arrival and admission**
Management should, where appropriate, make provision for the safe parking and access of spectators with disabilities. Wherever possible separate entrances should be provided for spectators with wheelchairs. Management should also adopt fair and reasonable admission policies, and ensure that such policies are clearly explained in advance, so as to avoid congestion or confusion at entry points.

Management should also brief staff, whenever possible, not to sell tickets to ambulant or semi-ambulant people with disabilities in areas of the ground which are not likely to be accessible.

e. **Special vehicles**

Where special vehicles (or invalid cars) used by disabled people are to be admitted, management should ensure that their passage and place of parking do not disrupt the safety or viewing standards of other spectators. Nor should the location of such vehicles restrict access to the ground by emergency vehicles, or block any emergency evacuation routes, including those leading to the playing area or area of activity.

f. **Provision of amenities**

Sufficient support services and facilities for disabled spectators should be made available. This will include the provision of lower counters in ticket offices and catering outlets, induction loops where required, and adequate provision of toilet facilities. This last recommendation is not purely a matter of amenity. Long queues for toilets, or congestion around spectators in wheelchairs, can cause safety problems for all spectators, disabled and able-bodied. Further guidance is available in the FSADC publication, *Toilet Facilities at Stadia* (see Bibliography).

g. **Awareness**

Management should recognise that the best source of information about the needs of disabled spectators are the spectators themselves. Sensitive and non-intrusive liaison should ensure therefore that any potential needs or concerns are brought to the attention of stewards and, if necessary, any other personnel, such as first aid or medical staff.

This is particularly important when evolving emergency evacuation procedures. For example, in certain situations it may be essential for spectators in wheelchairs to be carried bodily. This will require special training by stewards.

Management should also be aware that the presence of spectators who have partial impairments may not be apparent until an emergency arises.

h. **The needs of elderly spectators**

Although many elderly people do not consider themselves to have disabilities, it is often the case that they experience impaired vision, hearing or mobility, or may be semi-ambulant.

Given that the number of elderly people as a proportion of the population has increased, and continues to increase, this may be reflected in the number of elderly people attending sporting events.

Management should therefore be aware of their needs, particularly when planning and training stewards for emergency evacuation procedures.

Chapter Fourteen

Spectator accommodation –
Temporary demountable structures

14.1 Responsibility for safety

As stated in the Introduction, whether or not a sports ground is issued with a safety certificate, responsibility for the safety of spectators lies at all times with the ground management. The management will normally be either the owner or lessee of the ground, but may not necessarily be the promoter of the event.

This responsibility extends to any temporary demountable structure erected at the sports ground. Management cannot delegate the responsibility to the event promoter, to the designers of the structure, or to the contractors responsible for assembling the structure.

Ground management should therefore put in place procedures for ensuring the safe design, assembly and usage of any such structures. If the management does not itself possess sufficient expertise in specific matters relating to temporary demountable structures, it should require the event promoter or contractor to produce certificates from competent persons of the appropriate qualification and experience.

14.2 Need to meet standards

The construction and configuration of temporary demountable structures – such as grandstands, standing decks, hospitality suites and marquees – vary considerably, as do the materials used in their construction. Some structures may be erected for a single event only and may be commissioned at short notice. Structural components are lightweight, rapidly assembled, readily dismantled, and reusable.

Nevertheless, the fact that a structure is designed for temporary use does not justify acceptance of lower margins of safety than those required for permanent structures.

The design and construction of temporary demountable structures should, wherever possible, meet the standards for new construction, as specified in the *Guide*.

It is recognised, however, that there is a considerable amount of proprietary stock currently in use. When used at sports grounds this should at least meet the standards of the *Guide*, and should satisfy all relevant British Standards.

The principles of the *Guide* in respect of entry and exit systems, barriers, fire safety, and provision for disabled spectators are also applicable to temporary demountable structures. The need for lightning protection should also be noted (see Section 17.9).

Reference should also be made to *Temporary Demountable Structures – Guidance on Procurement, Design and Use*, published by the Institution of Structural Engineers (see Bibliography).

14.3 Independent design check

Prior to assembly, the design of a temporary demountable structure should be subject to an independent check by a chartered structural engineer of the appropriate skills and experience. The supplier of a temporary demountable structure may appoint the structural engineer responsible for the independent design check.

In the case of proprietary systems, the results of an independent design check should remain valid provided no subsequent modifications are made to the system. If significant changes are made, further independent design checking will be required; for example if the proprietary structure is supported by tubular scaffolding.

All temporary demountable structures should be erected and used in strict accordance with their approved design criteria. Any changes in lay-out, dimensions or loading will necessitate a new, independent design check.

Furthermore, ground management is responsible for ensuring the integrity of such structures after their assembly, and before spectators are permitted to occupy them.

14.4 Design performance and suitability

Temporary demountable structures should be designed in three-dimensional form, to be robust and stable, and to support design loadings for the required period with an adequate margin of safety. Guidance is available from the Institution of Structural Engineers (see Section 14.2). The following main points should also be considered:

a. By virtue of their lightweight construction and use, temporary demountable structures are often exposed to a greater risk of accidental damage, such as by vehicles, unauthorised removals and alterations. This fact should be carefully considered when assessing stability and when considering the management of such structures (see Section 14.11).

b. The robustness of temporary demountable structures should be such that the effects of accidental damage are not disproportionate, thereby leading to progressive collapse.

c. Having assessed the structure's overall stability, where necessary, ballast and/or anchorage to the ground should be provided to ensure adequate resistance to overturning.

14.5 Dynamic loads

Because of their lightweight construction, the need for rapid assembly of joints and fixings, and, in certain situations, the nature of their foundations or supports, temporary demountable structures are relatively sensitive to dynamic excitation.

Dynamic loads generated by spectator movements vary considerably according to the activity taking place. For example, spectator movement that is synchronised – such as hand-clapping, foot-stamping or swaying from side to side – can excite a natural frequency of the structure, which in turn can lead to a significant and potentially dangerous movement of the structure.

Management should be aware of this and ensure that spectator movement is monitored and, if necessary, controlled, both by vigilant stewarding and by management of the event itself (see also Section 14.11). Guidance on dynamic loads is also available from the Institution of Structural Engineers.

14.6   Consultation

Even when not formally required to do so under the terms of a safety certificate, management should consult the relevant authorities regarding enforcement responsibility, and any special local regulations, certificates, licences or permissions. Consultation should also take place with the fire authority concerning access for fire-fighting purposes.

14.7   Location

The choice of location for a temporary demountable structure may be pre-determined or limited, but factors which need to be considered include:

a.   access/egress for spectators

b.   access/egress for emergency vehicles

c.   the ground's load-bearing capacity, its slope, unevenness and drainage (see Section 14.8)

d.   the availability of mains services

e.   the proximity of overhead power lines, and of surrounding buildings in relation to the risk of fire

f.   exposure to the elements.

14.8   Ground conditions

It is the responsibility of management to ensure that the ground conditions are suitable for the type of temporary demountable structure being proposed. Where the supports of a temporary demountable structure make contact with the ground or foundation surface it is necessary to distribute the loadings so that differential settlement and overall bearing pressures are within acceptable limits.

It may also be necessary to fix anchors at the support points in order to resist uplift.

The ground conditions should be assessed by a visual examination, augmented, as necessary, by excavating trial pits, or by a ground investigation. For example, there may be soft spots due to the presence of unconsolidated fill, peat, land drains or previous excavations. Unequal settlement beneath supports could set up high stresses and deformations in the frame. Soft spots should be located, filled and compacted or bridged with grillages.

Care should also be taken that changes in the weather do not materially alter the ground conditions to the detriment of the structure's stability.

14.9   Assembly and dismantling

The assembly and dismantling of temporary demountable structures should be carried out by competent persons, experienced and trained in the proper performance of such work, in accordance with the manufacturer's written instructions, or any drawings and specifications prepared for a particular structure.

Work should be carried out only where lighting is sufficient to allow it to be safely and properly performed and checked. No assembly or dismantling work should be carried out to the danger of members of the public in the vicinity.

Assembly and dismantling should be carried out in a proper manner, using correct parts, and appropriate tools. Care should be taken with the handling of components to avoid damage or distortion. All components should be closely examined during assembly and dismantling for signs of wear, deformation or other damage, and where necessary replaced by sound components of matching material, properties and dimensions. Temporary repairs using makeshift components are not acceptable. Care should also be taken to ensure all components are correctly aligned. They should not be bent, distorted or otherwise altered to force a fit.

On completion, assembly work should be checked, with particular attention given to fastenings and connections.

14.10   Temporary demountable standing accommodation

Where temporary demountable structures are provided for standing spectators, it is particularly important to provide good sightlines. This is to minimise the risk of crowd movement and sway, and also to reduce the likelihood of spectators migrating to areas that offer better views (which in turn might lead to overcrowding).

The provision of continuous crush barriers between gangways, as recommended in Section 10.8, will also help to prevent migration.

In all other respects the crush barriers should meet the requirements of Chapter 10, including the design loads specified in Table 2. If the structure cannot accommodate the maximum design loads given in Table 2, the spacing of the crush barriers should be reduced accordingly so that they do meet the requirements.

Segregation fences should not be fitted to temporary demountable structures used for standing.

14.11   Management of temporary demountable structures

The special characteristics of temporary demountable structures require that management adopt specific strategies to ensure the safety of spectators. Such measures include the following:

a.   Management should ensure that the structure is used strictly for the purpose for which it was designed. If used for any other purpose, or modified in any way, it should be the subject of an independent design check before it can occupied by spectators.

b.   Stewards should be briefed to pay close attention to the circulation and behaviour of spectators around the structure, so as to ensure that no one is allowed to climb up or underneath any part of the structure, or behave in such a way that any elements or components may be damaged or removed.

c.   At events where there is a possibility of synchronised spectator movement, stewards, assisted by public address announcements, should ensure that spectators are suitably warned. If potentially dangerous synchronised movements do occur, the event organiser should ensure that the movement is halted and, if appropriate, any part of the event which stimulates the movement is curtailed.

d.   The occurrence of high winds immediately prior to or during an event may require management to consider prohibiting the public from occupying the temporary demountable structure, or, if necessary, cancelling the event.

e.   Management should ensure that maintenance is carried out in strict accordance with written instructions, which should be provided by the designer or manufacturer.

14.12   Designs of marquees

There are many different designs of marquees, but generally they fall into two categories: pole marquees or framed marquees.

The design of large marquees should be subject to an independent check by a chartered structural engineer of appropriate skill and experience. The term 'large marquee' applies to pole marquees of a span greater than 12m (40 feet), and framed marquees of a span greater than 9m.

All marquees should be capable of withstanding all forces to which they may be subjected, particularly wind (including uplift), taking into account the period of exposure and the time of year.

For guidance on marquees, reference should be made to the Codes of Practice developed and regulated by the Made-Up Textiles Association (see Bibliography).

14.13   Inspection of marquees

In common with all temporary demountable structures, marquees should satisfy the principles of this *Guide* in respect of entry and exit systems, barriers, fire safety, and provision for spectators with disabilities.

In addition, before use marquees should be subjected to a thorough inspection, taking into consideration the following points:

a.   anchorages should be suitable for purpose and hold fast

b.   bracing wires should be in place and properly tensioned

c.   all ropes, including wire ropes, should be sound

d.   the fabric should be tensioned and not prone to ponding

e.   exposed ropes and stakes adjacent to entrances and exits should be marked or roped off

f.   all locking pins and bolts should be in place and secure

g.   eaves connection joints should be securely locked home

h.   the fabric should have no unrepaired tears

i.   flooring should be evenly laid, securely fixed, with no tripping points

j.   roof linings should not drop significantly below eaves

k.   timber uprights and ridges should be free from splits caused by damage

l.   walls should be securely pegged and/or secured

m.   poled marquees should have a full complement of side uprights, anchor stakes, pulley blocks and guy ropes

n.   the main upright should be independently guyed.

Responsibility for ensuring the inspection is carried out lies with the management.

14.14   Surveillance and maintenance of marquees

The management and contractor should agree beforehand procedures for the surveillance and maintenance of marquees. The agreement should be reached on the basis of a risk assessment which takes into account all relevant factors, such as the use to which the marquee is put, the period of exposure, weather conditions and the time of year.

14.15   Marquees in abnormal conditions

Provision should be made for the dismantling, either partial or total, of a marquee should abnormal conditions arise that could lead to any collapse or distortion. Where such dismantling in any way affects the stability of the marquee, or the safety of members of the public, the work should not commence until the immediate area has been cleared of all but essential staff.

14.16   Other temporary demountable structures

For guidance on other uses for temporary demountable structures at sports grounds, see Chapter 19 (Media Provision) and Chapter 20 (Alternative Uses for Sports Grounds).

Chapter Fifteen

Fire safety

15.1 Achieving safety from fire

Safety from fire is achieved in two stages. The first stage is to conduct a fire risk assessment of all structures and areas of spectator accommodation within the sports ground, as explained further in Section 15.2. This assessment will identify and establish the existing levels of fire risk.

The second stage is to reduce those risks, wherever possible.

In order to achieve this second stage, management should:

a.   adopt measures designed to minimise the fire risk (see Section 15.9)

b.   ensure that measures are taken to restrict the rate of early fire growth and fire spread (see 15.10)

c.   provide and protect sufficient emergency evacuation routes (see 9.11, 15.10 and 15.16)

d.   provide appropriate fire detection and warning systems (see 15.12)

e.   provide appropriate fire extinguishing and/or first aid fire-fighting equipment (see 15.13–15.15)

f.   ensure that all staff receive appropriate training in fire safety and the use of fire-fighting equipment (see 15.9).

Once the above measures have been taken and the level of fire risk has been reduced, it is then possible to determine the appropriate times for both normal egress and emergency evacuation for each area of spectator accommodation. These times will then form part of the capacity calculation, as explained in Chapter 1.

When considering fire safety, it should be noted that:

g.   the maximum travel distance for seated spectators is 30m from the seat to the nearest exit from the viewing area (see Section 11.7), and for standing spectators 12m from the standing position to a gangway or point of entry to the exit system (see 12.4)

h.   the maximum normal egress time for a sports ground is eight minutes (see 9.7)

i.   the maximum emergency evacuation time varies between two and half minutes and eight minutes, according to the level of fire risk (see 9.9 and 15.4–15.6).

However, it is stressed that, rather than relying solely on a short emergency evacuation time, management should always aim to introduce measures which will minimise the outbreak and spread of fire.

In addition to these factors, achieving safety from fire also requires the preparation of contingency plans (see Sections 2.14 and 2.15), and the provision of a suitable system of internal and external communications (see Chapter 16).

15.2 Fire risk assessment

In order to determine the fire risk to staff, and to staff and spectators on match or event days, ground management should conduct a fire risk assessment of all accommodation within the sports ground, at least once a year (see also Sections 2.3 and 15.7).

This requires assessment of the risk of a fire occurring, and the danger to life should a fire occur.

It is not possible to give detailed guidance for fire risk assessment, because circumstances and conditions vary so widely. However, management should consider the points raised in the following sections, and the basic aims of a risk assessment, which are:

a. to identify parts of the ground where fire is likely, and assess the level of risk (see Sections 15.3–15.7)

b. to identify the location of combustible materials and any sources of ignition which might cause a fire (see 15.9)

c. to identify reasonable steps that can be taken to minimise the fire risk (see 15.9)

d. to identify people especially at risk and ensure that their needs in an emergency situation are provided for in the management's contingency plans. People especially at risk might include:

    i. children, semi-ambulant spectators and people with disabilities who might need help to escape, and/or may have difficulties in using escape routes, particularly stairs

    ii. staff or stewards who may have to assist others.

Once the risks have been identified, it is then possible to assess the level of risk for each area of spectator accommodation.

15.3 Levels of risk

The fire risk assessment should assess all structures and installations at the ground, including all areas of spectator accommodation, taking into account their form of construction, usage, facilities and location. This assessment will determine for each structure or area of accommodation the appropriate level of fire risk; that is, low risk, normal risk or high risk.

The assessment should also take into account the availability and location of a place or places of safety, and the proximity of other buildings or installations which might themselves carry a risk of fire.

Examples of each level of fire risk follow in Sections 15.4–15.6.

The level of fire risk will determine the emergency evacuation time, which in turn will form part of the calculation of the final capacity of the ground or sections of the ground (see Chapter 1).

If the fire risk assessment indicates that the area's holding capacity is too large to enable all spectators to evacuate the area and reach a place of safety within the emergency evacuation time appropriate to the level of risk, or if undue congestion or psychological stress is likely to result, the capacity should be reduced accordingly.

Note also that the conditions within a particular ground may call for interpolation between the emergency evacuation times referred to in the following sections.

In all cases, the advice of the fire authority should be sought.

15.4   Categorisation of low fire risk

A low fire risk seated or standing area at a sports ground is likely to be one where:

a.   the risk of a fire occurring is low, and

b.   in the unlikely event of a fire, the potential for the fire, heat or smoke generated by it to spread is negligible, and

c.   there is a minimal risk to life.

Such structures might include open terraces and stands constructed of non-combustible materials with fully protected catering outlets.

For low risk seated and standing areas, the emergency evacuation time for all spectators to reach a place of safety should be no more than eight minutes.

15.5   Categorisation of normal fire risk

A normal fire risk seated or standing area is likely to be one where:

a.   the risk of a fire spreading is low

b.   should a fire occur it is likely to be confined to a room or its place of origin

c.   there is in place an effective fire suppression or containment system.

For normal risk seated and standing areas, the emergency evacuation time for all spectators to reach a place of safety should be no more than six minutes.

15.6 Categorisation of high fire risk

The type of spectator accommodation most at risk from fire is the covered stand. A high fire risk seated or standing area is likely to be one where one or more of the following characteristics apply:

a.   the construction consists of combustible materials

b.   structural features could promote the spread of fire, heat and smoke

c.   there are voids under seating decks, floors or terraces where waste or litter may accumulate

d.   there are several storeys, with exiting systems from the upper levels routed through hospitality areas

e.   concourse areas have no fire separation between retail and/or catering facilities and the emergency evacuation routes

f.   highly flammable or explosive materials are present

g.   people in the seated or standing area are at risk from an incident occurring in an adjacent premise.

For high risk seated and standing areas, the emergency evacuation time for all spectators to reach a place of safety should be no more than two and a half minutes.

It is stressed that the list of characteristics summarised in Sections 15.4–15.6 above are for general guidance only. Any fire risk assessment must take into account all relevant local circumstances.

15.7 Fire risk assessment for new or refurbished stands

A fire risk assessment should be carried out for all newly constructed or refurbished grounds or stands, even though these will have been designed and constructed in accordance with the current relevant Building Regulations and/or British Standards, and as such should have a low level of risk. As part of the design process the designer should also carry out a fire risk assessment to identify areas where a fire might occur.

The management should also carry out a fire risk assessment of the new construction, as soon as possible after the premises are occupied. This is because, once completed, many modern stands have added facilities and furnishings which increase their fire loading and potential for a fire.

15.8 Recording, monitoring and reviewing the fire risk assessment

The findings of the risk assessment should be recorded and taken into account when planning and managing fire safety arrangements at the ground. The location of all people especially at risk (see Section 15.2), together with any special arrangements put into place to ensure their safety if a fire occurs, should also be recorded.

The risk assessment should be continually monitored to ensure that the fire safety arrangements remain adequate, and should be reviewed in the following circumstances:

a.   there is a significant change of staff

b.   there is a change to the safety management arrangements

c.   building or refurbishment works are planned or in progress

d.   there is a significant increase of combustible materials, or sources of heat in the ground.

Where the review indicates that the risk to people has changed, a new fire risk assessment should be carried out.

As stated in Section 15.1, having completed a fire risk assessment, the next stage is to reduce those risks, wherever possible. The following sections detail how this may be achieved.

15.9   Minimising fire risk

The following measures and practices should be considered when seeking to minimise fire risk:

a.   **Sources of ignition**
As stated in Section 15.2, the fire risk assessment should identify all potential sources of ignition at the ground. Where possible, those sources should be removed or replaced with safer forms. Where this cannot be done, the ignition source should be kept well away from combustible materials, be adequately guarded or made the subject of management controls. Ignition sources may include:

i.   cooking appliances

ii.   central heating boilers

iii.   room heaters

iv.   light fittings

v.   certain electrical apparatus, especially if not maintained

vi.   smoking materials (see Section 15.9.c).

b.   **Staff training, awareness and security**
It is essential that management ensures the training of all staff in first aid fire-fighting, so that, if necessary, they can tackle a fire without endangering life until the fire brigade arrives. The advice of the fire authority should be sought when drawing up such a training programme.

Staff should otherwise be aware at all times of the need to guard against fire, including the possibility of arson.

c.   Smoking

Management should adopt and enforce a clear policy on smoking, for both staff and spectators. Stewards and safety personnel should not smoke during an event. In stands which are constructed of, or contain, combustible or flammable items or materials, smoking should be discouraged or even prohibited.

d.   Flares and fireworks

Management should adopt and enforce a clear policy prohibiting spectators from bringing flares or fireworks into the sports ground.

e.   Voids

Voids under seating decks or terraces, or under the flooring itself, are often used for the unauthorised storage of combustible materials. They may also accumulate waste or litter. To counter this, all voids should either be sealed off or be kept entirely open to allow easy access for inspection and the removal of the combustible materials.

Voids which are unusable, for example, where the viewing deck is built over a slope, should, if practicable, be filled with a non-combustible material.

f.   Waste and litter

The accumulation of waste and litter (such as programmes and food and drink packaging) should be avoided. All parts of the ground should therefore be inspected before, during and after each event. Any accumulation of waste or litter should be removed without delay or kept in a fire-resistant container or room, pending removal.

Sufficient waste and litter bins should be provided and arrangements made for their frequent emptying during a match or event.

g.   Furnishings, upholstered seating and cushions

The use of furnishings, upholstered seating and cushions which are easily ignited or have rapid spread of flame characteristics should be avoided. If present, they should be taken into account when determining the acceptability of escape routes.

Further guidance on the suitability of various types of furnishings and synthetic materials is provided in the *Guide to Fire Precautions in Existing Places of Entertainment and Like Premises* (see Bibliography).

When stored in bulk, certain types of cushioning (which is distributed or hired for event use), and foam mats (used at athletics events) pose a risk of a rapid fire growth and should therefore be stored in a fire-resistant container or room.

h.   Storage

Rooms or buildings used for the storage of waste, litter, upholstered seating or hazardous materials should:

i.   be accessible directly from the open air

ii.   ideally, be well away from public areas

iii.   if forming part of a stand or structure, be separated from any other part of the building by construction having a fire resistance of at least one hour

iv.   if measuring 6m or more in depth, be provided with an alternative means of escape

v.   be kept locked shut when not in use.

i.   High fire risk areas

High fire risk areas should be separated from any other parts of spectator accommodation by a construction having a fire resistance of at least one hour. Such areas may include:

i.   kitchens

ii.   catering outlets

iii.   hospitality areas

iv.   office accommodation

v.   boiler rooms, oil fuel stores and general stores

vi.   enclosed or underground car parks.

j.   Catering facilities

Wherever possible, all catering facilities should be located in permanent structures. If located within other structures they must be separated by fire-resistant construction and provided with adequate ventilation.

Flues should be separated as they pass through the structure, have an adequate degree of fire separation, and terminate at a point where the emissions can disperse in the open air.

For further guidance on catering facilities at sports grounds, refer to the *Guide to Control over Concessionaire Facilities and Other Services at Sports Grounds*, published by the District Surveyors Association (see Bibliography).

k.   Fuel or power supply

Special care should be taken to ensure that any fuel or power supply used for cooking or heating, in particular LPG cylinders, is safely stored and used, in accordance with the advice of the authority responsible for enforcement of the Health and Safety at Work etc. Act 1974. (For further details refer to Bibliography.)

l.   Hazardous materials

If it is necessary to utilise hazardous materials, such as fuels (whether in containers or within fuel tanks and machinery), fertilisers, weed killers, paints or gas cylinders used for medical purposes, they should be stored in a fire-resistant room.

15.10   Restriction of fire growth and spread

It is vital to ensure that, in the event of a fire, the rate of fire growth is restricted in its early stages. It should also be noted that most measures which restrict the rate of fire growth in its early stages will also serve to restrict the fire spread in its later stages. These measures include:

a.   Viewing accommodation should be separated from adjacent areas or voids by a construction which has a fire resistance of at least half an hour. This is so that any fire underneath or in an adjacent area cannot easily break through into the spectator accommodation.

Where stands incorporate hospitality facilities, any additional separation must be determined by the level of fire risk.

b.   Where a stairway, vomitory, passage or any other part of an emergency evacuation route passes up, down or through a stand or other structure used by spectators, unless it is in the open air, it should be in a fire-resistant enclosure separated by a construction having a fire resistance of not less than one hour. For further guidance on vomitories and concourses, see Chapter 8.

c.   Walls and ceiling linings within spectator accommodation, together with ceiling linings beneath the floor of that accommodation, should have a flame spread classification of not less than Class 1 when tested in accordance with the current relevant British Standard. Walls and ceiling linings in emergency evacuation routes and circulation areas should have a flame spread classification of Class O.

d.   Any door forming part of the enclosure to an escape route should be self-closing and have a fire resistance of not less than half an hour.

e.   Where the roofs of buildings are close together or connected to each other, smoke or flame can easily spread. This risk should be eliminated by fire prevention measures, or by adequate fire separation.

f.   For some roof configurations, venting systems may offer a means of reducing the spread of fire (including the movement of flames under the roof) and the spread of smoke and toxic gases. The science of fire and smoke venting is, however, complex and advice from the fire authority should be sought on whether venting systems would be advantageous in a particular case.

g.   Where the roof contains flammable materials it should be replaced by non-combustible materials. Where this is not practicable, the roof should be underdrawn with non-combustible board.

h.   Shops, or catering outlets containing deep fat fryers or hot food cooking facilities, should be separated from other internal areas or spectator accommodation areas by a construction which has a fire resistance of at least one hour. Where roller shutters are used these should be capable of operating both manually and by fusible link. Where a fire detection or fire alarm system has been installed, the roller shutter should also be designed to close on the activation of the system.

15.11 Fire resistance in existing constructions

Existing stands and others areas of spectator accommodation will vary considerably according to age, condition and the materials used in their construction. It may therefore be difficult in some cases to improve the fire resistance of an existing structure to any significant extent. But it should be done wherever possible, even though, in some cases, substantial alterations may be needed to provide reasonable protection from fire.

Where not possible, alternative compensatory measures will need to be considered. These might include:

a. provision of an early fire warning system

b. improvements to the exit and emergency evacuation systems

c. installation of a suitable fire suppression system

d. a reduction of the travel distances

e. a reduction of the final capacity.

15.12 Fire warning and fire detection systems

All buildings to which the public or staff have access and which might pose a fire risk should be provided with a manually operated electrical fire warning system to alert staff. Consideration should also be given to the installation of an automatic fire detection (AFD) system in all high-risk fire areas (see Section 15.9.i) and also in any unoccupied areas that contain a normal fire risk.

These systems should:

a. be designed to accommodate the emergency evacuation procedure

b. give an automatic indication of the fire warning and its location. If this warning is directed to a part of the ground other than the control point (for example, to the secretary's office), there should ideally be a repeater panel sited in the control point

c. be designed, installed, maintained and tested in accordance with the advice given in the current British Standard

d. be approved by the fire authority.

Where the public address system is part of the fire warning system it should be connected to an auxiliary power source to ensure the continued use of the system in the event of fire or other emergency.

Whichever warning or detection systems are in place, however, if a fire occurs the fire brigade should always be called immediately.

The procedures adopted to notify the brigade should also form part of the management's contingency plans and of staff training.

15.13 Automatic fire extinguishing systems

Consideration should be given to the provision of automatic fire extinguishing systems in high-risk fire areas, such as large store-rooms and enclosed or underground car parks situated under or adjacent to spectator accommodation.

a.   Automatic fire extinguishing systems should be designed, installed, maintained and tested in accordance with the advice given in the current British Standards.

b.   Activation of the system should be automatically communicated to the control point.

c.   The system should be approved by the fire authority.

d.   The system may be installed instead of an AFD system.

15.14 Fire-fighting equipment

All sports grounds should be provided with appropriate fire-fighting equipment. For the majority of grounds, first aid fire-fighting equipment will be sufficient. However, at some larger grounds it may be necessary to provide a suitable water supply for fire-fighting, in the form of hydrants.

Advice on the type, the level of provision and the siting of fire-fighting equipment should be sought from the fire authority.

Responsibility for the provision of appropriate fire-fighting equipment lies with the management. It is also the responsibility of management to check that all fire-fighting equipment is in the correct position and in satisfactory order before each event.

15.15 First aid fire-fighting equipment

This refers to equipment such as fire extinguishers, fire blankets, buckets of sand and hose reels intended for use by safety staff or employees prior to the arrival of the fire brigade. When providing such equipment, the following should be considered:

a.   Hose reels, where appropriate, should be sufficient to provide adequate protection to the whole floor area, and should be installed in a suitable position by entrances, exits and stairways.

b.   Where hose reels are not provided, sufficient portable fire extinguishers should be installed to give adequate cover. The number and type will depend upon the size, lay-out, fire separation and risk in each structure.

c.   Fire blankets and appropriate fire extinguishers should be provided in all catering facilities and outlets.

d.   First aid fire-fighting equipment should be located so that it cannot be vandalised but is readily accessible to staff in the event of fire.

e.   All first aid fire-fighting equipment should be designed, installed, maintained and tested in accordance with the advice given in the current British Standards.

15.16 Emergency evacuation and places of safety

As stated in Section 9.7, a clear distinction should be made between the emergency evacuation time and the normal egress time at the end of an event.

The emergency evacuation time is a calculation which, together with the appropriate rate of passage, is used to determine the capacity of the emergency exit system from the viewing accommodation to a place of safety, in the event of an emergency (see also 9.9).

As stated in Section 15.3, the fire risk assessment should take into account the availability and location of a place or places of safety.

A place of safety is a place which people can reach safely via the escape route, and which will be safe from the effects of fire. It may be a road, walkway or open space adjacent to, or even within the boundaries of, the sports ground.

Within a large sports ground there may also be a need to designate a place or places of comparative safety where people can be safe from the effects of fire for 30 minutes or more, thus allowing extra time for them to move directly to a place of safety.

Such places of comparative safety may include:

a.   an exit route that is protected throughout its length by a construction having a fire resistance of one hour

b.   a stairway that is in the open air and protected from fire breaking out onto or below it

c.   the pitch or area of activity. As stated in Section 9.12, however, this should be considered only in certain circumstances and only after consultation with the fire authority.

It should also be noted that if the fire risk assessment indicates that an emergency evacuation exit could be affected by fire, that exit may have to be discounted when calculating the capacity of the emergency exit system (see Section 9.14).

15.17 Other fire safety considerations

When considering fire safety in the overall context of the design and management of sports grounds, reference should also to be made to the following sections:

a.   Section 5.8 (access for emergency vehicles)

b.   Chapter 9 (egress and emergency evacuation)

c.   Chapter 13 (particularly the sections dealing with the emergency evacuation of spectators with disabilities)

d.   Chapter 17 (particularly Section 17.3 concerning emergency lighting and 17.13 on the use of lifts for evacuation and fire-fighting).

Chapter Sixteen

Communications

16.1 Management reponsibility

Clear, efficient and reliable communications are an integral part of any safety management operation. This applies regardless of the type of sports ground or the nature of the event.

It is stressed that good communications are not solely dependent on the provision of advanced equipment or modern systems. The skills, awareness and efficiency of management, stewards and other personnel form a vital part of all links.

The management responsibility for communications can be summarised as follows:

a.   to provide, operate and maintain the necessary means of communication

b.   to provide, equip, maintain and manage the operation of a control point

c.   to keep open and maintain all necessary lines of communication, in both normal and emergency conditions

d.   to ensure that all safety personnel and stewards are competent and suitably trained in the practice of good communications, with or without equipment, as conditions allow.

16.2 Lines of communication

Whatever the *means* of communication utilised (see next section), there are essentially six *lines* of communication needed at all grounds. These are:

a.   communications between members of the safety management team, from the safety officer to stewards and all other safety personnel

b.   communications between the safety management team and all points of entry (including the monitoring of counting systems) and all points of exit

c.   communications between the safety management team and the police, other emergency services and medical agencies

d.   communications between the safety management team and spectators, inside and outside the ground

e.   communications between the safety management team and other members of staff

f.   communications between the safety management team and officials in charge of the actual event.

16.3   Means of communication

This chapter provides guidance on the principal means of communication, in terms of their technical and operational requirements.

Precise requirements will depend on the type of ground, the nature of the sport, and the number of people in attendance. Professional advice and expertise should therefore be sought from competent persons of the appropriate skills and experience. In general, the provision of all communication systems should also be determined after consultation with the emergency services, and, where a safety certificate is in force, the local authority. Communication systems should also conform to current, relevant British Standards or Codes of Practice.

The principal means of communication outlined in this chapter are as follows:

a.   radio communications

b.   telephone communications (internal and external)

c.   public address systems

d.   closed circuit television systems (CCTV)

e.   scoreboards, information boards and video boards

f.   signs

g.   written communications (via tickets, signs and printed material)

h.   inter-personal communications.

16.4   Provision of a control point

Regardless of the type or size of a ground, a control point should be provided, and equipped to meet the reasonable requirements of the ground. Such a facility should form the hub of the safety management's communications network.

In previous editions of the *Guide* and related publications, the control point has been referred to as the 'police control room', 'police box' or 'central control point'. At larger grounds, particularly football grounds, the control point is currently referred to using terms such as 'stadium control room' or 'ground operations centre'. But whatever the term employed, it is emphasised that the provision and equipment of the control point is the responsibility of management.

If the police and other emergency services are required to be present at the ground, all decisions relating to the location, design and equipment of the control point must be made in consultation with representatives of those services. This is in order to ensure that the control point will also meet the needs of the police and others in both normal and emergency conditions. Where a safety certificate is in force, consultation concerning the control point should also take place with the local authority.

Further guidance on the planning, staffing, design and equipment of control points is available in the FSDC publication, *Stadium Control Rooms* (see Bibliography). Although written primarily for football grounds, the publication contains much general advice applicable to all sports grounds.

16.5 Functions of a control point

As stated in Section 16.4, the control point should form the hub of the safety management's communications network.

It is needed for the following five main functions:

a. to monitor the safety of people inside the ground and its immediate vicinity

b. to co-ordinate responses to specific incidents and emergencies

c to provide, if required, a monitoring facility for the emergency services

d. to monitor public order

e. to assist the management in the staging of events.

16.6 Location of control points

The location of the control point should, as far as possible, meet the following requirements:

a. It should command a good, unrestricted view of the whole ground; that is, the whole playing area or area of activity, and as much of the viewing accommodation as possible. (It is recognised, however, that this may not be possible at certain grounds; for example, multi-tiered large grounds or those staging horse or motor racing, or where there are multiple areas of activity.)

b. It should be conveniently accessible for all authorised personnel in normal and emergency conditions, without depending on circulation routes or emergency evacuation routes used by large numbers of spectators.

c. It should be capable of being readily evacuated in an emergency.

d. Its presence should not restrict the views of any spectators. Nor should it have its own views restricted by the close proximity of spectators.

e. Its location should take into account any long-term plans for the ground, to ensure that, wherever possible, construction work and new structures will not disrupt its operation.

16.7 Command of control points

In normal conditions, command of the central point and its communication systems should be the responsibility of a representative of the ground management, who will usually be the safety officer (see Sections 2.9 and 2.10).

If the police are on duty in the control point, there should be a clear, unequivocal understanding of the division of responsibilities between their personnel and the ground's own safety management team. This understanding should be recorded as part of the written statement of intent (see Section 2.20).

16.8   Design of control points

For both new construction and existing grounds, as stated in Section 16.4 it is important to match the size, facilities and equipment of the control point with the reasonable requirements of the sports ground.

It should be recognised, however, that a control point is often occupied for long periods and that under the relevant legislation it may even be classified as a workplace. As such, both for the efficacy of the ground's safety management operation and for the health and safety of its occupants, the facility should be designed and fitted with due regard to these considerations. (For details of relevant guidance, see Bibliography.)

Advice on health and safety concerns should be sought from competent persons of the appropriate skills and experience, particularly concerning the use of computerised equipment and the provision of proper seating. The design and general arrangement of the control point should also be agreed in consultation with representatives of the local authority and the emergency services, if there is any likelihood that they will be involved in its operation.

Guidance on the equipment of control points follows in Section 16.9. Concerning the design, the following considerations should be taken into account:

a.   **Access**

Access to the control point should be strictly controlled, and entrance restricted to authorised personnel only. The facility should not be used by any individual purely for the purpose of viewing the event.

If possible, a lobby area (or an adjoining room at larger grounds) should be provided so that consultations can take place without disrupting operations within the control point. The fitting of a glazed panel in the door will also enable personnel working inside the control point to check the identity of anyone seeking to enter.

b.   **Space for personnel**

There should be space, including properly designed and equipped work stations where required, for all personnel working in the facility on a regular basis. In addition, space should be provided for personnel who may, in the course of their duties, need to visit the facility; for example, police officers, management, representatives of the emergency services, voluntary aid societies and representatives of other relevant authority.

However, as stated in Section 16.14, it is not recommended that the general public address announcer is stationed inside the control point, unless positioned in a separate booth.

c.   **Space for equipment**

As the hub of the communications network, the control point should have sufficient space to hold safely all the necessary equipment, such as radio, telephone and CCTV monitoring equipment, and any equipment related to the monitoring of turnstiles and entry points. Allowance should also be made for all necessary wiring and trunking, together with storage space, which should be provided as necessary in order to maintain orderly working conditions.

d. Maintenance

Allowance should be made for the safe and convenient maintenance, and the removal for repair, of all pieces of equipment. The routine cleaning of all windows should be possible.

e. Sightlines

The arrangement of space should be such that those who need to see outside the control point can do so without having to stretch or strain, and without other personnel having to move from their workstations. Where possible, the installation of raised viewing areas at the rear of the control point may help in this respect.

f. Glazing

The design and type of glazing installed should take into account the need to avoid both glare from the sun and internal reflections during non-daylight hours. Wherever possible glazing bars should not restrict views.

g. Sound proofing and absorption

Where necessary the control point should be sound-proofed against excessive noise, so that all communication inside can be conducted at normal voice levels. However, it may not be desirable to sound-proof the facility totally. In order to gauge the mood of spectators, personnel inside should still be able to hear a certain level of crowd noise.

As an aid to communications within the facility, the use of sound-absorbing flooring and ceiling materials should also help to reduce self-generated noise levels.

h. Lighting, temperature and ventilation

In order to ensure ideal working conditions (and therefore efficient safety management), the lighting, temperature and ventilation of the control point should be carefully controlled. This is particularly important where computer or CCTV monitors are used, and in small facilities where the presence of electrical equipment can lead to heat and condensation.

i. Fire safety and electrical fittings

If several items of electrical equipment are installed, an appropriate fire extinguisher should be provided.

All fixed and portable systems should be provided in a safe condition, and be maintained as such. Cables should be fixed wherever possible. The use of extension leads and multiple adapters should be avoided.

j. Amenities

For the smooth and uninterrupted functioning of the control point, wherever possible it should be self-contained, with its own kitchenette and toilet facilities.

Wherever this is not possible, provision should be made to ensure that such amenities are close at hand. If they are not and prolonged absences result, the safety management operation may be adversely affected.

k. **Security**

In view of the importance of the control point to a ground's safety management operation, the security of its contents should be a matter of priority at all times. This may even be a factor in the location of the facility. Wherever there is concern, advice should also be sought from local crime prevention officers and relevant insurers.

l. **Flexibility**

The control point should be designed to be flexible for changing circumstances. For example, consoles and workstations should not be tailored too closely to individual pieces of equipment. This is because faulty or outdated pieces of equipment might be replaced by differently sized models. In addition, allowance should be made for extra equipment and/or personnel brought in for a particular event, such as a special match or concert (see Chapter 20).

16.9   Equipment of control points

As stated earlier, it is important to match the equipment of the control point with the reasonable requirements of the sports ground. Certain means of communication included in the following sections may not therefore apply to all sports grounds.

However, regardless of the means of communication utilised in individual circumstances, it is essential that the six lines of communication summarised in Section 16.2 are available to personnel working in the control point.

The means employed may include communication by radios, telephones, coded announcements over the public address system, computers, and written and spoken messages, provided that the lines of communication remain open in all normal conditions, and are clear, efficient and reliable.

The following sections provide guidance on the communications network as operated to and from the control point (but see Section 16.14 concerning public address systems), and should be read in conjunction with Diagram 14.

16.10   Radio communications

Depending on the scale of the stewarding operation and the sports ground, radio usually forms the main means of communication between the control point and stewards (or stewards' supervisors). If telephone links are not provided, radio might also be used for communication with other personnel such as the crowd doctor, turnstile controllers, members of the emergency services and car park or traffic controllers.

When considering radio communications, the following points should be taken into account:

a.   Radio links may operate from either a radio base station or simply by hand-held radios. Where appropriate, if a base station is provided, it should be located adjacent to the police communicator's workstation, to assist in the exchange of information.

b.   A separate command channel between the control point and key safety personnel, such as the chief steward and supervisors, may be desirable.

c.   If possible there should also be a back-up radio channel within the system.

d.   Any police radio facilities available for the maintenance of law and order should augment, and not be regarded as a substitute for, the ground's own communications system.

e.   The police will advise on the extent of their own radio requirements, which may be more extensive than the system needed for the ground's own safety needs. The police system may also require extra space to be provided in the control point – for example, for more than one police communicator – and for the provision of a voice record facility.

f.   Consideration should be given to the provision of space for any ambulance or voluntary aid society radio equipment, in the event of this equipment being operated from within the control point or from an adjacent room.

g.   Personnel who operate two-way radios require an environment in which they can hear comfortably and avoid having to raise their voices. Good quality equipment, including the provision of appropriate headsets and microphones, should therefore be considered.

h.   The location of aerials should take into account the possibility of radio interference.

16.11   Telephone communications – internal

Ideally, but particularly at larger grounds, two forms of designated telephone systems should be provided; internal and external (see next section).

To complement (or in certain cases to take the place of) radio communications, the internal telephone system should provide the link between the control room and key points around the ground.

Where possible, the internal system should meet the following requirements:

a.   To ensure that lines are kept clear for safety communications only, the system should be independent of any other internal telephone system operating at the ground.

b.   It should be possible for the operator in the control point to select which line to talk to without being blocked by other calls.

c.   Telephone lines provided for emergency use should meet the current relevant British Standard; that is, no person who has need of the system should have to travel more than 30 metres to reach an emergency telephone.

Diagram 14. Communications to and from the control point

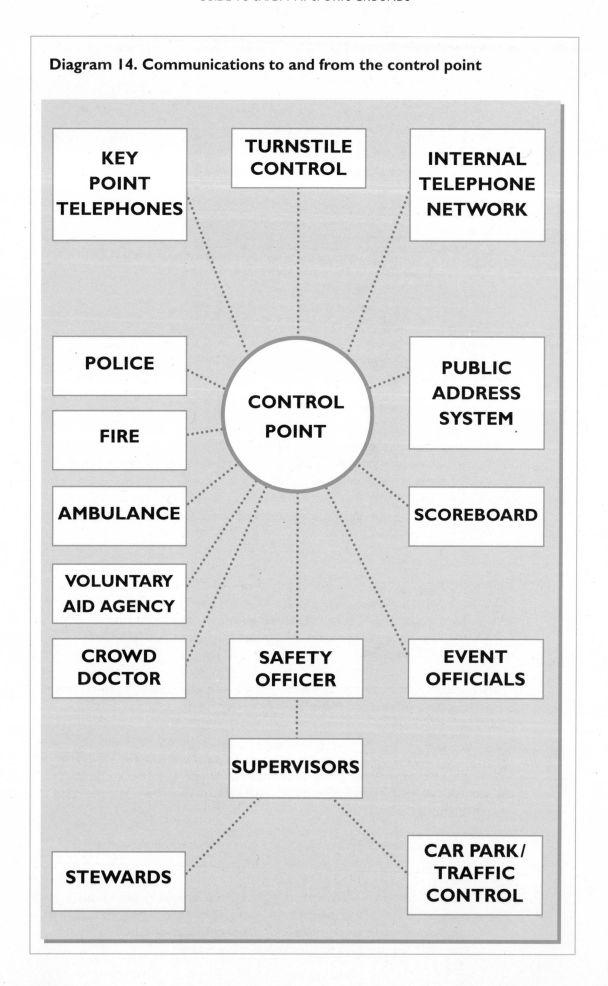

d.   Key points of the ground linked to the control point by telephone might include:

    i.   the turnstiles (or banks of turnstiles)

    ii.   all steward control points

    iii.   the public address operating booth

    iv.   the office of the Secretary, Clerk of the Course or equivalent senior official

    v.   the referee or event official's room

    vi.   lighting control points

    vii.   the crowd doctor

    viii.   the first aid room

    ix.   any police room

    x.   any rendezvous points.

e.   For safety-related communications, the use of mobile telephones should be discouraged.

16.12   Telephone communications – external

In addition to, and independent of, the internal system, telephone lines should also be available for direct and immediate telephone communication between the control point and the fire brigade and/or other emergency services. External telephone lines designated for emergency purposes should not be used for any other purposes.

16.13   Public address systems – guidance and specifications

Other than direct personal contact with staff and stewards (see Section 16.30), or through the circulation of written material (see Section 16.29), the public address system will usually provide the main form of communication between the management and spectators.

There are a number of current British Standards with which public address systems at sports grounds should comply. In addition, reference may be made to two publications.

Although written for football grounds, the FSADC publication *Stadium Public Address Systems* contains much general advice applicable to all sports grounds. The Sound and Communications Industries Federation have also published a Code of Practice. (see Bibliography).

In general, the public address system should meet the following requirements:

a.   **Audibility, clarity and intelligibility**
The system should be audible, clear (that is, free from distortion), and intelligible, so that broadcast messages can be heard under reasonable conditions (including emergencies), by all persons of normal hearing in any part of the ground to which the public has access.

b. Zoning

The system of the public address system should generally be designed to broadcast to individual areas outside and inside the ground, to groups of areas, and to the whole ground. The system should also be capable of broadcasting to the pitch, if that forms part of the management's emergency evacuation procedure.

Whether zoning is possible or not, however, at smaller sports grounds it may be preferable to make important announcements to the whole ground. Experience has shown that in these situations spectators sometimes think that they might have missed an announcement because the sound intended for one zone has carried partially into another. In such circumstances an assessment should be made before establishing any firm policy.

c. Override facility

As explained in Section 16.14, it is recommended that the public address system should not be operated from the control point. However, it should be designed so that an operator – either from the management or police, as agreed in the contingency plans – can override the system in order to broadcast emergency messages, either to the whole ground or to sections only.

Similarly, if there are areas of the ground which have the facility for turning down the output from the public address system – such as hospitality boxes or lounges – the system should be designed to override these volume controls automatically when emergency messages are broadcast.

d. Fire warning

Emergency use of the public address system as part of the fire warning system requires full compliance with the current relevant British Standard.

e. Back-up power supply

The back-up power supply to the public address system should be such as to enable it to continue to function at full load in an emergency, such as a fire or a failure of the mains supply, for up to three hours (see Sections 16.24 and 17.11).

f. Back-up loud hailers

In the event of a failure of the public address system, loud hailers should be available for the use of stewards and police in all parts of the ground, including the control point, for directing or instructing spectators. It is vital that that all personnel are trained in their use, and that the batteries are kept fully charged.

g. Inspections and tests

The public address system should be inspected and tested annually and an inspection certificate obtained. Where a safety certificate is in force, the inspection certificate should be available for inspection by the local authority.

16.14 Public address systems – operation

As stated in Section 16.1, good communications are not solely dependent on the provision of advanced equipment. This is particularly true of public address systems. The operation of the system, and the skills of the operators, are equally important.

The following considerations should be taken into account:

a. Provision of a separate booth

It is recommended that the general public address announcer should not be stationed within the control point, although it should be possible for personnel in the control point to override the system in the event of an emergency (see Section 16.13.c).

If a separate operating booth or facility is provided, it should command a good view of the playing area or area of activity, and be linked to the control point by telephone, via a land line. Ideally, this link should also include the provision of a clearly visible red light, so that the general announcer can see instantly when someone in the control point is trying to make contact.

This latter form of communication will not be necessary if the public address booth is located immediately adjacent to the control point, in which case there should be a sliding glass window, so as to enable more immediate contact to be made.

(The decision as to whether the booth should be adjacent to, or some distance from, the control point will depend on several factors. Further guidance can be found in the FSADC and FSDC publications on *Stadium Public Address Systems* and *Stadium Control Rooms* – see Bibliography.)

Whatever arrangement is provided, it is vital that public address announcements can be heard clearly in the control point. Management may also wish to control the sound level of the system from the control point, rather than leave control to the general announcer.

b. Agreement on emergency announcement procedures

As stated in Section 16.13.c, in addition to the provision of an override facility, there should be an agreed operational policy stating whether a representative of the management's safety team or a representative of the police broadcasts announcements in the event of an emergency. This agreement should be recorded in the management's contingency plans.

c. Pre-announcement signal

Important announcements relating to crowd safety should be preceded by a loud, distinct signal to catch the attention of the crowd, whatever the level of noise in the ground at the time.

The following recommendations should be considered:

i.   Experience has shown that a three-event two-tone chime (that is, 'bing bong bing') is most effective. This signal should be different to, and distinct from, any other signals which may be in general use on the public address system.

ii.   While the pre-announcement signal is being relayed, it is essential that the public address system's control panel clearly indicates that the microphone is temporarily muted. Ideally there should be two coloured lamps; one which indicates 'wait' and the other 'speak now'.

iii.   All ground officials, stewards, police, fire, ambulance and any other emergency personnel should be made aware of the pre-announcement signal.

iv.   The signal should be tested before the start of each event.

v.   The signal may also be sounded as part of a general announcement on safety procedures, to be broadcast to spectators before selected events.

vi.   The signal should be explained in every event programme printed for circulation to spectators.

d.   **Tone and content of annnouncements**
In the event of an emergency it is essential that clear, accurate information is given to spectators at the earliest possible time. Messages should be positive, leaving those to whom they are addressed in no doubt as to what is required of them. The messages should be scripted in advance with the agreement of the police, fire authority and, where a safety certificate is in force, the local authority. It may also be appropriate to pre-record certain standard messages, for use in emergencies.

In all cases it is recommended that the announcer practices using the public address system, while assessors comment on the audibility, tone and effectiveness of their delivery. It is also important that the announcer is familiar with the layout of the sports ground and the agreed evacuation procedures.

Management should ensure that for certain international events announcers able to speak the appropriate language are in post at the ground, and are briefed on the use of the system and the content of any safety announcements.

16.15   Closed circuit television – provision

The installation of closed circuit television systems (CCTV) is strongly recommended as an effective method of monitoring crowd movement and behaviour, particularly at larger sports grounds.

The primary advantage of CCTV is that it allows personnel in the control point to identify incidents – either by viewing the monitor directly or after receiving reports – and then, by use of the system, to make a more detailed appraisal.

However, a CCTV system should never be considered as a substitute for good stewarding or other forms of safety management.

16.16 CCTV – assessment of need

When considering the installation of a CCTV system, or the upgrading of an existing system, management should undertake a detailed assessment of the needs of the ground as a whole and in particular those specific areas that need to be closely monitored, in order to assess the likely benefits of having such a system.

The areas to be assessed will include those immediately outside the ground, plus all turnstile areas, entry routes, concourses, areas of seated and standing accommodation, and exit routes. Ideally the system will cover all these areas. The assessment should also take into account when specific areas need to be monitored; that is before, during and/or at the end of an event.

If it is decided to install a new CCTV system, or upgrade an exisiting one, a detailed specification should be drawn up to meet the operational requirements of the management, before contractual negotiations and procurement commence.

As outlined in the following sections, there are essentially three stages in the drawing up of a specification for CCTV systems:

a.   risk assessment

b.   statement of operational requirement

c.   tender document.

16.17 CCTV – risk assessment

In order to establish which areas need to be covered by CCTV, a detailed risk assessment of every part of the ground is required.

This assessment should identify the level of risk in each area. For example, a turnstile area at the end of a confined space may be assessed as a high risk, and a hospitality lounge a low risk.

The assessment should also take into account the nature of the risk, the likelihood of an incident occurring and the potential consequences.

Such an assessment will help management to establish whether alternative methods can be adopted to monitor areas of risk, or, if CCTV coverage is considered necessary, the level of coverage required.

The risk assessment should be recorded in the form of a plan of the ground, identifying the following points for each area:

a.   the type of risk; for example, overcrowding, crushing or the existence of a steep slope

b.   the level of risk

c.   whether CCTV is required

d.   the image required for monitoring purposes in the control point; for example, a general view, long shot, or closer view showing head and shoulders

e.   the number of images that might need to be viewed in detail and simultaneously, in the event of an incident or incidents (this may determine the number of cameras in a specific area)

f.   whether the image should be monochrome or colour

g.   the levels and types of lighting in specific areas, in both normal and emergency conditions.

Generally, the risk assessment requires no technical knowledge of CCTV. Only in respect of points (f) and (g) is there a need for some technical expertise. It is, however, recommended that the risk assessment is undertaken with the assistance of the relevant authorities, and, where appropriate, the certifying authority.

16.18   CCTV – operational requirement and tendering

The findings of the risk assessment, together with the annotated ground plan and any associated paperwork, should be combined to provide a clear statement of the CCTV system's operational requirement.

Additional points which should be considered are as follows:

a.   The images provided should be sufficiently clear and distinct to enable personnel in the control point to monitor effectively the areas covered.

b.   The system should make provision for video recording all CCTV coverage.

c.   Where a CCTV system is to be used for other purposes – for example, for 24-hour site security – care should be taken to ensure that the equipment is suitable for extended use. Otherwise, prolonged use may result in the system's failure at a crucial period during an event.

The statement of operational requirement should form the basis of any tender documents prepared for contractors to bid for the installation of the CCTV system.

However, the statement must be supported by additional technical specifications detailing aspects of the expected use and performance of the installation; for example, the need for weather protection of cameras, the quality of monitors, and the facilities required for video recording.

Advice on the drawing up of tendering documents is available in the Home Office publication *Guidance Notes for the Procurement of CCTV for Public Safety at Football Grounds* (see Bibliography).

16.19   CCTV – operation

Where CCTV cameras are installed the images produced must be capable of being monitored and recorded by personnel in the control point.

Personnel operating the system should be skilled in the interpretation and use of the data provided.

The positioning of monitors requires careful consideration to ensure that the images are not adversely affected by light or glare from windows or from overhead lighting.

Whilst it may be desirable to monitor the CCTV system from other locations – for example, a security office – it is essential that total control of the system is maintained by personnel in the control point.

An auxiliary power supply should be provided to ensure continued operation of the CCTV system in the event of a power failure.

16.20 Monitoring the number of spectators entering the ground

As stated in Section 6.1, all spectators entering all sections of the ground, including VIP and lounge areas, should be accurately counted at their time of entry, and their number controlled in order to ensure that overcrowding does not occur.

Whether manual, mechanical or computerised, the counting system used should be designed to ensure that personnel in the control point are informed immediately when a predetermined number of spectators has been admitted through each turnstile, or bank of turnstiles serving each section of the ground (see Section 6.5).

In addition, the following points should be considered.

a. Where a computerised counting system is installed, the display monitor should be sited in the control point, where it can be viewed by the safety officer and, if present, the police commander.

b. In the absence of computerised screen displays or read-outs, an efficient system of communication must be established between the turnstiles and the control point; using runners, land-lines or radios, with clear, written records kept at regular intervals using wipe boards and/or pro-formas.

c. All read-outs or written records should indicate the section of the ground, the number of spectators occupying that section and the time of the count.

d. All read-outs or written records need to be immediately available to the safety officer and, if present, the police ground commander.

e. Contingency plans should cover the failure of the computerised system.

16.21 Fire warning systems

The fire alarm master panel should be in a location that is both accessible and visible to the fire service. If this is not in the control point, a fire alarm repeater panel should also be located in the control point.

The repeater panel should run silently, or have a mute facility, so that if it goes off it will illuminate a prominent red or flashing light rather than sound out. This is so that there will be no extra noise to disrupt communications within the control room. If the repeater panel is located elsewhere, it will require a designated individual to monitor it constantly during events (see also Section 15.12).

16.22 Scoreboards and other display boards

Where electronic scoreboards or video display boards are in use, management should pre-arrange and script the contents of all safety-related and emergency messages. These should be displayed in co-ordination with the broadcast of prepared public address announcements.

Operation of the scoreboard or video display board should be from a place other than the control point; for example, from the same booth or room as used by the general public address announcer.

The contents and graphics of the messages should be agreed in consultation between the management, the police, the emergency services and, if a safety certificate is in force, the local authority.

16.23 Electronic securing systems

At grounds where electronic securing systems – also known as automated exit gate release systems – are installed, a designated exit gate supervisor should be stationed in the control point.

As stated in Section 9.16, the sole duty of this person is to operate and monitor the main console or computer display installed as part of such systems.

Written records of the operation should be maintained, and made immediately available to the safety officer and, where appropriate, the police's ground commander.

16.24 Auxiliary power

It is essential that power is maintained to provide the continuous operation of all control point functions and selected communications systems in the event of a power failure, fire or other emergency.

Auxiliary power should therefore be provided, sufficient at the very least to enable emergency lighting, the public address system, CCTV and all other safety-related installations to function for a minimum of three hours after the failure of the normal supply.

It is essential to test the necessary communication systems to ensure that they do continue to function normally when the auxiliary power takes over.

As stated in Sections 2.14 and 2.15, management should also prepare contingency plans to cover the possibility of a power failure. These should include, as stated in Section 16.13, the provision of loud hailers.

If, as recommended above, the auxiliary power is capable of supplying the entire load for the ground for a minimum of three hours, it may be possible to continue the event, provided it is scheduled to finish and the ground be cleared of spectators within this period, and no other emergency exists. In such cases, the auxiliary power supply must itself be provided with additional back-up power.

16.25 Displayed communications within the control point

Depending on the size and type of the ground, a certain amount of information will need to be displayed inside the control point. This is best achieved by the use of display and deployment boards. Such boards might display the following:

a. a plan of the ground and its immediate approaches

b. a plan showing the location of fire alarm points and fire-fighting equipment

c. a list of key point telephone extensions

d. a wipe board for the deployment of stewards

e. a wipe board for the deployment of police officers

f. a wipe board showing the location of ambulance service, voluntary agency and crowd doctor

g. where no computerised or mechanical read-outs are available, a wipe board to display the number of spectators passing through the turnstiles.

16.26 Documentation to be stored in the control point

As an aid to communications within the control point, storage space should be provided for documentation that might be required for instant reference. Such documentation is likely to include:

a. a copy of the ground's contingency plans (see Sections 2.14 and 2.15)

b. relevant details of the emergency plan (see Section 2.16)

c. where appropriate, a copy of the safety certificate, and any other records required as a condition of the safety certificate

d. where possible, copies of detailed scaled drawings of each section of the ground (see Section 4.15).

16.27 Signs – forms and categories

A vital part of the communications system is the provision of sufficiently large, clear, legible and suitably positioned signs.

There are essentially three forms of signs, as follows:

a. **Safety signs**
    Safety signs appear in five different categories, and should meet the shape and colour requirements specified:

    i. Prohibition signs; for example, 'No Smoking'
        (circular shape, with a black pictogram on a white background, red edging and a red diagonal line through the pictogram)

ii.   Warning signs; for example, 'Low Headroom' or 'Uneven Steps'
*(triangular shape, with a black pictogram on a yellow
background, with black edging)*

iii.   Mandatory signs; for example, 'Spectators must not cross this line'
(circular shape, with white pictogram on a blue background)

iv.   Emergency Escape or First Aid signs
*(rectangular or square shape, with a white pictogram
on a green background)*

v.   Fire-fighting equipment signs
*(rectangular or square shape, with a white pictogram
on a red background).*

All signs in this category should be easily seen and understood. In conditions of poor natural light it may be necessary to provide either artificial illumination and/or to make the signs using reflective material.

It is emphasised that safety signs are not a substitute for other means of controlling risk. They are to warn of any risk that may remain after all engineering controls and safe systems of working have been put in place.

The provision of signs that communicate a hazard warning or safety related message may, in certain situations, be mandatory under the Health and Safety at Work Act 1974, and in such cases should conform to the guidance provided within the Health and Safety (Safety Signs and Signals) Regulations 1996.

Further guidance on these regulations and on safety signs in general is available from the Health and Safety Executive (see Bibliography).

b.   Information signs
These are signs communicating information relative to the ground, to the event, or to specific restrictions. Such signs include:

i.   Ground plans; it is recommended that simplified ground plans are displayed at suitable locations, such as by ticket offices and main entrances, and, where appropriate, in places where they might benefit supporters of visiting teams. The ground plans should display any colour-coded information relating to ticketing and entry requirements.

ii.   Ground regulations, including information on prohibited items.

iii.   Directional signs, both outside and inside the ground.

iv.   Seat and row indicators.

Signs in this category should not use predominant colouring which could lead to their being confused with safety signs. Neither should they be placed in such a way that they obscure or dominate safety signs.

c. **Commercial signs and hoardings**
Care should be taken that signs and hoardings in this category are located in such a way that they do not obscure or detract from safety or information signs; for example, by being too close, by blocking the line of vision, or by the over-use of predominant colours utlilised in the safety or information signs.

16.28 Signs – general provision and maintenance

The provision of signs at sports grounds should meet the following general requirements:

a. All signs should be securely fixed, including temporary signs used on an event basis only.

b. Signs should not be fixed in such a way that they restrict spectator viewing or impede the circulation of spectators.

c. All signs should be kept clean.

d. Handwritten signs should be avoided.

e. It might be necessary to confirm with the appropriate authority that signs do not contravene the fire resistance or fire loading requirements of particular areas of a ground, such as emergency evacuation routes or concourses.

16.29 Tickets and programmes

Wherever possible, the written information provided for spectators should be used as a means of communicating safety-related information.

As stated in Section 2.25, the back of the ticket itself should provide a clear plan of the ground.

That part of the ticket retained by the spectator after passing through a ticket control point or turnstile should clearly identify the location of the accommodation for which it has been issued. Colour coding of tickets, corresponding to different sections of the grounds, should be considered.

As stated in Section 6.10, the design of the ticket should also ensure that the key information printed – such as turnstile, block, seat and row number – is clear and easy to read for the spectator, turnstile operators and stewards.

Clear and concise information about the ground's layout and safety procedures should also be printed in the event programme.

The management may also wish to issue periodically written material that provides further information of interest and relevance to spectators; for example, concerning changes of procedure or future arrangements. Such material may be issued with tickets.

16.30 Inter-personal communications

As stated in Section 16.1, it is stressed, finally, that good communications are not solely dependent on the provision of equipment or systems.

In all exchanges between members of the safety management team, individuals should recognise the need for clear, concise and constructive communication. Training and briefing should ensure that there is no confusion as to the use of specific terms, or to the meaning of instructions or directions.

It should also be remembered that for many spectators the only direct contact they have with representatives of management may be with staff or stewards. It is therefore crucial that any information imparted to spectators is clearly given, accurate and in accord with the policies of the safety management team.

False or confusing information, rudeness or unhelpfulness are all examples of poor communication, and are thus a weak link in the safety chain.

Chapter Seventeen

Electrical and mechanical services

17.1 Introduction

This chapter covers a number of electrical and mechanical installations likely to be in place at a sports ground, many of which are either safety-related or have their own safety implications. However, reference to other electrical and mechanical installations and systems may also be found elsewhere in the *Guide*, as follows:

a. public address, CCTV and emergency telephone systems: see Chapter 16

b. fire alarm and detection systems, and catering installations: see Chapter 15

c. turnstile monitoring systems: see Chapter 6.

Further reference may be made to the *Guide to Electrical and Mechanical Services at Sports Grounds*, published by the District Surveyors Association (see Bibliography).

17.2 The importance of maintenance

All electrical and mechanical installations at a sports ground are liable to gradual deterioration, particularly those situated in outdoor or exposed environments. It is therefore vital that management ensures that such installations are properly maintained by competent persons with the appropriate skills and experience.

It is imperative that maintenance procedures for both new and existing installations are properly understood, and that maintenance is carried out in accordance with:

a. the written instructions and schedules provided by the manufacturer

b. where appropriate, the current relevant British Standards

c. where a safety certificate is in force, the requirements of the local authority.

17.3 Inspections and tests

Unless specified to the contrary by the manufacturers' written instructions or other documentation, all electrical and mechanical installations should be inspected annually by competent persons, and an inspection certificate supplied to ground management.

17.4 Event-day staffing

Management should ensure that there is a competent person or persons either on site or readily available on an event day to deal with any problems which might arise in relation to the electrical or mechanical installations at the ground.

17.5   Anti-vandalism

A number of electrical and mechanical installations associated with safety systems, including auxiliary power units, may be vulnerable to vandalism. This should be taken into consideration when fixing and securing such installations.

17.6   Electrical installations

All electrical installations should comply with current regulations. New electrical installations should also comply with current British Standards, and wherever practicable, existing installations should be upgraded to comply with those standards.

An Electrical Installation Completion Certificate prescribed by the Institution of Electrical Engineers (IEE) should be retained by the management. Each Completion Certificate should be accompanied by a current Periodic Inspection Report. Any new part to the electrical installation should, in the first instance, have a separate Completion Certificate. Further guidance is available from the IEE (see Bibliography).

17.7   Circuit diagram

Main electrical circuit diagrams should be provided, clearly labelled to indicate:

a.   all main switches, circuit breakers and fuseways in distribution boards and the circuits which they control

b.   the location of all switch rooms and distribution boards.

The circuit diagram should be kept in a location easily accessible to technical staff, be protected from defacement or damage, and be updated as necessary.

17.8   Protection of cables

All cables should be sited so that they are, as far as practicable, inaccessible to the public. Where necessary, cables should also be enclosed throughout their length in a protective covering of material which has sufficient strength to resist mechanical damage. The following wiring systems are acceptable:

a.   mineral insulated metal sheathed cables

b.   steel wire or tape armoured cables

c.   insulated cables in screwed metal conduit

d.   insulated cables in metal trunking.

Notwithstanding the above, alternative wiring systems may be acceptable; for example, insulated cables in rigid PVC conduit which complies with the current relevant British Standard. However, PVC conduit or PVC served cables should not be used in confined areas (such as catering outlets or emergency evacuation routes), because of their fire smoke hazard. The use of PVC conduit should also be discouraged in exposed areas, because of its susceptibility to vandalism.

Where wiring systems do not meet the above requirements, consideration should be given to a programme of phased replacement.

17.9 Lightning protection

Lightning protection for structures, both permanent and temporary, should be provided in accordance with the current relevant British Standard. The lightning protection should be tested annually by competent persons, and a certificate supplied to the ground management. Floodlighting towers should be bonded to earth in accordance with the current British Standard.

17.10 Lighting

The lighting in all parts of a sports ground accessible to the public should allow them to enter, to leave and move about the ground in safety. This is particularly important in relation to entry and exit routes and stairways used by the public.

At all times when the daylight in any section of a ground accessible to the public is insufficient, or if the ground is to be used in non-daylight hours, adequate artificial lighting should be provided. This lighting should be sufficient to illuminate all signs, in accordance with current European Union Directives (see also Section 16.27).

Consideration should also be given to the lighting required for CCTV systems to operate satisfactorily (see Sections 16.15–16.19).

The minimum level of illumination should be as recommended by the Chartered Institute of Building Services Engineers. For details of guides produced by CIBSE, see Bibliography. For guidance on emergency lighting, see Section 17.13.

17.11 Provision of auxiliary power

As stated in Sections 2.14 and 2.15, management should prepare contingency plans to cover the possibility of a power failure.

Where appropriate, auxiliary power should be provided, sufficient at the very least to enable emergency lighting, the public address system, CCTV and all other safety-related electrical installations to function for at least three hours after the failure of the normal supply.

An auxiliary power system designed to supply emergency and safety systems should be independent of any other wiring systems.

17.12 Auxiliary power equipment

Auxiliary power equipment should be located in a secure room or building to which the public does not have access. The room or building should be of a construction having a fire resistance of not less than one hour.

Auxiliary power equipment should be installed, maintained and tested in accordance with the manufacturers' written instructions and current British Standards. As stated in Section 4.9, it should be inspected and tested 24 hours before each event, and should also be capable of operating on the failure of a single phase.

For further guidance on auxiliary power, see Section 16.24.

17.13 Emergency lighting

At sports grounds used to stage events in non-daylight hours, emergency lighting for use in the event of a failure of the general lighting should be provided in all parts of the ground to which the public have access, including and along all exit and emergency evacuation routes, with exit signs clearly illuminated.

There is no British Standard code for emergency lighting that is applicable to sports grounds. Instead, installation and inspection should generally comply with the current British Standard for the lighting of premises used for entertainment, other than cinemas and certain other specified premises.

Emergency lighting at sports grounds should meet the following requirements:

a.   Where emergency lighting systems are not separate from the normal lighting system, a risk assessment should be carried out to determine the adequacy of the chosen system in emergency conditions.

b.   The emergency lighting system should operate automatically on the failure of the normal lighting system.

c.   Where the emergency lighting is a non-maintained system, such lighting should be designed to operate on the failure of a circuit or sub-circuit.

d.   Along all exit and emergency evacuation routes, the emergency lighting should afford a level of illumination sufficient to enable people to leave the premises. For guidance on the level of illumination required, reference should be made to the CIBSE *Emergency Lighting* guide (see Bibliography).

e.   Unless, exceptionally, two entirely independent supplies can be obtained from outside sources, the emergency circuit should be connected to a source of auxiliary power located on the premises.

f.   If a generator is used, it should be able to operate the full emergency lighting load within not more than five seconds of start-up.

g.   The system should be capable of maintaining the necessary level of illumination for a period of three hours from the time of failure of the normal supply.

17.14 Passenger lifts

Passenger lifts should be maintained and tested in accordance with the manufacturers' written instructions and schedules and the current relevant British Standard.

The following general requirements should be considered:

a.   Lift alarms should be audible under event conditions.

b.   For new lift installations, consideration should be given to providing a duplicate alarm in the ground's control point.

c. Lifts for the use of spectators with disabilities should be provided in the circumstances described in Section 13.14.

d. As stated in Section 13.17, a lift provided for passenger use in the normal operation of the sports ground may be used for evacuation purposes only if it meets the requirements of an evacuation lift, as specified in the current relevant British Standard. Among other requirements, this means that it should be able to operate in reasonable safety when there is a fire in the building.

e. Where provided, a fire-fighting lift may also be used for emergency evacuation (see Section 13.17).

f. Among the recommendations for the safe-guarding of evacuation lifts, as required by the current relevant British Standard, the following points should be noted:

    i. An evacuation lift should be situated within a protected enclosure consisting of the lift well itself and a protected lobby at each storey served by the lift. The protected enclosure should also contain an escape stair.

    ii. Except for lifts serving two storeys only, evacuation lifts should be provided with a switch which brings the lift to the final exit storey (usually ground level), isolates the landing call buttons and enables an authorised person to take control.

    iii. The primary electrical supply should be obtained from a sub-main circuit exclusive to the lift. It should also have a secondary supply from an independent main or emergency generator and an automatic switch to change over from one to the other.

    iv. Any electrical sub-station, distribution board or generator supplying the lift should be protected from the action of fire for a period of not less than that of the enclosing structure of the lift shaft itself.

17.15 Gas-fired installations

All natural gas and liquefied petroleum gas (LPG) installations (see also Section 15.9.j), including heating and cooking appliances, pipework and meters, should comply with current gas safety legislation, as follows:

a. The Gas Safety (Installation and Use) Regulations 1994, as amended, covering matters related to meters, appliances, and the pipework connecting appliances to meters. These regulations allow only CORGI registered installers to carry out work on these parts of gas installations.

b. The Pipework Safety Regulations 1996, covering matters related to service pipework connecting meters to gas distribution mains.

17.16 Boilers and other heating devices

As stated in Section 15.9, rooms containing boilers may be considered as high-risk fire areas. For this reason, boilers (and other heating devices) should meet the following requirements:

a.   Boilers should be installed by a competent person in accordance with current British Standards. They should be housed in a fire-resistant enclosure, and, where appropriate, separated from areas of spectator accommodation by a construction having a fire resistance of at least one hour.

b.   To prevent over-heating, boilers, generators, air heaters and other similar appliances should be fitted with a fusible link or similar device that will automatically cut off energy supplies.

c.   Boiler or generator rooms should have adequate air supply for the safe operation of the appliances, and be generally ventilated.

d.   The location of both combustion air intakes and ducts, and flue pipes and exhaust systems for boilers and generators, should not prejudice the means of escape for spectators, and should not cause a nuisance by emission into spectator accommodation.

e.   Where it is necessary for ducts and pipes to pass through areas occupied by spectators, they should be of the same fire resistance as the room to which they are connected, until they reach a safe place of emission or supply.

17.17 Oil storage and supply

As stated in Section 15.9, the storage of oil constitutes a high fire risk. Oil storage and oil supply systems should therefore comply with the current relevant British Standards. To reduce the risks on event days, the amount of oil stored within the boiler or generator room should be limited to essential requirements.

17.18 Ventilation, air conditioning and smoke control systems

The installation of any mechanical ventilation, air conditioning or smoke control systems should be subject to detailed design and installation by competent persons with the appropriate qualifications and experience.

The provision of such systems will form an important part of any fire risk assessment (see Chapter 15).

Where provided to help facilitate safe evacuation (for example, smoke extraction in a concourse), they should be linked to an auxiliary power supply.

Chapter Eighteen

First aid and medical provision

18.1 Management responsibility and consultation

The measures described elsewhere in the *Guide* should, if followed, help to prevent a serious accident. However, for ground management to discharge fully its safety responsibilities it should ensure that proper first aid and medical provision are available for all spectators.

In all areas of first aid and medical provision, management should consult with the local ambulance service trust and in Scotland the local Health Board. Where a safety certificate is in force the consultation arrangements should be made through the local authority.

Management should also consider drawing up a written medical plan for spectators.

18.2 Provision of first aiders

Responsibility for the provision of suitably trained first aiders lies with management.

As stated in the Glossary, a suitably trained first aider is one who holds the standard certificate of first aid issued by the voluntary aid societies to people working as 'First Aiders' under the Health and Safety (First Aid) Regulations 1981.

The provision of first aiders should meet the following minimum requirements:

a.   No event should have fewer than two first aiders.

b.   At sports grounds with seated and standing accommodation there should be at least one first aider per 1,000 spectators (that is, of the number of spectators anticipated for the event).

c.   At all-seated grounds the ratio should be one first aider per 1,000 up to 20,000 spectators, and thereafter one per 2,000 (of the number of spectators anticipated for the event).

d.   For events where the need for first aiders may be greater than above, management should consult with the local ambulance service trust and in Scotland the local Health Board.

e.   First aiders should:

   i.   be aged not less than 16 years old

   ii.   have no other duties or responsibilities

   iii.   be in post at the ground prior to spectators being admitted

   iv.   remain in position until all spectators have left the ground.

18.3 First aid room

It is the responsibility of ground management to provide a room or rooms designated for the provision of first aid to spectators. This should be in addition to the sports ground's own medical room, and should complement the facilities provided by the ambulance service in attendance on event days.

The first aid room should be provided in consultation with the local ambulance service trust, the local authority, the crowd doctor (see Section 18.6), and representatives of the appropriate voluntary aid society.

It should be designated a non-smoking area, and meet the following requirements:

a. Size

  i.   The recommended minimum size of the room is 15 sq m. Where the authorised capacity of the ground exceeds 15,000, this size should ideally be increased to at least 25 sq m.

  ii. The room should be large enough to contain a couch, with space for people to walk around, and an area for treating sitting casualties. If the authorised capacity of the ground exceeds 15,000 and a room of at least 25 sq m is provided, an extra couch should be provided.

  iii. The room should provide sufficient room to store all the appropriate equipment and materials (see Section 18.4).

b. Fittings and facilities

The first aid room should have the following fittings and facilities:

  i.   heating, lighting (including emergency lighting), ventilation and modern electric sockets

  ii. a stainless steel sink plus facilities for hand washing

  iii. a supply of hot and cold water, plus drinking water

  iv. toilet facilities, which should be accessible to wheelchair users

  v.   a worktop

  vi. a couch or couches as detailed in Section 18.3.a above

  vii. telephone lines allowing internal and external communication. The external line should be a direct line; that is, not routed via a switchboard.

c. Design and location

The first aid room's location and design should:

  i.   be easily accessible to both spectators and the emergency services and their vehicles

  ii. be clearly signposted throughout the ground, clearly identified, and its location known to all stewards

iii.   be designed in such a way as to facilitate easy maintainance in a clean and hygienic condition, free from dust

iv.   have a doorway large enough to allow access for a stretcher or wheelchair

v.   include an area in close proximity where patients, relatives and friends can be seated while waiting.

18.4   First aid storage, equipment and materials

The first aid accommodation should contain suitable storage for first aid materials and equipment. This should include blankets, pillows, stretchers, buckets, bowls, trolleys and screens.

Suitable arrangements should be provided for the disposal and replacement of equipment, including containers for sharp items.

Management should ensure that a defibrillator is provided for all events at which an attendance of over 5,000 is anticipated. If the management itself does not possess a defibrillator, it should ensure that one is provided by either the voluntary aid society, the crowd doctor or the ambulance service in attendance.

18.5   Upkeep and inspection of the first aid room

Ground management is responsible for the upkeep of the first aid room, its equipment and materials.

As stated in Section 18.9, management should also ensure that the first aid room, equipment and materials are inspected before an event.

All first aid facilities should also be available at any time for inspection by the ground management and, if a safety certificate is in force, by the local authority.

18.6   Crowd doctor

At an event where the number of spectators is expected to exceed 2,000, a crowd doctor, trained and experienced in immediate care, should be present. This doctor's first duty must be to the crowd.

The whereabouts of the crowd doctor in the ground should be known to all first aid and ambulance staff and to those stationed in the control point, who should be able to make immediate contact with him or her.

The crowd doctor should be at the sports ground prior to spectators being admitted and remain in position until all spectators have left the ground.

If a crowd of less than 2,000 is anticipated, arrangements should be in place to summon immediately a suitably trained and experienced crowd doctor to deal with medical emergencies. This arrangement should be known to those stationed in the control point.

The crowd doctor should be aware of:

a. the location and staffing arrangements of the first aid room and details of the ambulance cover

b. the local emergency plans for dealing with major incidents and how these relate to contingency plans for the ground (see Chapter 2).

18.7   Ambulance provision

Management should make arrangements for the provision of at least one fully equipped ambulance at all events with an anticipated attendance of 5,000 or more.

The ambulance(s) should be from the NHS or, if from elsewhere, approved by the local ambulance service trust.

While the requirements for every event should be examined on an individual basis Table 5 provides a general guide for ambulance service provision which, in most cases, should be considered reasonable.

Ground management should be aware that should a serious incident develop the NHS ambulance service has the capability and command structure to build rapidly on the above resources in order to ensure the protection, treatment, care and medical evacuation of any casualties. Management should also be aware that in the event of a major incident, access to NHS resources may be delayed if no NHS ambulance is in attendance, or if crews from an NHS ambulance service other than the local one are on duty.

Where necessary, provision should be made for a representative of the local ambulance service trust and/or the voluntary aid society to have access to the control point, and, if further required, working facilities within the facility.

The ambulance(s) should be at the sports ground prior to spectators being admitted and remain in position until all spectators have left the ground.

18.8   Major incident plan

As stated in Sections 2.14–2.16, ground contingency plans should be compatible with the emergency or major incident plan prepared by the local emergency services.

The major incident plan should identify areas for dealing with casualties in multiple casualty situations, and identify access and egress routes, and a rendezvous point, for emergency service vehicles.

Consultation should therefore take place between ground management, the police, fire and ambulance services, and the local authority, in order to produce an agreed plan of action for all foreseeable incidents.

All first aid and medical staff likely to be on duty should be briefed on their role in the major incident plan, preferably before they undertake event-day duties. A copy should be kept in the first aid room.

Table 5. Ambulance provision according to anticipated attendance

anticipated attendance	ambulance provision
5,000 to 25,000	I accident and emergency ambulance (with a paramedic crew), plus: I ambulance officer
25,000 to 45,000	I accident and emergency ambulance (with a paramedic crew), plus: I ambulance officer I major incident equipment vehicle and a paramedic crew I control unit
45,000 or more	2 accident and emergency ambulances (with paramedic crews), plus: I ambulance officer I major incident equipment vehicle and a paramedic crew I control unit

Notes to Table 5

■ A paramedic is a person who holds a current certificate of proficiency in ambulance paramedical skills, issued by the Institute of Health Care and Development (IHCD), and who has immediate access to the appropriate level of specialist equipment, including drug therapy, as stipulated and approved by the relevant Paramedical Steering Committee.

■ A paramedic crew, as a minimum, consists of a paramedic plus an ambulance technician, trained to IHCD standards.

18.9   Inspections and records

a.   Before the start of the event
Management should ensure that:

    i.   sufficient first aid staff are present, and at their posts

    ii.   they are properly briefed

    iii.   first aid equipment and materials are maintained at the required level

    iv.   appropriate medical and ambulance provision are in place.

b.   During and after the event
Management should ensure that:

    i.   first aiders remain in position until stood down by the safety officer

    ii.   management, ambulance officers, first aiders and the crowd doctor should participate in a de-briefing, with comments and any follow-up actions being recorded by the management

    iii.   a record is kept of the numbers and posts of all first aiders in attendance at the event, plus the name of the crowd doctor

    iv.   a record is kept of all first aid or medical diagnosis and treatment provided during the event (while preserving medical confidentiality), showing the onward destination of casualties; that is, whether they remained at the event, returned home, went to hospital or to their own family doctor

    v.   records are kept readily available for inspection, where appropriate, by the relevant authorities (while preserving medical confidentiality).

Chapter Nineteen

Media provision

19.1 Management responsibility

Management is responsible for ensuring that media activities do not interfere with or negate the normal safety operation of the ground, and do not hamper the safety, comfort or viewing standards of spectators.

Guidance on the safety implications of broadcasting sports events is available from the Health and Safety Executive (see Bibliography).

19.2 Pre-event planning and briefing

Management should ensure that all arrangements for media coverage are agreed with the companies concerned in good time before the event, and that the safety officer is able to prepare pre-event briefings accordingly. Where appropriate, any temporary arrangements may also need to be discussed and, if a safety certificate is in force, agreed with the local authority, at a pre-determined period before the event.

Pre-event planning and briefings should include proposed arrangements for any associated pre-match, half-time or mid-event entertainment. If appropriate, safety personnel should also be assigned to the role of liaison with the media personnel, and for monitoring the media provision during the event.

If any media provision results in restricted views for any areas of spectator accommodation, tickets for those areas should not be sold, and access to them not permitted for spectators during the event.

Media personnel unfamiliar with emergency procedures at the ground and, where appropriate, specific requirements and conditions of the safety certificate should be fully briefed and informed by the safety officer.

19.3 Pre-event inspections

In particular, the management should consider the following:

a. Vehicles should not be parked in such a manner as to obstruct ingress to and egress from the ground by spectators or emergency vehicles.

b. Cables should not run along or across gangways, or passageways, or otherwise obstruct the movement of spectators. Where laid in front of pitch perimeter exits, cables should be buried or installed in a cable duct. The use of rubber matting is not recommended.

c. Camera gantries should be securely constructed and should not obscure the view of spectators.

d. Where cameras overhang gantries located above spectator areas, protective measures, such as netting, should guard against falling objects.

e. Where cameras or camera gantries are located in spectator areas, or where sightlines are restricted as a result of their location, capacities should be reduced accordingly. As stated in Section 19.2, management should also ensure that tickets for the affected areas are not sold.

f. The precautions listed above apply also to loudspeaker systems and other media installations; for example, video screens, stages or studios.

g. The output from loudspeaker systems should not drown out police and stewards' radios, or the public address system. Provision should be made for an override switch (normally in the control point), so that the loudspeaker output can be interrupted if necessary.

h. Temporary advertising boards or hoardings should be constructed safely and not obscure spectators' views, nor obstruct access gates or openings in pitch perimeter barriers.

i. Temporary scaffolding, for example for cameras or temporary television studios, should be installed in accordance with the recommendations made by the Institution of Structural Engineers (see Section 14.2 and Bibliography).

j. Temporary barriers protecting media installations should accord with the recommended loadings given in Table 1 of Chapter 10.

19.4 Roving media personnel

Management should make provision for the positioning of photographers, camera operators and any other roving media personnel, so as to ensure that the sightlines of spectators are not restricted more than momentarily.

Stewards should be instructed to move any media personnel whose activities create obstructions to either spectators' views or to the safety management operation.

19.5 Identification

All media personnel, and in particular all roving media personnel, should be clearly identified, but in such a way that their clothing cannot be confused with stewards or other safety personnel.

19.6 New construction

It is recommended that the design of new sports grounds and stands takes into full consideration the requirements of the media; for example, for the concealed routing of television and radio cabling, and for the avoidance of viewing restrictions when planning camera positions, advertising hoardings and any temporary installations.

Chapter Twenty

Alternative uses for sports grounds

20.1 Introduction

The increased use of grounds for events other than the specific sport or sports for which they are designed requires management to consider a number of issues. This should be done well in advance, in consultation with the emergency services and, if a safety certificate is in force, with the local authority.

In all cases, it is stressed that the provision of safe accommodation for spectators and the maintenance of safety standards remains the responsibility of ground management.

Where an event is being arranged by an outside organisation, close liaison will be needed between that organisation and the ground management to agree who is responsible for specific safety duties and to ensure that each party understands its responsibilities. The agreement should also be recorded in a written statement.

If doubts arise as to the suitability of the ground itself – its lay-out or structures – or to the management's ability to adapt its safety management operation to different circumstances, the event should not take place.

This chapter highlights some of the main concerns relating to safety, and offers guidance on safety and design considerations for new construction.

It should be noted that this chapter applies not only to the staging of such events as pop concerts or mass gatherings, but also to the staging of sports other than the sport or sports for which the ground was designed. This might include such events as a boxing match staged at a football ground, or a rugby match staged at an athletics stadium.

Further guidance on the use of temporary demountable structures can be found in Chapter 14.

20.2 Provision for spectator accommodation

Where the required provision for spectator accommodation is likely to differ from the standard arrangements for the ground, management should ensure that the safety of spectators is not compromised. In particular, management should consider the following:

a. If spectators are to be seated on the pitch or area of activity, the total number allowed should take into account the ingress or egress capacity of the entrances and exits available around the pitch or area, and to the arrangements made for emergency evacuation.

b. If spectators are to stand on the pitch or area of activity, suitable arrangements for their safety should be provided. This will include the provision of firm underfoot conditions, barrier protection where necessary (for example, around temporary structures), and effective stewarding and monitoring.

c. If there is to be a free movement of spectators between the stands or terraces and the pitch or area of activity, all entry points should be controlled and the numbers monitored.

d. Areas of fixed viewing accommodation from which the event cannot be safely or comfortably viewed in full, because of the erection of temporary structures – such as stages, temporary demountable stands, advertising hoardings or camera platforms – should, wherever possible, be taken out of use and, in any case, discounted from any capacity calculation. Management should ensure that such arrangements do not preclude the attendance of disabled people.

20.3 Profile of likely spectators or audience

Different sports and events attract different groups of people. Some may attract more women, children, disabled or elderly people than is the norm for the core sport or sports staged at the ground. Provision for their safety and welfare should therefore be considered in advance. Contingency plans for the ground might also have to be adapted accordingly.

In particular, the following considerations should be addressed:

a. Many of the people attending the event might be unfamiliar with the layout of the ground, thus requiring extra signs and stewarding at key points.

b. The response of many people to instructions, controls and emergency evacuation procedures might be slower than is the norm for regular attenders.

c. Toilet and catering arrangements might have to be adapted. If temporary facilities are brought in, their siting and service arrangements should not block any circulation routes, particularly those required for egress or emergency evacuation.

20.4 Briefing of event personnel

Many events will involve the participation of personnel – including technical staff, contract stewards, officials, media personnel and even participants – who are unfamiliar with the ground and its safety management arrangements. Ground management should therefore ensure that such people are suitably briefed and familiarised in advance.

Pre-event agreements should make absolutely clear to all concerned the chain of command, and the division of responsibilities.

20.5   The staging of pop concerts

Before considering the staging of a pop concert at a sports ground, management should seek guidance from competent persons of the appropriate experience.

Detailed advice is also available in the *Guide to Health, Safety and Welfare at Pop Concerts and Similar Events*, issued jointly by the Health and Safety Commission, the Home Office and The Scottish Office (see Bibliography).

Particular concerns to be addressed are as follows:

a.   **The suitability of spectator accommodation**
It is stressed that not all areas of a ground may be suitable for safely accommodating audiences at a concert.

Before an area of spectator accommodation is used, whether it is permanent or temporary, an evaluation of the structure must take into account the dynamic loading likely to result from the movements of a concert audience (see Sections 4.5 and 14.5).

b.   **The suitability of systems**
Clearly conditions during a pop concert will differ greatly from those experienced during a routine event at the sports ground. Management should thus ensure that all systems will function under such conditions. For example, radio communications might be more difficult owing to the high noise levels.

Provision should also be made for any imported sound system to be interrupted by safety announcements made from the central control point.

c.   **Keeping gangways clear**
Particular care may need to be taken to ensure that spectators do not sit or stand in gangways in order to gain an improved view.

d.   **Lighting**
At certain types of events reduced lighting levels form part of the performance, in order to place greater emphasis on the stage. Care may therefore need to be taken in order to ensure that the safety of spectators is not prejudiced.

20.6   Fireworks displays

Any firework display should be arranged and located in such a way that spectators and surrounding residents are not at risk, and that there is no threat to structures at the ground or to surrounding industrial or commercial premises (particularly those where petroleum products may be stored).

Management should also ensure that the smoke from any fireworks will disperse and not become concentrated under stand roofs.

Similar precautions should be made if fireworks or flares form a part of any other event to be staged.

20.7   Designing for alternative uses

For new construction:
The design of a new sports ground, or section of a ground, should take reasonable account of all likely uses of the ground, with particular emphasis on:

a.   The arrangements for emergency evacuation (particularly from and to the playing area).

b.   The design of seated areas. As stated in Section 11.11, if it is intended to stage events for which a greater level of accessibility and comfort will be required – such as concerts or mass gatherings – the dimensions of seat depths should be increased. Extra comfort levels for the actual seats might also be considered in particular areas.

c.   Circulation routes should be designed in such a way that, if necessary, a free movement of people can be safely managed for particular events. This will require the installation of flexible dividing structures.

d.   To avoid congestion in concourses, the design of toilets should be flexible to cater for differing ratios of males and females. Further guidance is available in the FSADC publication, *Toilet Facilities at Stadia* (see Bibliography).

Annexes

Annex A

Assessment of capacity – worked examples

Introduction

This Annex includes seven worked examples of how to apply the guidance on capacity calculations to different types of standing accommodation. The method of calculation is explained more specifically in Chapter 1 and Diagrams 1 and 2. Reference should also be made to Chapters 10 and 12, and to Section 9.6 (concerning rates of passage).

The examples are as follows:

Worked example 1

A terraced standing area with a continuous crush barrier configuration and conforming to the relevant recommendations of the *Guide* (as described in Section 10.8 and Diagram 8).

This example also shows how network plans can be drawn up to analyse exit and emergency evacuation systems.

Worked example 2

A terraced standing area with a non-continuous barrier configuration (see Section 10.9).

Worked example 3

A terraced standing area with a non-continuous barrier configuration, with barriers which do not conform with the spacing or loadings specified in Table 2 of Chapter 10.

Worked example 4

A terraced standing area with crush barriers along the front only.

Worked example 5

A terraced standing area with a rail along the front which does not conform with the loadings specified in Table 2 of Chapter 10.

Worked example 6

A level standing area (see Section 12.20).

Worked example 7

A racecourse enclosure where, on the front slope, or lawn, both viewing and circulation take place, and where there is a free movement of spectators between this front area and a rear covered terrace (see Section 12.21).

Worked example 1

A terrace with a continuous crush barrier configuration

Example 1 shows a terraced standing area incorporating all the main recommendations of the Guide. The terrace measures 21m from front to back (not including lateral gangways at the front and rear), and is 74m wide.

It is enclosed on three sides and entered from the rear via 12 turnstiles and two 3.6m wide stairways. The rear lateral gangway is also 3.6m wide. From the rear spectators move down five radial gangways, each 1.2m wide. The front lateral gangway is 2.4m wide.

Normal egress is via the two stairways and from either side of the front lateral gangway. There are five pitch perimeter gates, each 1.2m wide, for forward evacuation in an emergency.

All crush barriers have been tested to a horizontal imposed load of 5.0 kN/m length.

The crush barriers are continuous between each radial gangway, each row being spaced 3m apart.

The gangways are 14m apart.

The gradient of the terrace is 25° and 'C' values range between 120mm at the front to 90mm at the rear.

The terrace is fully covered and there are no restricted views.

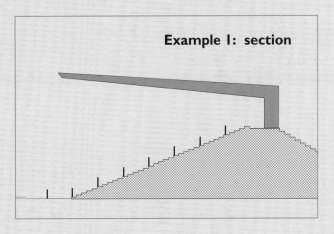

Example 1: section

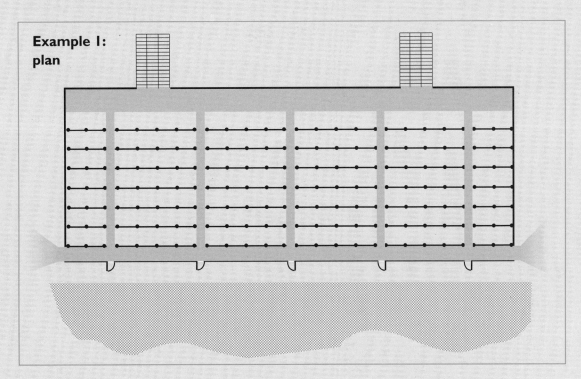

Example 1: plan

Stage one: available viewing area

Areas available behind barriers
There are four sections of terracing 14m wide, plus two end sections 6m wide.

Thus total length = (14 x 4) + (6 x 2) = 68m

There are seven rows of barriers, each spaced 3m apart (i.e. within recommended maximum of 3.1m for 25° terrace – as per Table 2).

Thus depth of terrace = 7 x 3 = 21m

The available viewing area is therefore:

68 x 21 = 1428 sq m

No discounts need be made for restricted views or partial roof cover.

Required gangway provision
No calculation need be made in this instance because there are designated gangways, and these have been considered in the previous calculation.

Total available viewing area
The total available viewing area is therefore

1428 sq m

Stage two: appropriate density

Physical condition
The terrace's physical condition is of a high standard. There are no sightline problems or concerns over the size of terrace.
Therefore (P) = 1.0

Safety management
The club's safety management is of a high

standard. There are no problems with crowd dispersal or behaviour.
Therefore (S) = 1.0

Appropriate density
Therefore the appropriate density is:

1.0 x 47 = **47 per 10 sq m**

Stage three: holding capacity

The available viewing area = 1,428 sq m
The appropriate density = 47 per 10 sq m

Applying the formula:

$$\frac{1428}{10} \times 47 = 6,711.6$$

Therefore the holding capacity is 6,711

Stage four: entry capacity

There are 12 turnstiles serving the terrace. Each has a flow rate measured at 660 persons per hour, which is the maximum allowable for the purposes of calculation.

Therefore the entry capacity of the terrace is

12 x 660 = **7,920**

Stage five: exit capacity (see network plan overleaf)

There are two stairways, 3.6 m wide. The overall stairway width is therefore 7.2 m.

There is an exit at each end of the front lateral gangway, 2.4 m wide. The overall front lateral exit width is therefore 4.8 m.

The normal egress time for the terrace is set at eight minutes.

Applying a rate of passage of 73 persons per metre width per minute for the two stairways and 109 persons per metre width per minute for the two front lateral exits (see Section 9.6), the exit capacity is therefore:

$(7.2 \times 73 \times 8) + (4.8 \times 109 \times 8) = 8,390.4$

Therefore the exit capacity is 8,390

Stage six: emergency evacuation capacity (see network plan)

The terrace is non-combustible and the exit routes are good. Therefore the upper emergency evacuation time of eight minutes should be deemed acceptable.

In addition to the normal exits (see Stage Five) there are also five gates in the pitch perimeter barrier, providing emergency access onto the pitch. Each is 1.2 m wide.

Therefore the total number of available exit widths available in an emergency is:

Stairways: 7.2 m
Front lateral exits: 4.8 m
Pitch perimeter gates: 6.0 m

Therefore the emergency exit capacity is:

$(7.2 \times 73) + (4.8 \times 109) + (6.0 \times 109) =$

$(525.6) + (523.2) + (654) = 1,702.8$

$1,702.8 \times 8$ (minutes) $= 13,622.4$

The emergency evacuation capacity is therefore **13,622**, a figure larger than the holding capacity of 6,711.

It is thus necessary to calculate in what time (T) the holding capacity can be evacuated.

$1,702.8 \times T = 6,711$ Therefore $T = 3.94$

The emergency evacuation time is 3.94 minutes; that is, within the eight minutes required.

(Note, as stated in Section 9.9, that while in practice spectators may evacuate onto the pitch or area of activity in an emergency, this should not form part of the emergency evacuation time for newly constructed grounds or sections of grounds.

In this example, therefore, the width of the five pitch perimeter gates (6.0m) would be discounted from the emergency evacuation capacity, which would thus be:

$(525.6) + (523.2) = 1,048.8$

$1,048.8 \times 8$ (minutes) $= 8,390.4$

As can be seen, however, this is still greater than the holding capacity of 6,711 and could still be evacuated in less than eight minutes.)

Stage seven: final capacity

After calculating each of the previous stages, the smallest of all the figures produced is taken as the final capacity.

In this example, the smallest figure is the holding capacity.

No further calculations are necessary. This figure represents the maximum capacity possible under present conditions.

The final capacity of the terrace is therefore 6,711

Example 1: network plan to analyse the exit system

As stated in Section 9.8.d, where there are a number of exit routes and/or a choice of alternative exit routes for spectators to follow the system should be analysed in the form of a network. Represented below is a network plan drawn up to analyse the exit system of the terrace shown in Example 1. The plan should be viewed in conjunction with the calculations laid out on the preceding pages, and with Section 9.6, concerning rates of passage.

The purpose of the plan is to analyse each part of the exit system to ensure that it has the capacity for all spectators to flow freely through it within eight minutes. The figures listed below are a useful part of that analysis, but need to be considered in the context of all local circumstances, such as adjoining circulation routes, facilities and patterns of spectator movement.

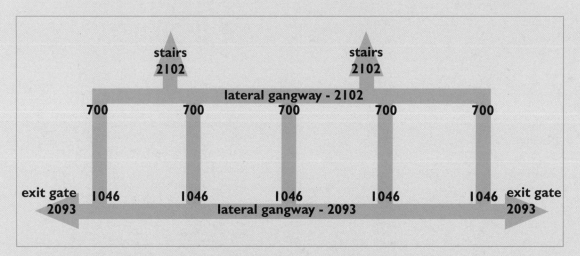

Radial gangways

Each radial gangway is 1.2 m wide and exits at both front and rear. However, the exits to the rear include passage via stairways. As stated in Section 9.6 therefore, the lower rate of passage (73 persons per metre width per minute) applies. Exit to the front is via a level, lateral gangway, for which the higher rate of passage (109 persons per metre width per minute) applies.

Therefore the exit capacity of each radial gangways is:

Exit to rear via radial gangways = 1.2 x 73 x 8 (minutes) = **700**
Exit to front via radial gangways = 1.2 x 109 x 8 (minutes) = **1,046**

Rear lateral gangway

The gangway is 3.6 m wide and exits in two directions, including stairways. Therefore the exit capacity of the rear lateral gangway is 3.6 x 73 x 8 (minutes) = **2,102**

Front lateral gangway

The gangway is 2.4 m wide and exits in two directions, both level. Therefore the exit capacity of the front lateral gangway is 2.4 x 109 x 8 (minutes) = **2,093**

Stairway capacity

Each stairway at the rear of the terrace is 3.6 m wide. Therefore the exit capacity of each stairway is 3.6 x 73 x 8 (minutes) = **2,102**

Exit gate capacity

Each exit gate is 2.4 m wide. Therefore the exit capacity of each gate is 2.4 x 109 x 8 = **2,093**

Example 1: network plan to analyse emergency evacuation routes

A network plan is also useful for analysing emergency evacuation routes. For the terrace shown in Example 1, as the plan below illustrates, these evacuation routes consist of all the normal exit routes (as shown in the previous network plan), plus five exit gates onto the playing area. Because this is a modern standing area which has been categorised as a low fire risk, the maximum emergency evacuation time of eight minutes is deemed acceptable.

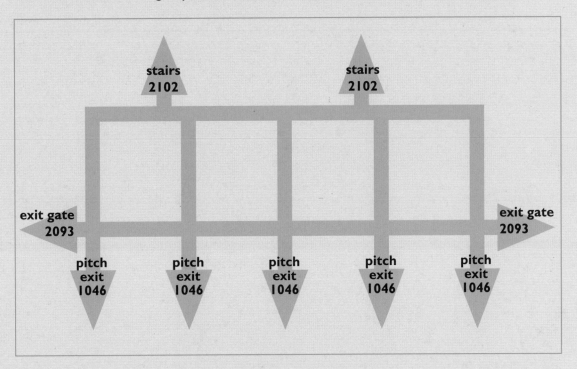

From the above network plan it can be seen that:

The maximum emergency evacuation capacity of the rear stairs = 2 x 2,102 = **4,204**

The maximum emergency evacuation capacity of the front exit gates = 2 x 2,093 = **4,186**

The maximum emergency evacuation capacity of the pitch exits = 5 x 1,046 = **5,230**

(Note, as stated in Section 9.9, that while in practice spectators may evacuate onto the pitch or area of activity in an emergency, this should not form part of the emergency evacuation time for newly constructed grounds or sections of grounds – see Stage Six.)

Worked example 2

A terrace with non-continuous crush barriers

Example 2 shows a terraced standing area. Its overall area (excluding the rear concourse) measures 21m deep x 74m wide. The area is enclosed on two sides and is entered from the north-east corner by a 3.3m wide stair, via six turnstiles. Spectators move from the stair along a rear concourse of the same width, from which they descend onto the terracing.

The terrace is separated from the perimeter track by a pitch perimeter barrier with four gates of 1.1m width for forward evacuation in an emergency. There are no radial or lateral gangways.

Barriers are laid out in a non-continuous configuration, according to the conditions specified in Section 10.9: that is, the alignment of gaps between successive rows of barriers form angles of less than 60°; there are no more than two consecutive gaps in any line, and these gaps measure at least 1.1m but no more than 1.4m in width.

All crush barriers are in satisfactory condition, having been tested to a horizontal imposed load of 5.0 kN/m length. Each crush barrier is 4m long. The depth of the spacing between lines of barriers is 3m except for that between the pitch perimeter barriers (line A) and the next line (line B), which is 4m, and that from the rear line (line F) to the edge of the rear lateral gangway, which is 5m.

Normal egress is by a stairway 3.3m wide in the north-east corner, and by an additional stairway of 2.2m width in the north-west corner.

The terrace is in reasonably good order, but with a few suspect patches. The gradient is 25°. 'C' values range from 80mm at the front to 45mm at the rear. The bases of floodlight pylons encroach on the viewing area, causing restricted views behind each base. The terrace is uncovered and therefore no discount need be made for partial roof cover.

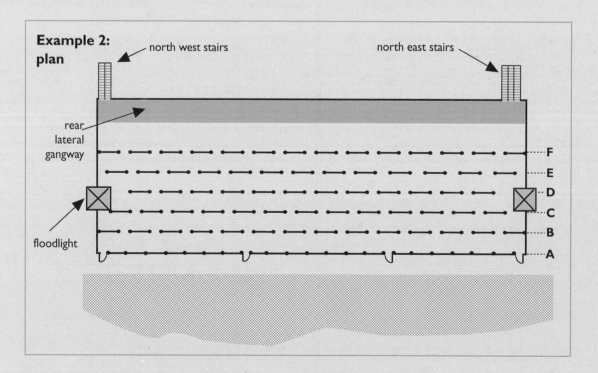

Example 2: plan

north west stairs

north east stairs

rear lateral gangway

floodlight

F
E
D
C
B
A

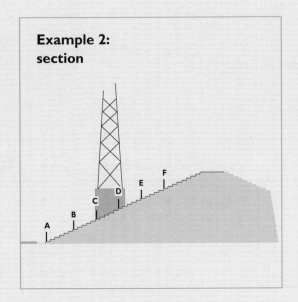

Example 2: section

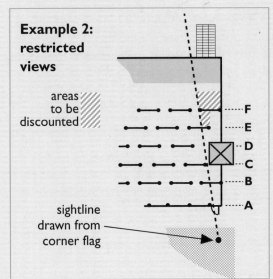

Example 2: restricted views

areas to be discounted

F
E
D
C
B
A

sightline drawn from corner flag

Stage one: available viewing area

Areas available behind barriers

Line A (pitch perimeter barriers):
Length: 74m less 4 exits at 1.1m each = 69.6m.
Depth: 4m, between front barrier and Line B.
But permitted distance between lines of crush barriers tested to 5.0 kN/m length on a gradient of 25° is 3.1m.

Available viewing area: 69.6 x 3.1 = 215.76 sq m

Line B:
Length: 14 barriers each of 4m length = 56.0m
Depth: 3m, between Lines B and C, i.e. within the permitted 3.1m.

Available viewing area: 56.0 x 3.0 = 168 sq m

Line C:
Length: 13 barriers each of 4m length = 52.0m
Depth: 3m, between Lines C and D, i.e. within the permitted 3.1m.

Available viewing area: 52.0 x 3.0 = 156 sq m

Line D:
Length: 12 barriers each of 4m length = 48.0m
Depth: 3m, between Lines D and E, i.e. within the permitted 3.1m.

Available viewing area: 48.0 x 3.0 = 144 sq m

Line E:
Barriers as per Line C (i.e. 156 sq m), but flood-lights create restricted views from areas behind part of each end barrier (see diagram above). These areas measure 6.75 sq m on each side.

Deductions: 6.75 sq m x 2 = 13.5 sq m

Available viewing area: 156 – 13.5 = 142.5 sq m

Line F:
Length: 14 barriers each of 4m length, but floodlights create restricted views from areas measuring 14 sq m behind each end barrier.

Length therefore: (14 – 2) x 4 = 48.0m.

Depth: 5m, between row of Line F and edge of lateral gangway, i.e. greater than permitted 3.1m. Only 3.1m allowed therefore.

Available viewing area: 48.0 x 3.1 = 148.8 sq m

Sub-total of available viewing area:
The sub-total of the available viewing area is therefore:

215.76 + 168 + 156 + 144 + 142.5 + 148.8 =

975.06 sq m

215

Required gangway provision

The *Guide* recommends radial gangways no greater than 24m apart for areas of standing accommodation. This terrace has no designated radial gangways. Therefore the area which should be taken up by radial gangways must be deducted from the sub-total of the available viewing area (as shown in the diagram right).

(Note that the gangways as shown are purely notional and are illustrated for the purpose of calculation only.)

Area of notional gangways

The minimum width for gangways is 1.1m. In this example four gangways would be needed in order to fall within the 24m maximum spacing.

Therefore the area to be deducted for notional gangways is:

4 x 1.1 x 21m (terrace depth) = **92.4 sq m**

Available viewing area:

The notional gangway provision for the terrace should be deducted from the sub-total of the available viewing area.

Thus: 975.06 − 92.4 = 882.66 sq m

Therefore the available viewing area is 882.66 sq m

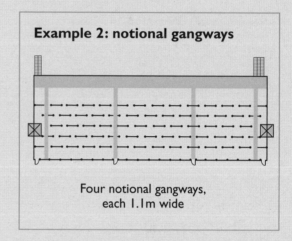

Example 2: notional gangways

Four notional gangways, each 1.1m wide

Stage two: appropriate density

Physical condition

The terracing is in reasonably good condition but there are areas of uneven treads, caused by settlement, plus other areas where the surface is beginning to crumble. Poor sightlines at the rear of the terrace also lead to excessive crowd movement.

After careful analysis and observation the (P) factor is therefore determined at 0.5.

Safety management

The stewarding is fairly good, although for large crowds the spread tends to be uneven, with a greater number of spectators standing in the half of the terrace nearer the entry point.

The (S) factor is therefore determined at 0.7.

Appropriate density

The lower figure from (P) or (S) is taken.

Therefore: 0.5 x 47 = 23.5

Therefore the appropriate density is 23.5

Stage three: holding capacity

The available viewing area = 882.66 sq m

The appropriate density = 23.5

Therefore, applying the formula:

$$\frac{A}{10} \times D = \frac{882.66}{10} \times 23.5 = 2074.25$$

Therefore the holding capacity is 2,074

Stage four: entry capacity

There are six turnstiles, each with a measured flow rate of 690 persons per hour.

Because this exceeds the maximum upper rate of 660 persons per hour, the figure of

660 is therefore applied instead:

Thus: 6 x 660 = 3,960.

Therefore the entry capacity is 3,960

Stage five: exit capacity

The width of the north-east stairway is 3.3 m.

The width of the north-west stairway is 2.2 m.

Given an egress time of eight minutes and a rate of passage for each stairway of 73 persons per metre width per minute (see

Section 9.6), this produces the following calculation:

(3.3 x 73 x 8 minutes) + (2.2 x 73 x 8) =

1,927 + 1,285 = 3,212

Therefore the exit capacity is 3,212

Stage six: emergency evacuation capacity

The terrace is non-combustible and the exit routes are good. Therefore the maximum emergency evacuation time of eight minutes should be deemed acceptable.

In addition to the normal exits (see Stage Five), there are also four gates in the pitch perimeter barrier, providing forward evacuation onto the pitch, at a rate of passage of 109 persons per metre width per minute (see Section 9.6). Each is 1.1m wide.

Therefore the total exit width available in an emergency is as follows:

Stairways: 5.5 m

Perimeter gates: 4.4 m

Therefore the emergency exit capacity is:

(5.5 x 73) + (4.4 x 109) = 401 + 480 = 881

881 x 8 minutes = 7,048

The emergency evacuation capacity is **7,048**, a figure larger than the holding capacity. It is thus necessary to calculate in what time (T) the holding capacity of 2,074 can be evacuated.

Thus: 881 x T = 2,074   Therefore T = 2.35

The emergency evacuation time is 2.35 minutes; that is, within the eight minutes limit.

Stage seven: final capacity

After assessing each of the previous stages, the smallest of all the figures produced is taken as determining the final capacity.

In this example, the smallest figure is the holding capacity of 2,074 (Stage Three).

No further calculations are necessary. This figure represents the maximum certifiable capacity possible under present conditions.

The final capacity of the terrace is therefore 2,074.

217

Worked example 3

A terrace with non-continuous crush barriers not conforming to Table 2

Example 3 shows a terrace of the same dimensions as worked examples 1 and 2 (21m deep x 74m wide) but with fewer crush barriers, whose spacing and loadings do not all conform with the requirements of Table 2 in Chapter 10. In addition, two crush barriers have failed. These are shown above purely for the purpose of illustration. In practice, as stated in Section 10.25, the failed barriers must be removed and replaced, or strengthened and then re-tested.

As the diagram shows, the available viewing area is restricted to those shaded areas behind the crush barriers and the pitch perimeter barrier. The depth of the areas to be used for the purposes of calculation depends on the loadings of each barrier, as detailed in Stage One.

The terrace gradient is 20°.

There are three lines of barriers. The first line (Line A) is formed by the pitch perimeter wall, which measures 74m in length, and includes four gates for forward emergency evacuation, each 1.1m wide. The pitch perimeter wall has been tested to 5.0 kN/m length (see Table 2).

The second line of barriers (Line B) consists of five crush barriers tested to 3.4 kN/m length. Two other barriers in this line have failed and are therefore discounted for calculation purposes.

The third line of barriers (Line C) consists of six crush barriers tested to 5.0 kN/m length.

As can be seen from the diagram and from cross-reference to Table 2, there is excessive space between Lines A and B, and between Lines B and C, while the space behind Line C is within the maximum distance permitted.

The terrace is uncovered and therefore no discount need be made for partial roof cover. The surface of the terracing is in reasonably good order, but with areas of crumbling concrete, owing to poor maintenance. There are no restricted views.

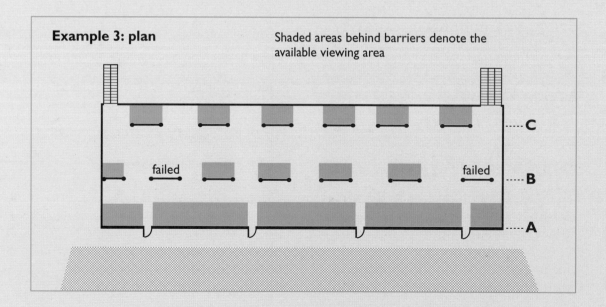

Example 3: plan

Shaded areas behind barriers denote the available viewing area

Stage one: available viewing area

Areas available behind barriers

Line A (pitch perimeter wall):
Length: 74m less 4 exits 1.1m each = 69.6m
Depth: 6m between Line A and Line B. But permitted distance behind barriers of 5 kN/m on a gradient of 20° is 3.4m.

Available viewing area: 69.6 x 3.4 = 236.6 sq m

Line B:
Length: 4 crush barriers at 6m each, plus 1 crush barrier at 3 m. Total = 27m.
Depth: 7m between Line B and Line C. But permitted distance behind barriers of 3.4 kN/m on a gradient of 20° is 2.3 m.

Available viewing area: 27 x 2.3 = 62.1sq m

Line C:
Length: 6 barriers at 6m each = 36m
Depth: 3m between Line C and rear of terrace. Permitted distance behind barriers of 5 kN/m on a gradient of 20° is 3.4 m. The actual distance, at 3m, is therefore acceptable.

Available viewing area: 36 x 3 = 108 sq m

No discounts need be made for restricted views or partial cover. The excessive space between barriers also means that no discount need be made for notional gangways.

Available viewing area is therefore

236.6 + 62.1 + 108 = **406.7 sq m**

Stage two: appropriate density

Physical condition
The terracing is in reasonable condition but there are areas where the surface is crumbling and where maintenance has been poor. The (P) factor is therefore determined at 0.8.

Safety management
The excessive spacing between barriers requires particular care in dispersing crowds. This does not happen, leading to surging. The

(S) factor is therefore determined at 0.5. (This may have to be reduced further if the failed barriers are removed but not replaced.)

Appropriate density
The lower figure from (P) or (S) is taken.

Therefore: 0.5 x 47 = 23.5

Therefore the appropriate density is 23.5

Stage three: holding capacity

The available viewing area is 406.7 sq m. The appropriate density is 23.5. Therefore, applying the formula:

$$\frac{A}{10} \times D = \frac{406.7}{10} \times 23.5 = 955.7$$

Therefore the holding capacity is 955

Replacing or strengthening the failed barriers to a loading of 3.4 kN/m would increase the holding capacity as follows:

Line B now = 39m (27 + 2 x 6m barriers). Available viewing area now 39 x 2.3 = 89.7

Total available viewing area now 434.3 sq m

In addition, concern over crowd dispersal is reduced and the (S) factor increased to 0.75.

Appropriate density now = 0.75 x 47 = 35.25

Therefore the holding capacity =

$$\frac{A}{10} \times D = \frac{434.3}{10} \times 35.25 = 1,530$$

Therefore, by replacing or strengthening the two failed barriers the holding capacity would increase from 955 to 1,530.

Worked example 4

A standing area with front barriers only

Example 4 shows a terraced standing area which has crush barriers along the front only. There are no other crush barriers. The front barriers have been tested to 5.0 kN/m length. There are four exit gates for emergency evacuation onto the pitch and no gangways.

The overall area measures 21m deep 74m wide. The terrace gradient is 20°. The terrace is uncovered and therefore no discount need be made for partial roof cover. The surface of the terracing is in good order, with steps conforming to the dimensions in Chapter 10. There are no restricted views.

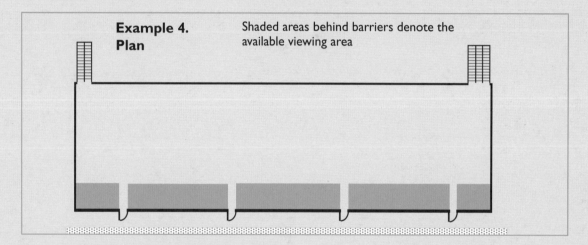

Example 4. Plan

Shaded areas behind barriers denote the available viewing area

Stage one: available viewing area

Length: 74m less 4 exits at 1.1m each = 69.6m
Depth: confined to the permitted distance behind the front barriers, which, for barriers tested to a horizontal imposed load of

5 kN/m length on a gradient of 20°, is 3.4m.

The **available viewing area** is therefore:

69.6 x 3.4 = **236.6 sq m**

Stage two: appropriate density

Physical condition
The physical condition is of a high standard. There are no sightline problems or concerns over the size of terrace. Therefore (P) = 1.0

Safety management
The safety management is good. However, it

is important to ensure that concentrations of spectators are not allowed to gather along the front barrier. Therefore (S) = 0.9.

Therefore the **appropriate density** is:

0.9 x 47 = **42.3 per 10 sq m**

Stage three: holding capacity

The available viewing area = 236.6 sq m. The appropriate density = 42.3 per 10 sq m.

$$\frac{236.6}{10} \times 42.3 = 1,000$$

Applying the formula:

Therefore the holding capacity is 1,000

Worked example 5

A standing area with no crush barriers

Example 5 shows a viewing slope which has no crush barriers. There is a rail measuring 74m along the front, but this does not meet the horizontal imposed load requirements specified in Table 2. In such circumstances, all relevant factors have to be considered; for example, the nature of the sporting event, the position of the standing area in relation to the pitch or area of activity (and therefore possibly the dispersal of spectators), the control of spectators entering onto the slope, underfoot conditions and the quality of the safety management.

The depth of the area is irrelevant, owing to the lack of barriers. The gradient is uneven, but does not exceed 25°. The slope is uncovered, so no discount need be made for partial cover. The surface varies, with sound steps only at the front 7m, and ash fill beyond.

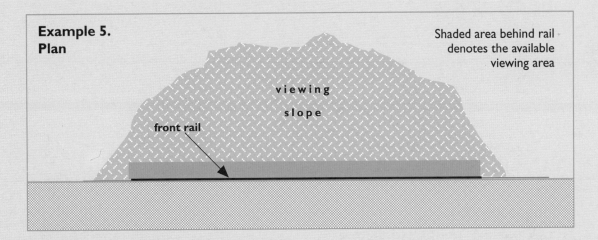

Example 5.
Plan

Shaded area behind rail denotes the available viewing area

viewing

slope

front rail

Stage one: available viewing area

Because there are no crush barriers meeting the Table 2 requirements, the available viewing area is confined to 1.5m behind the front rail.

Therefore the **available viewing area** is:

1.5 x 74 = **111 sq m**

Stage two: appropriate density

Physical condition
Conditions are poor, drainage is inadequate, but there are no concerns over sightlines or the size of terrace. Therefore (P) = 0.4.

Safety management
The safety management is not of a high

standard, but is adequate for the number of spectators who typically choose to stand in this area. Therefore (S) = 0.5.

Therefore the **appropriate density** is:

0.4 x 47 = **18.8 per 10 sq m**

Stage three: holding capacity

The available viewing area = 111 sq. m
The appropriate density = 18.8 per 10 sq m

$$\frac{111}{10} \times 18.8 = 208$$

Therefore, applying the formula:

Therefore the holding capacity is 208

Worked example 6

A level standing area

Level standing areas, with or without a front crush barrier, pose inherent problems, particularly because spectators lining the front of the area restrict the viewing of those spectators immediately behind.

Experience has shown that a concentration of four persons deep is the maximum for safe viewing from level areas.

Based on a level standing area 74m wide, the calculation should therefore be similar to that used for worked example 5; that is, the available viewing area will be a maximum of 1.5m x 74.

As in all such calculations, careful consideration should also be given to the (P) and (S) factors. For example, if observation identifies crowds of more than four deep forming, the (S) factor should be reduced for the purpose of calculation.

Worked example 7

An enclosure used for viewing and circulation

Example 6 shows an enclosure at a small racecourse, with a covered terrace for standing spectators behind a turfed viewing slope, or 'lawn', as described in Section 12.21.

Entry to the enclosure is mainly from access routes behind and to the sides of the covered terrace. In addition, there are gates in the fences on either side of the lawn, offering transfers to and from adjacent enclosures. Although there is a free movement of spectators between the two standing areas, the holding capacity of each should be assessed separately.

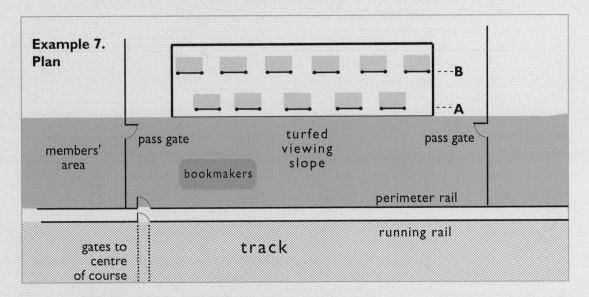

**Example 7.
Plan**

members' area   pass gate   turfed viewing slope   pass gate

bookmakers

perimeter rail

running rail

gates to centre of course   track

Covered terrace
The covered terrace measures 35 m wide x 8 m deep. There are two lines of non-continuous crush barriers, each barrier being 3 m long, and tested to a horizontal imposed load of 5 kN/m length. There are no defined gangways. Spectators enter the terrace from the front. The gradient is 20°. Sightlines are good for the finishing line, if not for the racecourse as a whole, but there are no views which could reasonably be considered as restricted.

Viewing slope
The turfed viewing slope measures 50m wide x 15m deep, and slopes down to the track rail, which has been tested to a horizontal imposed load of 1 kN/m length. Part of the slope is allocated to bookmakers. The gradient of the slope is even and does not exceed 10°.

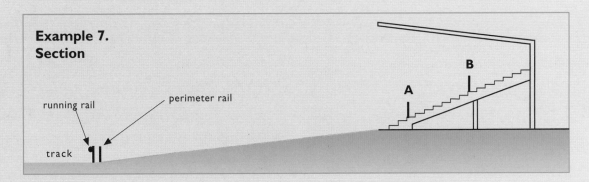

**Example 7.
Section**

running rail   perimeter rail   A   B

track

223

Stage one: available viewing area of covered terrace

Areas available behind barriers

Line A:
Length: 5 x 3m = 15m
Depth: 3.5m between Line A and Line B. But permitted distance between lines of crush barriers tested to 5.0 kN/m length on a gradient of 20° is 3.4m (see Table 2).

Available viewing area: 15 x 3.4 = 51 sq m

Line B:
Length: 5 x 3m = 15m
Depth: 4m between Line B and rear of terrace. Table 2 permits 3.4m behind crush barriers tested to 5.0 kN/m length on a gradient of 20°.

Available viewing area: 15 x 3.4 = 51 sq m

The available viewing area of the covered terrace is therefore

51 + 51 = **102 sq m**

No discounts need be made for restricted views or partial cover, or for notional gangways (the space between the barriers being deemed sufficient).

Stage two: appropriate density of covered terrace

Physical condition
The terrace underfoot conditions are good, but there are no defined gangways. The (P) factor is therefore determined at 0.8.

Safety management
The stewarding and safety management is good and able to monitor and manage the free movement of crowds reasonably well between the viewing slope and the terrace. The (S) factor is therefore determined at 0.9.

The appropriate density is therefore:
0.8 x 47 = 37.6

Therefore the appropriate density of the covered terrace is 37.6

Stage three: holding capacity of covered terrace

The available viewing area is 102 sq m.

The appropriate density is 37.6.

Therefore, applying the formula:

$$\frac{102}{10} \times 37.6 = 383$$

Therefore the holding capacity of the covered terrace is 383.

Stage one: available viewing area of viewing slope

The viewing slope, or lawn, measures 50m in width – between the side fences – and extends 15m from the front of the covered terrace down to the perimeter rail.

There are acceptable sightlines from all areas of the viewing slope.

The area allocated to bookmakers occupies approximately 30 sq m.

The available viewing area of the viewing slope is therefore

(50 x 15) – 30 = **720 sq m**

Stage two: appropriate density of viewing slope

Physical condition

Although the bookmakers' area has been discounted from the available viewing area, there is a need to allow the circulation of spectators around this area. Further allowance should be made for the free movement of spectators between the viewing slope and the covered terrace, and towards other spectator facilities underneath and beyond the covered terrace (such as bars, lounges and Tote areas).

In view of this free movement and the general use of the viewing slope for circulation, and taking into account the turfed underfoot conditions, a (P) factor of 0.3 is considered appropriate.

Safety management

The safety management and stewarding of the viewing slope is good, and the same (S) factor as for the covered terrace – that is, 0.9 – is therefore applied.

Appropriate density

The lower figure from (P) and (S) is taken.

Therefore: $0.3 \times 47 = 14.1$

Therefore the appropriate density of the viewing slope is 14.1

Stage three: holding capacity of viewing slope

The available viewing area is 720 sq m

The appropriate density is 14.1.

Therefore, applying the formula:

$$\frac{720}{10} \times 14.1 = 1,015$$

Therefore the holding capacity of the viewing slope is 1,015

Example 7: further comments

Once separate holding capacities have been calculated, when added together, in practice this creates an overall capacity of 1,398 for the whole enclosure. However, it is still important for the racecourse management to take reasonable measures to ensure that neither area within the enclosure is filled beyond its holding capacity.

■ Where larger attendances are expected, stewards should be trained to monitor the numbers entering the enclosures, and to make a visual assessment of when individual areas are approaching their capacity, so that no further spectators are admitted.

■ Where attendances are generally low in relation to the capacity of the racecourse's various enclosures, the management controls may be less stringent.

■ Extra vigilance may be necessary if there is a significant migration of spectators from the open viewing slope to the covered terrace, for example in poor weather conditions, to ensure that the holding capacity of the terrace is not exceeded.

■ Although spectators at racecourses generally prefer a larger amount of space for viewing than for sports such as football or rugby, the management should still monitor and prevent any congestion of spectators behind, for example, the perimeter rail close to the finishing post.

Annex B

Glossary

Barrier

Any element of a sports ground, permanent or temporary, intended to prevent people from falling, and to retain, stop or guide people. Types of barriers used at sports grounds are further defined in Section 10.1.

Certifying authority

The local authority responsible for issuing a safety certificate under the Safety of Sports Grounds Act 1975 or the Fire Safety and Safety of Places of Sport Act 1987.

Circulation

Free movement of spectators within a sports ground.

Combustible

Able to burn.

Competent person

A person shall be regarded as competent where he or she has sufficient training and experience to take responsibility for an identified task. A competent person will have an awareness of the limitations of his or her own experience and knowledge.

Concourse

A circulation area providing direct access to and from spectator accommodation, via stairways, ramps, vomitories, or level passageways, and serve as a milling area for spectators for the purposes of refreshment and entertainment. It may also provide direct access to toilet facilities.

Contingency plan

A contingency plan is prepared by the ground management setting out the action to be taken in response to incidents occurring at the venue which might prejudice public safety or disrupt normal operations (for example, the loss of power to CCTV or PA systems).

Control point

A designated room or area within the sports ground from which the safety management structure is controlled and operated. Also known as a 'match control', 'event control' or 'stadium control' room.

Crowd doctor

A qualified medical practitioner, registered with the General Medical Council, who has received training in pre-hospital (immediate) care and major incident management.

Crush barrier

A barrier which protects spectators from crushing, positioned in areas of standing accommodation.

Datum

The finished level of the floor, seat row, terrace, ramp, landing, pitch line of stairs, or, in the case of barriers behind seats, the seat level.

Emergency plan   An emergency plan is prepared and owned by the emergency services for dealing with an event at the venue or in the vicinity (for example, a major fire or bomb alert). Also known as an emergency procedure plan, or major incident plan.

Exit   A stairway, gangway, passageway, ramp, gateway, door, and all other means of passage used to leave the sports ground and its accommodation.

Exit system   A set of different types of exits, linked to form a means of passage of spectators.

Fire resistance   Ability of a component of a building to resist fire for a stated period of time, when subjected to an appropriate test in accordance with the current relevant British Standard.

First aid fire-fighting equipment   Equipment such as portable fire extinguishers, fire blankets, buckets of sand and hose reel equipment, intended for use by safety staff or employees prior to the arrival of the fire brigade.

First aider   A person who holds the standard certificate of first aid issued by the voluntary aid societies to people working as first aiders under the Health and Safety (First Aid) Regulations 1981.

Flammable   Able to burn with a flame.

Guard   See Barrier.

Handrail   A rail normally grasped by hand for guidance or support.

Horizontal imposed load   The load assumed to be produced by the intended use (usually of a barrier).

Landing   A level surface at the head, foot, or between flights of stairways, or ramps.

Lateral gangway   Channel for the passage of spectators through viewing accommodation running parallel with terrace steps or seat rows.

Local authority   As defined by the Safety of Sports Grounds Act 1975.

(P) factor   The term used for the assessment of the physical condition of an area of viewing accommodation.

Pitch perimeter barrier   A barrier which separates spectators from the pitch or area of activity.

Pitch perimeter fence   A barrier higher than 1.1m, which separates spectators from the playing area or area of activity.

Place of comparative safety   A place where people can be safe from the effects of fire for 30 minutes or more, thus allowing extra time for them to move directly to a place of safety.

Place of safety	A place where a person is no longer in danger from fire or other emergencies.
Radial gangway	Channel for the passage of spectators through viewing accommodation, running with the slope between terrace steps or seat rows. For the purposes of design and assessment, the criteria applying to radial gangways may be different from those pertaining to stairways.
Ramp	An inclined surface linking two areas at different elevations.
Rate of passage	The number of persons per metre width per minute passing through an element of an exit system.
Risk assessment	See Section 2.3.
Robustness	The capability of a structure to withstand some misuse and to tolerate accidental damage without catastrophic consequences.
(S) factor	The term used for the assessment of the safety management of an area of viewing accommodation.
Side gangway	Channel for the forward passage of spectators between an end row of seats and a protective barrier at the edge of a structure.
Sightline	The ability of a spectator to see a predetermined point of focus (such as the nearest touchline or outside lane of a running track) over the top of the head of the spectators sitting immediately in front.
Spectator accommodation	The area of a ground or structure in the ground provided for the use of spectators; including all circulation areas, concourses and the viewing accommodation.
Spectator gallery	A gallery, usually attached to a hospitality area, from which spectators can view the event.
Sports ground	Any place where sports or other competitive activities take place in the open air and where accommodation has been provided for spectators, consisting of artificial structures or of natural structures artificially modified for the purpose.
Stairway	That part of a structure which is not a radial gangway but which comprises of at least one flight of steps, including the landings at the head and foot of steps and any landing in between flights.
Stand	A structure providing viewing accommodation for spectators.
Temporary demountable structure	Any temporary structure erected on a temporary basis at a ground, including stands, standing area, marquees, and media installations.
Terrace	An area of steps providing standing accommodation for spectators.

Viewing slope   A non-stepped, sloping area providing standing accommodation for spectators.

Viewing standard   The quality of view available to spectators, consisting of three elements: the sightlines, the presence of any restrictions to viewing, and the distance between the spectator and the pitch or area of activity.

Vomitory   An access route built into the gradient of a stand which directly links spectator accommodation to concourses, and/or routes for ingress, egress or emergency evacuation.

Annex C

Bibliography and further references

1.7 **Terraces – Designing for Safe Standing at Football Stadia**
Football Advisory Design Council, 1993
Available from: Publications Department, The Sports Council,
P. O. Box 255, Wetherby, West Yorkshire LS23 7LZ
Tel. 0990 210255

2.3 **5 Steps to Risk Assessment**
Health and Safety Executive, IND(G) 163

A Guide to Risk Assessment Requirements
Health and Safety Executive, IND(G) 218

Both available from: HSE Books, P. O. Box 1999, Sudbury CO10 6FS
Tel. 01787 881165   Fax 01787 313995
InfoLine tel. 0541 545500   Info Centre fax 0114 289 2333

2.5 **Management of Health and Safety at Work Regulations 1992**
Approved Code of Practice.
Health and Safety Executive. L21. 1992

A Guide to the Health and Safety at Work etc. Act 1974
Health and Safety Executive. L1. 1992

Successful Health & Safety Management
Health and Safety Executive. HS(G)65. 1991

All available from HSE Books, op. cit. Section 2.3

2.7 **Guidance Notes for Drawing Up a Statement of Safety Policy for Spectators at Football Grounds**
Football Licensing Authority, 1995
Available from: FLA, 27 Harcourt House, 19 Cavendish Square, London W1M 9AD
Tel. 0171 491 7191   Fax 0171 491 1882

Writing a Safety Policy: advice for employers
Health and Safety Executive HSC6
Available from HSE Books, op. cit. Section 2.3

2.14 **Football Club Contingency Planning**
Football Licensing Authority, 1994
Available from: FLA, op. cit. Section 2.7

2.27 **Sporting Events (Control of Alcohol etc.) Act 1985**

Criminal Law (Consolidation) (Scotland) Act 1995

3.6 **NVQ (for England and Wales) or SVQ (for Scotland) in Spectator Control**
Levels 2, 3 & 4, Occupational Standards
Awarded by City and Guilds or SCOTVEC
Details from: Sports, Playwork, Recreation Industry Training Organisation (SPRITO),
81–103 Euston Street, London NWI 2ET
Tel. 0171 388 3111

Stewarding and Safety Management at Football Grounds
Football League, Football Association and FA Premier League, 1995
Available from: Football League, Lytham St Annes, Lancs FY8 1JG
Tel. 01253 729421   Fax 01253 724786

4.8 **Guide to Surveys and Inspections of Buildings and Similar Structures**
Institution of Structural Engineers, 1991
Available from: ISE, 11 Upper Belgrave Street, London SW1X 8BH
Tel. 0171 235 4535   Fax 0171 235 4294

4.13 **Appraisal of Existing Structures**
Institution of Structural Engineers, SETO Ltd, 1996 (2nd edition)
Available from: ISE, op. cit. Section 4.8

8.5 **Toilet Facilities at Stadia**
Football Stadia Development Committee, 1994
Available from: The Sports Council, op. cit. Section 1.7

11.1 **Seating: Sightlines, Conversion of Terracing, Seat Types**
Football Stadia Advisory Design Council, 1991
Available from: The Sports Council, op. cit. Section 1.7

11.6 **Stadium Roofs**
Football Stadia Advisory Design Council, 1991
Available from: The Sports Council, op. cit. Section 1.7

11.17 **Stadia: A Design and Development Guide**
G. John and R. Sheard
Butterworth-Architecture, 1994

12.1 op. cit. Section 1.7.

12.25 op. cit. Section 1.7.

13.1 **Designing for Spectators with Disabilities**
Football Stadia Advisory Design Council, 1993
Available from: The Sports Council, op. cit. Section 1.7

Centre for Accessible Environments
Nutmeg House, 60 Gainsford Street, London SE1 2NY
Tel. 0171 357 8182

13.2 **Disability Discrimination Act 1995 – Code of Practice**
National Disability Council, 1996
Available from: HMSO Books, P. O. Box 276, London SW8 5DT
Tel. enquiries: 0171 873 0011   Tel. orders: 0171 873 9090

13.4 **Royal National Institute for the Blind**
224 Great Portland Street, London WIN 6AA
Tel. 0171 388 1266

National Federation of the Blind of the UK
Unity House, Smyth Street, Wakefield WF1 1ER
Tel. 01924 291313

13.5 One such training scheme is called **Sympathetic Hearing Scheme**
For details: Hearing Concern, 7–11, Armstrong Road, London W3 7JL
Tel. 0181 740 4447

13.19 op. cit. Section 8.5.

14.2 *Temporary Demountable Structures – Guidance on Procurement, Design and Use*
Institution of Structural Engineers, SETO Ltd, 1995
Available from: ISE, op. cit. Section 4.13

14.12 *Code of Practice for Marquee Hirers*
Made-Up Textiles Association, 1995
Available from: MUTA, 42 Heath Street, Tamworth, Staffordshire B79 7JH
Tel. 01827 52337   Fax 01827 310827

15.9.g *Guide to Fire Precautions in Existing Places of Entertainment and Like Premises*
Home Office / Scottish Home & Health Department, 1990
Available from: HMSO, op. cit. Section 13.2

15.9.j *Guide to Control over Concessionaire Facilities and Other Services at Sports Grounds*
District Surveyors Association. No. 3 in series Safety of Sports Grounds, 1996
Available from: DSA Publications, PO Box 23, Beckenham, Kent BR3 3TL
(order forms also available from local associations)

15.9.k *Keeping of LPG in cylinders and similar containers*
Health and Safety Executive. CS4. 1986

Small scale storage and display of LPG at retail premises
Health and Safety Executive. CS8. 1985

Both available from: HSE Books. op. cit. Section 2.3

16.4 *Stadium Control Rooms*
Football Stadia Development Committee, 1994
Available from: The Sports Council, op. cit. Section 1.7

16.8 Health and Safety legislation of relevance to stadium control rooms is:

Health and Safety at Work etc. Act 1974
Workplace (Health, Safety and Welfare) Regulations 1992
Health and Safety (Display Screen Equipment) Regulations 1992
Management of Health and Safety at Work Regulations 1992

HSE Books issue a number of guides which may also be useful in the planning and design of control rooms, particularly with reference to work stations, seating and VDUs. op. cit. Section 2.3

16.13   ***Stadium Public Address Systems***
Football Stadia Advisory Design Council, 1991
Available from: The Sports Council, op. cit. Section 1.7

Code of Practice
for the assessment, specification, maintenance and operation of sound systems
for emergency purposes at sports grounds and stadia, in pursuit of approval
by licensing authorities
Available from: Sound and Communications Industries Federation, 4b High Street,
Burnham, Slough SL1 7JH
Tel. 01628 667633   Fax 01628 665882

16.14   op. cit. Sections 16.4 and 16.13

16.18   ***Guidance Notes for the Procurement of CCTV for Public Safety at Football***
Grounds
A. J. Ford, Police Scientific Development Branch, 1990
Available from: Football Trust, Walkden House, 10 Melton Street, London NW1 2EJ
Tel. 0171 388 4504

16.27   ***Safety Signs and Signals***
Health and Safety (Safety Signs and Signals) Regulations 1996. Guidance on the regulations.
Health and Safety Executive. L64. 1996
Available from: HSE Books. op. cit. Section 2.3

17.1   ***Guide to Electrical and Mechanical Services at Sports Grounds***
District Surveyors Association. No. 4 in series Safety of Sports Grounds, 1996
Available from: DSA Publications, op. cit. Section 15.9.j

17.6   ***Guidance Note 3 on Inspection and Testing***
Institution of Electrical Engineers
Available from: IEE, Michael Faraday House, Six Hills Way, Stevenage, Herts SH1 2AY
Tel. 01438 313311   Fax 01438 742792

17.10   ***Code for Interior Lighting***
Lighting Guide: LG04 – Sport
Lighting Guide: LG06 – The Outdoor Environment
Chartered Institute of Building Services Engineers
Available from: CIBSE, Delta House, 222 Balham High Road, London SW12 9BS
Tel. 0181 675 5211

17.13   ***Emergency Lighting: TM12***
Available from: CIBSE, op. cit. Section 17.10

19.1   ***Safety in broadcasting sports events***
Health and Safety Executive, 1996. ETIS 1
Available from: HSE Books. op. cit. Section 2.3

20.5   ***Guide to Health, Safety and Welfare at Pop Concerts and Similar Events***
Health and Safety Commission, Home Office and The Scottish Office, 1993
Available from: HMSO, op. cit. Section 13.2

20.7   op. cit. Section 8.5.

Further references:

Safety at Sports Grounds Act 1975
Chapter 52. HMSO, 1975

Fire Safety and Safety of Places of Sport Act 1987
Chapter 27. HMSO, 1987

The Construction (Design & Management) Regulations 1994
CONDAM/CDM Regs. HMSO, 1994

Report of the Inquiry into Crowd Safety at Sports Grounds
Rt Hon. Lord Wheatley, May 1972. Cm 4952.

The Hillsborough Stadium Disaster: 15 April 1989
Inquiry by Lord Justice Taylor: Final Report. HMSO, 1990. Cm 962

Guidance on safety certificates
Football Licensing Authority, 1992
Available from: FLA, op. cit. Section 2.7

Specimen safety certificate and guidance notes for designated grounds
District Surveyors Association. No 1 in series Safety of Sports Grounds
Available from: DSA Publications, op. cit. Section 15.9.j

Guide to during performance inspections of specified activities at sports grounds
District Surveyors Association. No 2 in series Safety of Sports Grounds
Available from: DSA Publications, op. cit. Section 15.9.j

Specimen safety certificate and guidance notes for regulated stands
District Surveyors Association. No 5 in series Safety of Sports Grounds
Available from: DSA Publications, op. cit. Section 15.9.j

Annex D

Summary of new guidance

This section briefly summarises or highlights some of the key areas in which this fourth edition of the *Guide* differs from the previous edition. The list is not comprehensive and in all cases reference should be made to the full text of the *Guide*.

General issues

Risk assessment: in line with wider practice, the current *Guide* places greater emphasis on the need for assessment, particularly risk assessment.

Distinction between existing and new construction: the text of the *Guide* now makes specific recommendations for new construction.

Viewing standards: the *Guide* now provides more detailed guidance; for example, on sightlines and strategies towards partially and seriously restricted views.

Chapter 1. Calculating the safe capacity of a sports ground

Assessment of (P) and (S) factors: (P) and (S) factors have been introduced in order to help with the assessment of safe capacities. (P) factors relate to the physical condition of an area being assessed. (S) factors relate to the safety management of the area. Each is to be expressed as a factor of 1.0 (that is, between 0.0 and 1.0).

Restricted views: there is new emphasis on the effect of partial and restrictive views on the calculation of holding capacities.

Chapter 2. Management – responsibility and planning for safety

Awareness of new legislation and standards: there are new references to health and safety legislation, and to provision for disabled spectators.

Contingency planning: more detailed guidance is provided on the need for, and the issues to be addressed in, contingency plans.

Admission policies: there is new guidance on the effect of admission and ticketing strategies on crowd management.

Chapter 3. Management – stewarding

Standards and training: new guidance is provided on the role and training of stewards, and on a code of conduct.

Chapter 4. Management – structures, installations and components

Planned maintenance: emphasis on the importance of maintenance and good housekeeping.

Structural dynamics: new advice on the effect of dynamic forces.

Chapter 5. Circulation – general

Widths: recommended minimum for new construction increased to 1.2m (from 1.1m).

Chapter 6. Circulation – Ingress

Admission policies: new guidance on the impact of ticketing strategies on rates of admission.

Computerised counting system: to be installed wherever practicable (not only at specific football grounds).

Chapter 7. Circulation – stairways and ramps

Stair riser heights: for new construction, a maximum riser height of 180mm (from 190mm).

Stair widths: maximum extended to 1.8m (from 1.65m). Minimum of 1.2m recommended in new construction.

Handrails: for new construction, minimum height of 900mm (from 840mm). Maximum of 1.0m.

Chapter 8. Circulation – concourses and vomitories

Concourses: new general guidance on concourses which serve as gathering areas in addition to ingress and egress routes.

Chapter 9. Circulation – egress and emergency evacuation

Rate of passage: change in expression of flow rates from unit widths, per minute to metre widths per minute (that is, actual width).

Electronic securing systems: new guidance.

Discounting of exit routes: the decision now to be based on risk assessment.

Exit gates: recommended that all exit gates be numbered.

Chapter 10. Barriers

Barrier loadings: change in presentation of barrier loading tables, with certain changes in light of research.

Spectator galleries: new advice included.

Barrier configuration: continuous crush barriers recommended for new construction.

Pitch perimeter fences: to be discouraged in favour of other methods.

Barrier test regime: now subject to risk assessment instead of a four-yearly cycle.

Barrier test – proof cycle: reference to deflection of less than 2mm deleted.

Chapter 11. Spectator accommodation – seating

Sightlines: new emphasis on need to provide adequate and appropriate sightlines.

Seating row depth dimension: for new construction, minimum 700mm.

Chapter 12. Spectator accommodation – standing

Terrace tread depths: minimum dimension for new construction extended to 400mm.

Angle of slope: clarification of maximum recommended angle of 25°.

Partial cover: new guidance on the effects of migration.

Terrace tread depths: maximum dimension for new construction extended to 400mm.

Conversion of terraces to seating: need for awareness of design factors.

Chapter 13. Spectator accommodation – disabilities

Building Regulations: more detailed guidance owing to introduction of new Building Regulations.

Number of wheelchair spaces: for England and Wales, definition of a 'large stadium' clarified in relation to Part M.

Chapter 14. Spectator accommodation – temporary demountable structures

Design checks: more emphasis on independent design checks.

Structural dynamics: new advice on the effect of dynamic forces.

Chapter 15. Fire safety

Fire risk assessment: new emphasis, including guidance on levels of risk.

Places of safety: definition of places of safety and places of comparative safety.

Emergency evacuation onto pitch: for purpose of calculation, not recommended for new construction.

Chapter 16. Communications

New guidance: on control points, PA systems, CCTV and signs.

Chapter 17. Electrical and mechanical services

New guidance: on mechanical services.

Chapter 18. First aid and medical provision

Provision: more detailed guidance on numbers of first aiders and ambulances, and on provision of a crowd doctor.

Chapter 19. Media provision

New emphasis: acknowledgement of greater media presence and safety implications.

Chapter 20. Alternative uses for sports grounds

New emphasis: acknowledgement of wider usage of sports grounds for non-sporting events.

Annex E

Location of 3rd edition paragraphs

For the benefit of readers familiar with the previous edition of the *Guide*, this section shows where the former paragraph numbers (in left column) are now located in the current *Guide*.

Key: **A – Annex** **In – Intro** **P – Preface** **p – paragraph** **Del – Deleted**

1	In a/c	32	2.10	63	17.8	94	9.8	125	7.7
2	In d	33	4.8	64	17.9	95	9.2	126	7.9
3	P p3	34	2.16	65	17.10	96	9.2	127	7.9
4	P p4	35	2.12	66	4.13	97	9.7	128	7.9
5	P p5	36	3.13-3.16	67	4.13	98	9.8	129	7.9
6	P p6	37	1.2	68	4.13	99	9.10	130	7.9
7	P p7	38	2.29	69	4.9	100	9.12	131	7.9
8	In e/5.2	39	2.29/18.3	70	4.10	101	9.8	132	7.10
9	In c/5.1	40	2.25	71	4.9	102	9.8	133	Del
10	In c/g	41	4.3	72	4.10	103	9.8	134	7.12
11	In c/f	42	2.3	73	4.10	104	9.8	135	7.12
12	In c	43	2.30	74	4.12	105	9.8	136	7.12
13	In d	44	13.1	75	4.14	106	9.15	137	12.1
14	In a	45	13.4	76	Del	107	9.15	138	12.3
15	In a	46	13.5	77	6.8	108	9.15	139	12.9
16	1.1	47	13.5	78	6.2	109	9.15	140	12.9
17	In e	48	13.6	79	6.7	110	9.15	141	12.8
18	5.5	49	13.7	80	6.6	111	9.15	142	12.8
19	Del	50	Del	81	6.3	112	9.15	143	7.2
20	Del	51	13.14	82	6.8	113	7.2	144	12.4
21	Del	52	13.19	83	6.8	114	7.3	145	12.4
22	4.3	53	13.12	84	6.9	115	7.3	146	12.5
23	In f	54	13.19	85	6.9	116	7.3	147	12.4
24	In f	55	13.17	86	6.8	117	7.3	148	12.5
25	4.2	56	4.2/17.2	87	6.8	118	7.3	149	12.6
26	4.2	57	4.5	88	6.11	119	7.3	150	12.6
27	15.9	58	5.5/7.5	89	9.1	120	7.4/7.5	151	12.6
28	In d/2.1	59	4.7	90	Del	121	7.5	152	12.15
29	2.6	60	17.6	91	9.2	122	7.7	153	12.15
30	2.17	61	17.6	92	9.2	123	7.5	154	12.16
31	2.9	62	17.7	93	9.4	124	7.8	155	12.15

156	12.21	192	14.7	228	15.17	264	16.16	300	10.17
157	12.15	193	14.9	229	15.14	265	16.17	301	10.15
158	12.7	194	14.9	230	15.15	266	16.24	302	10.16
159	12.19	195	14.9	231	15.15	267	17.12	303	10.16
160	12.19	196	14.9	232	15.15	268	17.12	304	10.16
161	12.19	197	14.9	233	15.15	269	17.13	306	10.16
162	12.11	198	14.9	234	2.14	270	17.13	307	9.13
163	10.10	199	Del	235	15.9	271	17.13	308	10.16
164	10.11	200	14.12	236	9.10	272	17.13	309	10.16
165	10.7	201	14.13	237	9.10	273	16.13	310	1.1
166	10.8	202	Del	238	9.10	274	3.6	311	1.1
167	10.9	203	14.13	239	Del	275	3.6	312	1.3
168	10.7	204	Del	240	15.10	276	3.6	313	1.3
169	10.19	205	14.13	241	9.9	277	3.11	314	12.24
170	10.19	206	15.11	242	15.4-6	278	3.4	315	1.8
171	10.7	207	Del	243	15.4-6	279	3.15	316	Del
172	10.6	208	15.9	244	Del	280	3.16	317	12.23
173	10.19	209	15.9	245	9.12	281	3.9	318	1.10
174	Del	210	15.9	246	9.12	282	3.10	319	A A
175	11.1/12.1	211	15.9	247	9.12	283	Del	320	A A
176	11.2/12.3	212	15.9	248	5.8	284	Del	321	A A
177	11.7	213	15.9	249	5.8	285	Del	322	A A
178	9.7	214	15.9	250	16.1	286	2.19	323	A A
179	11.7	215	15.9	251	16.6	287	Del	324	A A
180	11.7	216	15.10	252	16.20	288	2.21	325	A A
181	11.7	217	15.10	253	16.14	289	Del	326	A A
182	11.9	218	15.10	254	16.13	290	Del	327	A A
183	11.9	219	15.15	255	16.14	291	2.22	328	A A
184	11.15	220	15.10	256	16.13	292	11.17	329	A A
185	11.11	221	15.10	257	16.14	293	Del	330	A A
186	11.12	222	15.10	258	16.13	294	2.23	331	9.5
187	11.14	223	15.12	259	16.10	295	2.23	332	9.6
188	14.1	224	16.12	260	16.7	296	2.26	333	9.6
189	14.2	225	15.12	261	Del	297	2.27		
190	14.4	226	15.12	262	16.8	298	2.27		
191	14.6	227	15.12	263	16.11	299	10.14		

Former Annexes

Annex A – now 2.6

Annex B – now Chapter 18

Annex C – now Sections 4.8–4.13

Annex D – now Sections 10.19–10.25

Annex E – now Chapter 3

Annex F – now Annex B

Index

Printed in the UK for the Department of National Heritage.
DNH JO133NJ.
C50 3/97 59226